TOM 'CHICO' ADRAHTAS

Forewords by Kelly Hrudey & Glenn Hall

Glenn Hall

THE MAN THEY CALL MR. GOALIE

GREYSTONE BOOKS

Douglas & McIntyre Publishing Group

Vancouver / Toronto

In memory of Sthenelaos M. Stanitsas, beloved papou

Greystone Books
A division of Douglas & McIntyre Ltd.
2323 Quebec Street, Suite 201
Vancouver, British Columbia
Canada v5T 4s7
www.greystonebooks.com

National Library of Canada Cataloguing in Publication Data
Adrahtas, Tom, 1955–
  Glenn Hall

  Includes index.
  ISBN 1-55054-912-X

  1. Hall, Glenn, 1931– 2. Hockey goalkeepers—
Biography. I. Title.
GV848.5.H34A37 2002   796.962′092   C2002-911006-8

Copyediting by Michael Carroll
Proofreading by Christine Kondo
Jacket and text design by Peter Cocking
Jacket photograph courtesy the Hockey Hall of Fame
Typesetting by Rhonda Ganz
Printed and bound in Canada by Friesens
Printed on acid-free paper ∞

We gratefully acknowledge the financial support of the
Canada Council for the Arts, the British Columbia
Ministry of Tourism, Small Business and Culture, and
the Government of Canada through the Book Publishing
Industry Development Program (BPIDP) for our
publishing activities.

Contents

Foreword

by Kelly Hrudey

———————

MANY OF US RETURN from work at the end of the day believing we truly gave our best effort. We feel proud, satisfied, fulfilled. Imagine, then, what it must feel like to have your actions so highly regarded that people feel you literally change your profession. Legendary goaltender Glenn Hall did just that while he played in the National Hockey League.

To me, what's amazing is that Glenn Hall surely must recognize his accomplishments and his contributions to the game of hockey. But as Tom Adrahtas remarks in his acknowledgments, "the person [Hall] least liked to talk about was himself." This may be the grandest compliment one person can give to another; it is also befitting of Glenn.

I first met Glenn in 1986 while I was playing for the New York Islanders. Coach Al Arbour, a man I highly respected, set up a meeting between Glenn and me to find out if there was any way Glenn could help me become a better goalie. Unfortunately Glenn was already helping the Calgary Flames, so my hopes of having him as my personal goalie coach went down the drain.

On one of our western road trips, however, Al arranged for Glenn to come to our practice to watch me and help me figure out my strengths and weaknesses. After practice the team was flying to Calgary, and I was to ride with Glenn to the Edmonton airport, a drive that takes about 40 minutes.

I was very nervous about meeting somebody I'd come to idolize, even though I couldn't remember ever watching a game he had played. I'd come to know his greatness through the media reports and the stories told to me by people in the industry.

One of the first people to talk to me about Glenn was my coach in Medicine Hat in the Western Hockey League (WHL). Vic Stasiuk was a wonderful man and a former Detroit Red Wing who played with Glenn Hall. After only two days of training camp, Vic called me into his office to inform me that I had made the team. But what would normally have been a five- or ten-minute meeting lasted close to two and a half hours as Vic told me story after story about how great Glenn Hall was as a player and as a teammate.

On our drive to the airport, I remember looking over at Glenn often from the passenger seat. It was hard for me to grasp just how lucky I was to be with this man. I didn't know what to say, but for some reason I was curious what he thought about the goalies of my generation. Much to my surprise he had nothing but complimentary things to say, even though looking back now I wonder whether the goalies of that period might not have been the weak link on many teams.

He told me how impressed he was with one young goalie the Flames had in their organization, a player by the name of Mike Vernon. I had faced Mike in the Alberta Midget Provincial finals in 1977 and also many times in the WHL and, to me, he was the toughest goaltender to play against. As Glenn predicted, Mike went on to a brilliant NHL career, including two Stanley Cup wins and a Conn Smythe Trophy.

I was hoping that just sitting there talking to Glenn would somehow transform me into a Vezina Award–winning goalie. He did his best. During the drive, he said the first thing he'd noticed about my game was my skating ability. We now had a huge connection because I always felt, like Glenn, that being an exceptional skater is the key to playing goal.

Reading this book brought back those memories. As I turned the pages, I couldn't help but feel that in some ways Glenn and I had similar childhoods. Although he grew up in a rural setting whereas I grew up in a city, his stories made me think back to all the road-hockey games played on the street in front of our house and the countless hours I spent at the community-league rink playing hockey. We, too, only took breaks to warm up our frostbitten toes, fingers, ears, and anything else exposed during those cold Edmonton winters.

Glenn also tells the story of how as a youngster he listened religiously to the radio broadcasts of his favorite team, the Toronto Maple Leafs, while dreaming the whole time of becoming a star player himself. It's no secret that to achieve greatness, one has to be passionate about that goal from a young age. By the time Glenn reached the NHL, greatness had become his standard and he was rewarded with a collection of league awards, a Stanley Cup, and a sure mention anytime the topic of best goaltender of all time comes up.

But Glenn's real greatness is the influence his style of play has had on the game. Glenn was able to dominate his goalkeeping position because of his unique "butterfly" style. So it's no wonder that today's goalies rule the game: many of their moves are similar to the moves Glenn used years ago.

At the time Glenn was criticized for his unorthodox style, as were Dominik Hasek and Patrick Roy after him. Today these three are among the most successful goalies of all time. And all because they stuck to their beliefs that they were the ones leading the way.

I chuckled when I read Glenn's comment, "I believe many of the so-called experts know little about goaltending," because most teams in the NHL now employ goalie coaches who agree that the styles that Hall, Hasek, and Roy use are the most effective.

In this book, Tom Adrahtas does an amazing job of relating not only Glenn's stories, but also the tales of his teammates, coaches, and others who fondly recall those early times. Glenn's reminiscences about the times he spent with his teammates fascinated me the most, because his stories are similar to the ones I have from my own playing days. I was pleasantly surprised to discover that even though we always seem to say how much times change, the closeness between the players has endured.

These days I don't bump into Glenn very often, but when I do I'm still as awed by him as when I rode in his pickup truck all those years ago. Personally I appreciate Glenn's modesty after all his success.

Is Glenn Hall the greatest goaltender of all time? Some will say absolutely; others will say no. What is certain after reading this book is how driven Glenn was and how passionately he approached everything he did in his life.

Foreword

by Glenn Hall

————————

I SUPPOSE I SHOULD start out by telling you why I wanted to write a book.

My first reason was to share the humor I found within the game. Because of the way the game is designed, there are emotional peaks and valleys to contend with. Without humor, the valleys would drag a person down.

I also had a story to tell. Being sick before games is generally considered to be a weakness, but I saw it as a strength. It was simply part of a preparation that forced me to play as well as I was capable of playing. Anything less was unacceptable to me.

I have been approached many times over the years to write a book, but I felt it should really have been done shortly after I retired, and that's where it stayed until I met Chico Adrahtas.

Not only was I amazed at what he knew about the way I played goal, but all that he knew about the other goalies who played during my time as well. When talking to sportswriters and others, I always felt they had researched previously written articles and material to find out how and how well I played. In most cases, they'd never seen me play. If they had, it was limited.

Chico knew why I made the moves I did; moves that were generally considered unacceptable at the time. Goaltending is such that if you do nothing other than stand in front of the net, there is a reasonable chance of stopping the puck. On the other hand, you can make a terrible move and stop the puck. It is for this reason that I believe many of the so-called experts know little about goaltending.

I want to thank Chico. He made it clear from the beginning that this would be a labor of love for him. Whether it worked out that way or not, I don't know, but thanks for your dedication, friendship, and total commitment in telling this story.

Looking back, I cherish all the memories and experiences of my hockey career. If indeed I have done well it is because of my family, my teammates, my coaches, and my friends, and this book is a way for me to thank them all. Thinking about it, I cherish all the memories and experiences in my life. Many of the people who were closest to me have passed on. Too many to mention and I don't want to run the risk of missing anyone so I won't name names. They know who they are. I miss you all and I dedicate this book to your memory.

I hope you enjoy reading the book as much as Chico and I enjoyed writing it for you.

Preface

———

IN THE SEEMINGLY neverending stream of polls and rankings that were so in vogue at the close of the millennium, we as a people became obsessed with making "best of" and "greatest ever" lists. Something compelled us to determine the top 100 movies of all time, history's most influential politicians, the greatest songs ever written, the top ten moments of the 20th century, and, of course, the top 50 athletes of the last 100 years. ESPN/TSN (Canada's The Sports Network) lost me when they counted a horse among those top 50 athletes.

It seems to me that it's a peculiarly male need to have to establish the absolute "best" by numerical rank. I wonder where that comes from? What purpose does it serve to state unequivocally that Michael Jordan was the greatest athlete of all time? Is it truly imperative to our existence to present an "objective" case that Wayne Gretzky was greater than Gordie Howe?

Maybe the male of the species is more comfortable defining the world in black and white, whereas the female of the species is naturally more appreciative of, and more at ease with, the nuances of the various shades of gray. I doubt women invest a great deal of emotion debating the difference in historical significance between Eleanor Roosevelt, Queen Elizabeth II, and Mother Teresa, whereas I am quite positive a nose or two has been broken by men over who packed a harder punch, Muhammad Ali or Rocky Marciano. Perhaps this male myopia is a manifestation of our natural competitive urges. Life would be so much simpler if everyone acknowledged that the only true absolutes are found in mathematics and physics.

The hockey world, of course, fell right in line with the rest of the planet when *The Hockey News* published its millennium list of the 50 greatest players of all time, selected by a so-called panel of experts. One can certainly debate the placement of some of the forwards and defensemen, but as a whole I think they did a reasonable job. However, as someone who has coached goalies for a long time and has observed the game closely for nearly 40 years, the one thing I can assure you is that the aforementioned prestigious panel didn't know their butts from their elbows about goalkeeping.

I saw Gretzky's entire career and I saw Howe from the early '60s on and I can tell you that you're comparing apples with oranges when you search for who was the greater of those two. Despite Gretzky's gaudy offensive numbers, that question just cannot be answered definitively. It is fair to say Gretzky would have been a superstar in the six-team National Hockey League and it is fair to say Howe would have been likewise in the 28-team league. It is certainly true Gretzky wouldn't have had the numbers he'd accumulated if he'd played in the Original Six era. The goaltending and team defense were better, and there would have been no Marty McSorley to protect him. The Howes, Bobby Hulls, and Maurice Richards never needed protection to establish their offensive wizardry. Although Gordie wouldn't have needed a McSorley had he played in the '80s, neither was he gifted with the extraordinary ice sight that made Gretzky so special. So the only right answer is to acknowledge they were the two best, different, unique, and gifted enough to dominate the eras they inhabited.

So why can't we just leave the discussion at that? Too easy. We could never be that reasonable because without a good argument, how would a TV special draw viewers or a magazine sell subscriptions?

Having said that, it is time to take a hard look at an assumption that has not been adequately challenged since the mid-'70s. The one thing every hockey greatest-ever list has in common is the presumption that hockey's greatest goalie was Terry Sawchuk. In *The Hockey News*' list, Sawchuk is first. A quick look over almost every major hockey publication of the past three decades ranks him the same. Recently, two biographies have been written about the man nicknamed "The Uke." *Sawchuk: The Troubles and Triumphs of the World's Greatest Goalie* is a wonderful read, written with the cooperation of the Sawchuk family, vividly capturing a talented but very troubled soul. But at the core of the book is the assumption, almost never challenged, that it is a fact that Sawchuk was the best. When Patrick Roy bypassed Sawchuk's all-time win record during the 2000–01 season, the debate began over where Roy's place in history would be. The ensuing publicity over the new record brought out the chorus of Sawchuk faithful, all of them sincere.

And all of them wrong.

Now perhaps from my introduction, you're expecting me to present a contrast between Roy and Sawchuk. Maybe from my tone you'd anticipate a measured comparison between the two, acknowledging the vast differences in the eras of the game that both men faced to such acclaim.

But you'd be wrong.

You see, when presenting my case regarding the folly of those inane lists and the absurd comparisons between athletes of divergent eras that result, I can do so logically because I can be emotionally detached.

Not so when it comes to goalkeeping. You see, goalkeeping is the ultimate mental challenge in all of sport. The athletes who accept the challenge of being the last line of defense in a sport played on ice, a game that requires them to face the routine threat of a vulcanized rubber disc hurtling their way at speeds of up to 100 miles per hour, are due very special scrutiny. The serious examination the position deserves begins only when you dig deeply enough behind the numbers and push hard enough past the easily held (and erroneous) assumptions of the lists. Most of these have been compiled by people who never played goal and therefore cannot understand the subtleties of the position enough to separate the good from the great, the great from the greatest.

So let me cut to the chase and dispel the myths. Simply stated, Glenn Hall was the greatest goalie of all time.

You wouldn't know it to look at those lists, and you wouldn't know it by reading some of hockey's more renowned historical works. Whenever Glenn Hall is referenced, he is usually ranked third behind Sawchuk and Jacques Plante. Unless the record is set straight, after Roy retires I would expect Hall to be pushed a notch farther down the list. The man they called Mr. Goalie is most widely remembered for his incredible ironman record of 502 consecutive starts in goal at the NHL level. But even that record, as acclaimed as it is, has never been given the proper historical perspective or credit. Hall, a native of the open spaces of western Canada, is also the man who invented the "butterfly style" of goalkeeping. If you listen to commentators today, you'd think this method—often dubbed the "Quebec style" because of Roy's repopularization of this system of puck-stopping defense—was the brainchild of someone whose primary language was French. The lack of historical credit given Hall stems from a number of factors, all of which I hope to set straight in this work.

Since history allows us the luxury of hindsight and perspective, I propose we define true greatness by the consistency, impact, and longevity of its gifts. In considering Terry Sawchuk, we will see that he was a brilliant talent and an innovator in his own way. He was the first goalie to play in a low crouch (dubbed the "Gorilla Crouch"), which afforded him greater lateral agility and quickness. That he strung together the best five consecutive years of goalkeeping in hockey history back in the early 1950s cannot be disputed. Those first five years of his career were remarkable. If you need a modern frame of reference, think Dominik Hasek at the end of the '90s, only with Stanley Cup victories added. From 1950 through 1955, Sawchuk recorded 195 of his once-record 447 wins, posted 56 of his record 103 career shutouts, earned five of his seven All-Star team mentions, and won three of his four Stanley Cups. But Sawchuk played in the NHL for 20 years, so nearly half of his career wins came in the first quarter of his career, as did over half of his shutouts and three-fourths of his Cup wins. He only made the All-Star team twice in his last 15 years of NHL play, and never the first team.

The years of Sawchuk's dominance were of the pre–slap shot/curved stick era. Although he did continue on successfully into the next era, and he played effectively—and in pockets brilliantly—into the late '60s, he never came close to duplicating the feats of those special five first years. But like so many historical figures who pass from this Earth too quickly, Sawchuk's legend increased exponentially after his untimely death at the age of 40 in 1970. It is interesting to note that in the press and in the hockey literature of the '60s, Sawchuk is often referred to as the greatest Detroit Red Wing goalie of all time, but he is almost never mentioned as the best goalie of his day, much less of all time.

The immediate heir to Sawchuk's hardware was Jacques Plante. From 1955 through 1960, "Jake the Snake" had the luxury of playing behind one of the great dynasties of all time, the Montreal Canadiens, and behind one of the greatest defensemen of all time, Doug Harvey. Plante was a special talent, brilliant and eccentric. He pioneered the modern face mask, was the first goalie to wander behind his net to set up pucks for his defense, and in an era of team players, he was a precursor to the boastful modern athlete. Plante was totally convinced he was the greatest, and was happy to share that opinion with anyone who would listen. In the '60s, the weaknesses in his game were exposed when a trade left him on a needy New York Ranger team. No longer able to rely on the great Canadien defense to sweep away rebounds and shut down threats from the weak side of the ice, Plante's almost scientific understanding of angle cutting was rendered ineffective and his goals-against average soared. After a three-year retirement, Plante reemerged late in the 1960s and put together some remarkable seasons at an age when most athletes are content to read their scrapbooks. By the time his career ended, Plante had amassed seven Vezina Trophies as the league's top goaltender, six Stanley Cups, seven All-Star team nods, and one Hart Trophy as the NHL's most valuable player. But outside of the 1955–60 time frame that the Habs so dominated the game, Plante won the Vezina only twice, was an All-Star only twice, and never played for a Cup winner again.

Both Plante and Sawchuk were nearing the end of their careers in the late '60s. At the same time and at the same age, Sawchuk had been relegated to a part-time, backup role while Plante was near the top of the league in goals-against average. Where Sawchuk's emotional demons left him often unknowable and distant from teammates, Plante's "no goal is my fault" ego and physical unreliability accomplished the same. In a sport where you were expected to dress if you weren't in intensive care, Plante's ailments, ranging from asthma to knee injuries (both real and, as Montreal, New York, and St. Louis management would contend, imagined) frequently kept him off the ice.

Both Sawchuk and Plante shared in the transition from old-school, pre-curved-stick-and-slap-shot hockey to the new era of the post-expansion game with some memorable athletes. Johnny Bower played in goal successfully and often superbly, first for New York and most notably later for Toronto. Unlike Sawchuk, Bower was indisputably better in the more challenging decade of the '60s than he was in the '50s when he had a hard time cracking an NHL lineup. A respected and popular teammate, Bower was an amazing physical specimen who played in the league until just after his 44th birthday. Lorne "Gump" Worsley worked behind miserable Ranger teams in the '50s and finally found respect playing for Cup-winning Canadien teams in the mid-1960s. But even the Gump was relegated to the minors for long stretches during both decades. Still, of all the Original Six goalies, Worsley, whose career spanned 21 NHL seasons, may yet be the most underrated.

Glenn Hall coalesced the very best traits of the four goalies I've mentioned. He played behind three NHL teams of vastly different abilities and commitments to defense. Like Sawchuk, he was a Calder Trophy (Rookie of the Year) winner. Unlike any of the goalies already mentioned, his goals-against average never once ventured above the 3.00 mark in 16 full seasons of play. He set the aforementioned record of 502 consecutive games, a record that will never be broken. There's another record he holds that will likely stand just as long, although it is less heralded. Hall earned a spot on more All-Star teams, 11 (7 first team, 4 second) than any goalie in history. He won three Vezinas and a Conn Smythe Trophy as the most valuable player in the playoffs, and he invented a puck-stopping style that was visionary and that is even more alive in the NHL of the new millennium than it was when he first employed it to howling criticism in the 1950s.

In today's NHL, the best goals-against average is rewarded with the Jennings Trophy, which didn't exist in the '50s or '60s. It goes to a club's goalies, but it is truly a team-defense award. The Vezina, which used to be awarded for goals-against average, is now given to the goalie considered to be the league's best, or in fact the first All-Star goalie. If you extend those standards back to the '50s, Hall would have held a record seven Vezinas, whereas Sawchuk and Plante would have had three each. Plante would have won the Jennings, not the Vezina, seven times, Sawchuk four, Hall three. Hall was the consummate team player, respected unconditionally by teammates (one Chicago writer said the respect Hall earned from teammates was of the same depth most people hold for a parent) and opponents, revered by his coaches. Said Scotty Bowman, "Goaltenders are a breed apart, and Glenn Hall is apart from the breed."

Glenn was not a self-promoter like Plante nor was he self-destructive like Sawchuk, and to a large degree those factors keep him third on those bothersome "all-time" lists.

Dave Dryden, a thoughtful and respected man who once shared the nets with Hall for the Black Hawks in Chicago, said of Mr. Goalie, "He was the best I ever saw play. There's no question. He always seemed kind of tragic because he didn't get the recognition he should have."

I write this book because it is time for Glenn Hall to receive that recognition, for the fans and students of the game to remember how great a player he really was, and to acknowledge how important a contribution to the history of the game he really made. Although his name is synonymous with that iron-man streak, it is not the sheer numbers that should most impress, it is the consistent excellence he achieved game in and game out. Showing up for work 502 times in a row wasn't important to a man with the fierce pride and high standards of excellence that Hall possessed. Playing 502 games in a row as close to perfection as possible was.

There is something to be said for the combination of character and ability, a most precious mixture that I fear is vanishing in a game of hits from behind and sticks carried at ear level. That combination is something everyone who cherishes this great game of ours should honor; it's something that finally sets Hall apart from all the others. Glenn's former teammate Billy McCreary told me, "You know, when you hear so much about the greatest 'this' and the best 'that' of all time, it's time people knew that Glenn was really the Joe DiMaggio of our game."

To take the high road is to acknowledge that it's not so important to establish a definitive "best ever." But we are talking about goalkeeping and I am a male of the species so I can't help but stress that Hall was simply the best. After all is said and done, there was only one "Number One, Mr. Goalie."

And I'd also take Eleanor Roosevelt over the Queen and Mother Teresa.

Prologue

November 13, 1969

"WE WANT HALL! WE WANT HALL!"

Exactly 15,993 different voices chant together this November evening in 1969, their shouts echoing off the cavernous ceiling of the St. Louis Arena.

"We want Hall! We want Hall!"

Just a few years earlier, this scene would have been unimaginable. At that time, the St. Louis Arena and the man the gathered assembly was saluting were both closer to permanent retirement than to boisterous acclaim. St. Louis was the model baseball town, insanely devoted to the games of summer. And the man now standing at center ice toiled for a hockey team in Chicago, a city that rivaled St. Louis in every aspect of life.

"We want Hall! We want Hall!"

All that changed when NHL expansion introduced Glenn Hall to St. Louis, and in no small way that introduction helped to make expansion successful. St. Louis, Missouri, is the most unlikely home to one of the greatest feel-good sports stories of the '60s, and Hall is the most unlikely candidate to receive such a public outpouring of affection. But the fans will not be denied: to them Hall is a hero and his Vezina Trophy award presentation is an excellent excuse to celebrate.

"We want Hall! We want Hall!"

ST. LOUIS HAD SEEN better days. Built along the banks of the mighty Mississippi, it was a bustling metropolis in the 1800s, a crucial port in the expansion west of the U.S. and a vital center for the country's riverway-based commerce. As the United States economy began to rely less on river traffic and more on land shipping, the town quickly evolved into a railroad hub, albeit geographically less significant than the hulking monolith of Chicago to the north. As Chicago grew, St. Louis's economic significance shrank, and by the middle of the 20th century it was well on its way to being a second-class city.

By the 1960s, there were a few bright spots. The city once known as "The Gateway to the West" was home to the Anheuser-Busch Breweries. There was a large aerospace presence in the form of the McDonnell-Douglas Corporation. The recently completed St. Louis Arch was a significant tourist attraction. But the downtown business section of the city had deteriorated badly. Businesses, and therefore jobs, were migrating to the city's outer ring of suburbs. City fathers were hoping that the sparkling new baseball temple, Busch Stadium, built within easy sight of the Arch and just off the edge of downtown itself, would help anchor a resurgence of building and growth in the business district.

Almost 15 miles due west of Busch Stadium stood a zeppelin of a structure, a building that could have been a metaphor for St. Louis itself. When the St. Louis Arena was completed in the late 1920s, it was a state-of-the art facility that seemed limitless in its potential. The cavernous hall of its interior boasted nearly 12,000 seats that arched back from the main floor, angling upward to form a viewing bowl that offered incredible sightlines to any event staged below. The powers-that-were in the Gateway City were sure they'd attract a huge share of the convention business to the building, and that the building would be booked to overflowing with sporting events, such as major boxing cards, figure-skating shows, college basketball tournaments, and perhaps even a team in the fledgling National Hockey League.

But just as Chicago had eclipsed St. Louis in size and importance, Chicago would also erect a structure that would dwarf the Arena in seating capacity and significance. At nearly the same time as the finishing touches were being put on the Arena, the same flourishes were being capped on the Chicago Stadium. More than 15,000 seats were contained within, an NHL franchise had already been secured as a tenant, and the size and location of the city itself made it a preferable draw for the conventions and sporting trade that the Arena was designed to attract.

Finding regular functions for the Arena became a challenge. Hockey would be played there on and off over the years but mostly at the minor-league level, which never came close to filling the building to capacity. Professional basketball tried to stake a claim at one point, but its lifespan was short. Livestock shows drew more visitors than roundball. In a town that had perhaps the most ardent baseball following in the nation, the "hot stove league" of baseball chat took priority during the winter months. The city would get and lose an NFL team. Bowling was popular enough that its Hall of Fame was erected not far from Busch Stadium.

By the mid-'60s, the Arena had fallen into disrepair mostly from sheer neglect. It was an antiquated, bloated barn, a shadow of the once impressive edifice that had stood as a symbol of hope and economic growth. Even the Arena's main tenant, the St. Louis Braves hockey team, would remind St. Louis natives of their inferiority to Chicago. The Braves were the principal farm club for the NHL's mighty Chicago Black Hawks. Chicago always found a way to eclipse St. Louis. If Chicago was the Second City, where did that leave St. Louis?

But for St. Louisians, there was still baseball. And there was no question who held the upper hand there. The St. Louis Cardinals were perennial World Series contenders whereas the Chicago Cubs hadn't been in a Series since the '40s and hadn't won one since Roosevelt, *Theodore* Roosevelt, was in office. St. Louis sports fans were used to the sweltering St. Louis summers, and could cite chapter and verse about the careers of slugger Stan "The Man" Musial and fireballing pitcher Bob Gibson.

You can bet that nearly none of those fans could tell the difference between a slap shot and a backhander. And you could bet the rent that even fewer cared. Fewer that is, until the NHL came to town.

"WE WANT HALL! WE WANT HALL!"

The chorus rings down on a middle-aged man wearing a conservative blue suit. Had you passed him in the hallway on the way to your seat, you might have mistaken him for an accountant or a salesman. You might have thought he'd come to the game straight from work and was ready to loosen his tie, unwind, and enjoy a cold one and the game.

But if you'd taken the time to look closely at his face, you'd have seen something different. You'd have seen scars, the occupational hazards of his trade. You'd have seen the halfmoon mark off the edge of his mouth. You'd have seen the line along his cheek. You would have recognized his eyes, eyes that give him a more than passing resemblance to Roy Rogers, eyes that are keen enough to track 100-mile-per-hour pucks while simultaneously detecting where every man in the wrong-colored sweater is standing.

And if you are familiar at all with the sport in this November of 1969, and especially if you are a St. Louisian, you would never mistake him for just another fan. His name now means as much to you as Musial's and Gibson's. His heroics during the past two seasons in this newly discovered sport of ice hockey have elevated him to legendary status.

He'd spent most of his career stopping pucks in the same Chicago Stadium that helped doom the St. Louis Arena, the same city of Chicago that always had the upper hand on your hometown of St. Louis, the same team that used your own team as a farm club, the team nobody on the NHL team wanted to be exiled to.

But when the NHL found its way to St. Louis against the longest of odds, things began to change. The new owners set to work restoring the building, and the management they hired set to work building a hockey team. The owners poured money into a building that already had a foundation, the management team chose the man in the blue suit as the team's foundation. The owners sold the baseball-mad town on hockey, the man in the blue suit gave them a credible product to sell.

That the man standing at center ice has come to St. Louis from Chicago means a lot. That he speaks openly about preferring St. Louis to Chicago means even more. That he came here at the age of 36, when he should have been content to collect a paycheck and bide his time until his pension kicked in, but plays with All-Star intensity and results earns your admiration. That he has helped put St. Louis on the hockey map with performances that are the envy of athletes ten years his junior earns your devotion.

So if he passed you in the hallway, you would recognize him, because chances are you are there this night in November to honor him. He retired at the end of the previous season to the tranquillity and calm of the farm he so often spoke of in near-poetic terms. The pressures both mental and physical had finally spelled "enough." The quiet man from western Canada, the man the St. Louis Blues had "stolen" from Chicago, to the Hawks' great chagrin and the Blues' great glory, is being presented with the Vezina Trophy this night, a trophy symbolic of goalkeeping excellence.

He returned from the farm for this event, returned to the scene of his final triumphs.

"We want Hall! We want Hall!"

You are screaming the chant at the top of your lungs, hoping to exhort him back to the ice, hoping to see him flash his trademark butterfly style at the edge of the crease, swallowing pucks, leaving teams frustrated in his wake.

Two years ago, you wouldn't have known a slap shot from a backhander. Two years ago, you wouldn't have known the greatest goalie who ever played the game from an accountant.

But tonight you know the difference.

"We want Hall! We want Hall!"

I

The Winter of Youth

AT FIRST GLANCE, you would think the populace of the tiny burg of
Humboldt, Saskatchewan, would have absolutely nothing in common with
the citizenry of the three enormous American cities where Glenn Hall would
spend his National Hockey League career: Detroit, Chicago, and St. Louis.
In 1931, Humboldt was a town of about 2,000 whereas Detroit, Chicago, and
St. Louis measured their populations in the hundreds of thousands. Humboldt was a branch line railroad town between Saskatoon and Winnipeg;
Detroit was already the automotive capital of the world, Chicago the railroad
hub of the United States, and St. Louis still a major river port and rail center.
Humboldt was a serene geographic dot in the vast western plains of Canada;
Detroit, Chicago, and St. Louis were sprawling metropolises, bustling with
activity from daybreak to the wee hours. But the people inhabiting all four
locations had some important experiences in common, the very same factors
that would help to shape Glenn Hall as a person and an athlete, factors that
would indeed have a profound effect on all who experienced them.

By 1931, North America was in the grip of the deepest economic depression the modern world had ever known. The reaches of the Great Depression
affected families as deeply in Humboldt as they did in Detroit, Chicago, and
St. Louis. The populations of all four towns found jobs to be scarce. Families
did whatever they could to keep food on the table, and tomorrow's meal was
seldom guaranteed. The challenges that Henry and Agnes (née Cruikshank)
Hall faced when they welcomed their second son, Glenn Henry, into the world
on October 3 of that year, were exactly the same as those faced by couples
raising families in the huge cities Glenn would play professional hockey in.

Henry Hall worked for the Canadian National Railways (CNR) as an engineer. In those days, engineers were known as "hogheads" for their hard-nosed, no-nonsense approach to their jobs. In a world that relied on the railroad for almost everything, it would seem that no job would be more secure than the one in which Henry was employed, even during hard economic times. But the CNR operated on a strict seniority system, and for almost a decade, his job assignments were scarce. To keep his wife, eldest son, Doug, and Glenn fed and clothed, Henry worked an assortment of jobs throughout the '30s, the longest of which saw him driving a cream truck. If the Halls felt any extra economic pressure raising their family, they never betrayed it to their sons, both of whom recall a peaceful upbringing in a home where a voice was never raised. "We were dirt poor in the 'Dirty '30s,' I suppose," recalled Glenn, "but we didn't really know it and we never went hungry."

As tough as times were financially, children of that era held something in common, no matter the size of the town or the family income, that offered a huge advantage over the children of today and the superior material privileges they enjoy. In the '30s, there was little or nothing in the way of organized sports. When kids were sent out of the house to play, that's what they did. They *played*. Parents were preoccupied with earning enough for tomorrow's supper, so the thought of supervised play time was ludicrous. Although parents were burdened with the sad reality of the Depression, they were also free of the real worry today's parents endure when they leave their children unsupervised. Kids who grew up in the '30s organized their own play time, invented games to play, made up the rules to play by, and improvised any equipment that was required. In the inner city of Chicago, a boy who wanted to roller-skate crushed two cans and molded them to his shoes. In St. Louis, woolen gloves became baseball mitts. In Detroit, long bits of string were collected and rolled tightly together to fashion a baseball. In Humboldt, two-by-six planks were placed around the slough to frame the local version of a rink. Frozen horse dung became pucks. Necessity was the mother of invention, and kids adapted without the "benefit" of a coach or a scoreboard.

Like millions of youthful Canadians, Glenn Hall's first hockey was shinny played on that local slough. The deep freeze of the forty-below Saskatchewan winters ensured that ice was a constant presence, and not too long after learning to walk, Glenn was on that ice. From the beginning, it was apparent that he was an exceptional athlete, and childhood friends and teammates remember Glenn as a skilled forward right from the age of seven. School recesses were spent on the pond, and while in school, the kids enjoyed the luxury of playing with a real puck. The slabs of lumber that the teachers used to create a rink did little to keep errant shots out of snowbanks, so the players stayed conscious of keeping all shots along the ice. If a puck was lost in the snow-bank, the search to retrieve it would eat up too much precious playing time.

"We played shinny and learned how to stickhandle. We had to learn be-cause there weren't more than two pucks in the whole town and if you had one of them, boy, you did a trick to keep it. *That's* learning how to stick-handle," said Hall. Learning creativity without the fear of making a mistake is a lesson today's coaches would do well to accept. The winters were so cold that on occasion, one of those oh-so-precious pucks would crack in half. Undaunted, the boys from Humboldt would nail it back together and the game would continue.

As with most Canadians, Glenn's first exposure to the NHL came via the airwaves. Game nights would be spent huddled around the radio, listening to the exploits of the Toronto Maple Leafs. Unless you spoke French, chances were that if you were a Canadian citizen you were a Leaf fan because of that radio exposure. The earliest hockey photograph of Glenn shows him in his forward gear, grinning widely and proudly wearing a Maple Leaf sweater.

There were two local grade schools in Humboldt: the public school that Glenn attended and the Catholic school, St. Gabriel's. Jim Kacourek, whose father worked with Glenn's at the CNR and who attended St. Gabriel's, was a friend of the Hall brothers. Jim recalled the winters of their youth.

"Saturday was hockey day," said Kacourek. "The two schools would play against each other and we'd play all day long. One of our teachers, R. J. Ward, would come out and serve as sort of a coach. Those were what you'd call the Peewee years. We formed a traveling team by combining the Catholic and public schools, and we'd play against the surrounding towns. Glenn was one of our best players, although he was still a forward. I'm convinced that if Glenn had stayed a forward, he'd have still made the NHL. That's how good a skater he was."

Glenn's brother, Doug, remembered that Glenn was much more passion-ate about recess than he was about his other time spent at school: "He wasn't an enthusiastic student. His grades were good, of course, but I don't think he ever put that great an effort toward his schooling. He was very intelligent though, but quietly so. He did have a great feeling for Shakespeare, and could quote the soliloquies accurately. But his real academic inspiration came from the poetry of Robert Service. He knew Service's writings word for word."

Robert William Service was Canada's most beloved poet in the early 1900s. A British citizen who tired of his family's banking business, he opted for a life of adventure that began when he hopped a tramp freighter to

Canada. Years spent in the Yukon and Klondike as the gold rush ebbed inspired him, and his first book, *The Songs of Sourdough*, sold widely. Service, of Scottish extraction like Glenn, captured the aura of the Far North in his work, and in turn captured the imagination of a generation of readers who became enthralled with the romance of the wild open land. Glenn's passion for Service's works reflected his own deep feelings for the open spaces of the West, a passion that would stay with him throughout his life. Like so many other Canadians of his day, Glenn could cite you chapter and verse of "The Shooting of Dan McGrew":

> *A bunch of boys were whoopin it up in the Malamute Saloon;*
> *The kid that handles the music-box was hitting a jag-time tune;*
> *Back of the bar, in a solo game, sat Dangerous Dan McGrew,*
> *And watching his luck was his light-o'-love, the lady that's known as Lou.*

Perhaps Hall's lack of overt participation in school stemmed from the slight speech impediment that gave his s's a soft "th" sound. Childhood friend Murray Parker, whose father, Leo, would be Glenn's first real coach, tells of the ribbing Glenn took for his lisp, "We'd always ask him to pronounce photosynthesis."

To respond to the teasing, Glenn developed a razor wit that all who know him well mark as one of his greatest attributes. Longtime friend and Peewee teammate Graham Crossman remembers Glenn as "a joy to be around. He had a tremendous sense of humor and was always pulling stunts on people."

The Hall brothers share some responsibility for undercutting Crossman's potential goalkeeping career. One morning, the boys found a discarded mattress and immediately recognized its potential as goal pads. They cut, pulled, and sewed until they'd fashioned a set of pads for Graham and convinced him to put them on for a round of shinny. Glenn picks up the story: "We put the pads on him and before he takes a single shot, Graham says, 'Now make sure you keep the shots low.' We say, 'Of course, don't worry about it.' So naturally the very first shot is up in the air and catches him something fierce. We had to 'borrow' a toboggan and cart him back to his house. Now as I recall I was all for knocking on the front door and telling his mother how he ended up unable to walk, but I think Doug convinced me to just rap on the window and leave him there on the toboggan as we ran away. Of course, it ended up not being that serious an injury. I mean, he did eventually have children . . ."

It was while playing Peewee hockey that Glenn took his first step inside the crease. Glenn was still a forward and the team captain, an honor of course, but not very meaningful if your team doesn't have a goalie.

Since there was no real coach of the team, the captain was relied upon to know the responsibilities of his teammates and to direct them when necessary. Years later, this experience would show itself in Glenn's almost extrasensory abilities to anticipate where a play was going and to read the ice in front of him. But his immediate concern was solving the crisis at hand: the team had no goalie. Glenn recalled, "I asked one of the guys, and then the next ten and they all said no." So, responding to his sense of duty as a leader, Glenn donned the big pads and not long thereafter was bitten by the goaltending bug. "I found it to be enjoyable. It's such an interesting position after all," he said.

STILL VERY SMALL for his age, Glenn did not take up much of the net, but because he was such a masterful skater his physical size was never an issue. The other talent apparent to those around him was his ability to catch pucks. The games of shinny helped hone that skill during the winter, when catching pucks without a real glove was the norm. During the summer, the boys would become accomplished baseball players. Brother Doug was better at the great American pastime, but Glenn would flash his glove skills at first base and occasionally in the outfield. If it was summer and it was Wednesday, Humboldt was shut down for the local ball tournaments. The same could be said for holiday weekends, when the local team would travel to tournaments in the surrounding towns. For the Hall brothers, summer also meant trips to their grandparents' farm, and it was there that Glenn first got a taste of the idyllic farming life that he would grow to enjoy immensely.

But it was during the harsh winter months that Glenn began to make a name for himself. He'd stepped up to the Juvenile level (the rough equivalent of today's Midget hockey) by the age of 14, his head barely at crossbar level when he stood straight up. By this time, he'd developed a full love for the position and eagerly awaited the next game. "It would be hard to sleep when you knew you had a game the next day," said Hall. "I was so excited just to play that I'd get completely worked up. You know it was just so great to think that we were going to travel to another town to play."

Still, playing in the NHL was nothing more than a pipe dream, and Hall never recalls thinking that far ahead: "I never even considered making a career out of it. And as far as the NHL was concerned, that was totally out of the question." The only exposure kids outside NHL cities got to the big time was over the airwaves or in the newspapers. Playing Juvenile for the town's team was plenty exciting. But soon enough, the drama would increase. The Humboldt Indians were the local Junior A team. Murray Parker, four years

Glenn's senior, and Murray's brother, Bob, were playing for the Indians when they lost their goalie, giving Hall his first real break.

"Halfway through the season, one of our players had gotten into some sort of a scrape with one of the locals," Parker recalled. "Our coach, Don McIntyre, kicked him off the team. Well, as it turns out, that player was rooming with our goalie. Our goalie tells McIntyre that if the player goes, he goes. My brother and I tell McIntyre to let him go and bring Glenn up. He was already better than our goalie anyway so we felt we were much better off with both of the guys gone."

For Glenn to play Junior while underaged, his parents had to give permission for him to do so, and with very little reluctance Hank and Agnes signed on. According to Parker, Glenn rewarded Coach McIntyre with a shutout in his debut performance. Hank was a devout fan, never missing a game, but it was tough on Agnes to watch her barefaced son face the hazards of the position. Glenn finished the season with the Indians and played the next entire year with the club. By the end of that second season, Hall was making a name for himself. Although he was late developing physically, he'd been inching his way toward his eventual height of 5 feet 11 inches, but he was still rail-thin. It was clear to his teammates that he had a special talent, but as remote as Humboldt was, Hall was never scouted by an NHL squad.

Glenn's second break came when a Detroit Red Wing scout gave Bob Parker some registration forms for an upcoming regional camp the Wings were putting on in Saskatoon. Parker handed an extra paper to Hall who filled it out and tagged along with Murray and Bob to the tryouts. The experience was an eye-opener, as established pros such as Black Jack Stewart and a young phenom named Gordie Howe participated in the scrimmages. The environment and the presence of NHL talent gave Glenn a dose of the butterflies, but they disappeared once he stepped on the ice. Being on the ice, and facing the shots, actually relaxed him.

Still, if you were a non-scouted attendee, you had to do something in this type of tryout to get noticed. For Glenn, that something happened via the combination of bad equipment and the astounding hand quickness that would become a Hall trademark. Glenn was given bulky, ill-fitting gloves by the Wings to use during the camp. During one of the scrimmages, his oversize catch glove slipped off his hand just as the opposing team was on the attack. One of the players lofted a shot toward the upper half of the net, and Hall thrust out his bare left hand, snaring the disc in mid-air. That's the type of thing that'll get you noticed, and Glenn was now on the Red Wing radar

screen while the player who'd been stopped was in for some merciless ribbing. Red Wing scout Fred Pinkney was in charge of the camp, and he was
impressed enough to phone the man who made all the decisions for the Red
Wings, the legendary Jack Adams.

Jack Adams had literally built the Detroit Red Wings. An accomplished
goal scorer as a player, he skated for two Stanley Cup winners before retiring
to coach the then Detroit Cougars. Adams built his franchise from the farm
out, investing a great deal of time in constructing a reliable feeder system. His
efforts took time but paid off handsomely. Six years after taking over, Detroit
won the first of 12 regular-season championships under his stewardship and
would win the Stanley Cup seven times. Adams was a product of his times,
and he ran the organization with an iron fist. In the days of athletes as inden-
tured servants, Jack Adams perfectly fit the mold of plantation boss. When
Adams took Pinkney's call about the young goalkeeping find, he had no way
of knowing how important that call would be, and Glenn Hall had no way of
knowing how intertwined his hockey future would be with the whims of the
man who would be known as "Trader Jack."

ESSAY: THE GOALKEEPER

If you cut to the chase, I would wager that almost every goalkeeper was first drawn to the position by the equipment. There's something absolutely mesmerizing about the pads and gloves, and they elicit a certain "moth to the flame" attraction for kids with stars in their eyes. But, as almost everyone who plays hockey has taken a turn in the goal, when it comes to actually becoming a goalkeeper, many are called, few are chosen. The few who endure past the aesthetics of the gear are bitten by the intricacies of the challenge the position presents. And the challenge is more intense and varied than any other position in all of sport.

The stories of goalkeepers whose nerves were shattered by the demands of the position are legion. Bill Durnan quit while still an All-Star, Wilf Cude threw a steak at his wife after hearing her levy a perceived criticism, Gerry McNeil walked out in mid-playoff, Roger Crozier's ulcers forced him to the sidelines mid-season, Terry Sawchuk walked out on Boston, and on and on. These stories make for good press and advance the legends and hockey lore, but they only obscure the real great story, which is not why goalies quit, but rather why it is they keep answering the bell.

Let's start by looking not at the equipment itself, but at what happens when you put it on. There's a transformation that begins, and it's something the athlete can feel. Before you strap on the leg pads, you could almost pass for any forward in the room. You're wearing your hockey pants, your skates are tied snugly, the long sleeves of your white, quilted long underwear tops stretch over your arms down to your wrists. But as you reach down and start to buckle those pads around the toes of your skates, you are no longer indistinguishable from your peers. By the time both pads are fastened securely to your legs, the transformation has begun in earnest.

The mind of the goalie changes now, thoughts of the game are inescapable. Visions of the attack you are sure to face dance in your head and . . . there is fear. The fear is real, and no amount of padding can protect you from it, because the fear almost never has to do with any form of physical threat.

The fear is of failing, of suffering the indignity of being beaten, of not being at your best. The goalie must wrestle with his mind as he pulls on his arm pads and chest protector and finally covers them with the sweater. Goalkeeping is such an extreme mental contest that the goalie's true priority is not mustering the courage to face 100-mile-per-hour shots, but rather mastering his own mind, taming his thoughts, training them to focus on only those that will create the right inner force for him to excel.

The athlete you see in the crease bears no resemblance to the man who walked into the rink that night. As he fields his warm-up shots, searching for a "feel" for the puck, he is now in a deep crouch, the rectangular glove gripping the thick goal stick, the extended first baseman's mitt swinging gently at his side, ready to make snakelike strikes at flying discs. His concentration is now so intense that he only has the vaguest sense of noise. His eyes become so focused it's as if he's borrowed against the sense of hearing to heighten his eyesight to superhuman acuity.

When the game starts, the goalie must learn to combine instinct with anticipation. The line between those factors is finer than razor-thin. A half second of bad anticipation can make you look like a fool, total reliance on human reflex can accomplish the same. Familiarity with an opponent establishes trends that you can defend, but what happens when he catches you by surprise—if this time he goes against his history and dekes to the backhand?

Then comes the breakaway. The ultimate one-on-one challenge. As the player moves in, the thoughts flood your mind. Goalies are taught a checklist of the fundamentals: challenge, stay square, never make the first move. As you fend off those thoughts knowing that entertaining any of them compromises the concentration absolutely necessary to win, you are revealed.

Yes, under 40 pounds of equipment you are stripped and revealed. Answer this challenge with your best effort and you are courageous, worthy of the honor of being a member of the Goalkeepers' Union. Second-guess yourself, admit you don't really believe in your talent by committing early and damn yourself to the stares of accusing teammates and worse, a sleepless night of second-guessing yourself, wondering what it is about you that made you become a goalkeeper.

But, oh, make that save! Feel the thick *thwack* of the puck being snared in the webbing of your catcher and see the scowl of frustration on the forward who has been denied. At that very instant, you understand the position and why you were meant to play it. The rush fills your insides with an indescribable joy, but unlike the goal scorer you cannot lift your hands in the air and rejoice outwardly, because you don't have the luxury of celebration. You must discipline your mind, steer it, rein it in, control it, and understand you are exactly as good as the next shot . . . and ultimately the shot after that, and the shot after that.

And finally, there is the element of time. That breakaway might have taken six seconds of real time from beginning to end. But for the goalkeeper, it seemed like minutes. Your mind has the ability to slow the attacks, you see the puck carrier, you sense where his passing options are, but you cannot cheat toward them. Your eyes and your mind work in perfect sync. It is when that happens, that perfect melding of body and mind, that you understand there is no other position to play, no other position that can create the precarious balance between excellence and mediocrity, no other position that is so essential to a team's success.

Everyone knows the goalie is the last line of defense.

But only the goalie understands the addiction.

2

Go East, Young Man

IN THE DAYS OF the Original Six hockey teams, the development of players was not left to draft or chance. Each of the top teams owned their own farm clubs all the way down to the Junior level, a system that was far superior from the standpoint of the National Hockey League teams.

First, the moment an NHL team induced a young player to sign with its Junior club, the team owned his rights until it deemed him expendable. For that player, there was no such thing as negotiating for a better deal when contract talks came up by using interest from a competing team as leverage. The young players themselves were glad for any crumbs thrown their way, hardly believing their great luck at potentially being paid to do something they loved so dearly. Second, at the farm clubs the players were coached by men hired by the NHL team, men who represented on-site the philosophy of that particular organization. Whatever skills and traits the organization thought were important were taught. Finally, because of the direct ties to the big club, the players were given a sense of what the sweaters they were being groomed to wear stood for. An important loyalty to the organization was being bred, and with it, a deep passion that was sure to induce an athlete's best efforts on a consistent basis. That type of loyalty exists only in lip service in today's world of free-agent vagabonds.

Jack Adams had built one of the NHL's most efficient farm systems for the Detroit Red Wings, and the foundation of his feeder program was located conveniently, just across the river from Detroit in the Canadian town of Windsor. The Junior A Spitfires were a consistently strong club in the vaunted Ontario Hockey Association, a league that was one of the richest breeding grounds for eventual NHL talent.

In the 1948–49 season, the Spitfires had fielded a particularly good team, which had been saddled with subpar goalkeeping. Jimmy Skinner, an affable Manitoban, helmed the squad, and in the fall of 1949, he made the trip from Windsor to the Red Wing main training camp held in Sault Ste. Marie, Michigan, to help out Detroit head coach Tommy Ivan. Wing scout Fred Pinkney had already informed Ivan about the goalkeeping "find," the skinny kid from Humboldt, they'd made in their Saskatoon camp. Skinner, still in the dark about his goaltending situation, had no sooner walked into the rink than he ran into Adams.

"Jimmy, what's wrong? You look worried," said the crusty general manager who ironically liked to be called Jolly Jack.

"I am worried. I've got a good team and a bad goalie and I don't want to go through another year like last season," replied Skinner.

Adams smiled and patted Skinner on the shoulder, "Don't worry, Jimmy. Tommy [Ivan] says we got a real good one out west who'll do the job for you."

When training camp started for the Spitfires and Hall took his turn in the cage, Skinner was not initially impressed. "Glenn wasn't what you'd call a real practice goalie, and I was plenty worried," Skinner recalled. "He sure didn't look great in those first practices. Tommy and Jack kept telling me not to worry, but I did. I did until the exhibition games started and then I saw what they were talking about.

"Right away, you could see that Glenn was different," explains Skinner. "Nothing like [Red Wing goalie Harry] Lumley, or [Boston Bruin Frank] Brimsek who were good position goalies who stood up well, and nothing like [Terry] Sawchuk who was good on the angles. Glenn was a reflex goalie. And he was the best reflex goalie. He had the best catch hand I ever saw. We didn't try to change his style. Oh, I'd remind him every so often to watch his angles, not give up the short side and the like. When I got Glenn, the only thing he needed was to grow up. You know, he was just a young kid, and like all the other Junior players, he just had to grow up a little. But he was a very good young man, respectful, and a team player all the way."

Glenn recalls Skinner fondly: "I really liked Jimmy. He taught us a lot about being prepared. He set a great example. Before and after a game he was loose and relaxed. But during a game he was focused. He had that 'rah rah' college mentality and he was very positive." Hall also remembers the pointers that Skinner gave him. His stick was always to be on the ice, he was to stand up as often as possible, and he was never to play a puck that was going to miss the net. He could live with those if he had to, but when Skinner took exception to Glenn's handling low shots to his catch side with his catch glove,

Glenn questioned him. Says Hall, "I asked him why I shouldn't do it that way. I was good with the glove and I was stopping the shots. He said, 'Well, what if you let one in?' and I said he should talk to me *after* I let one in."

Glenn did not let too many in that first year in Windsor, posting a 31–11–1 record for the Spits, good enough for a second-place finish. Windsor defeated the Toronto Marlies in the first round of the playoffs before succumbing to Guelph. Although his play was earning raves within the organization, it was during this season that he began a pre-game behavior that would take on legendary proportions and was nearly universally misunderstood as the actions of someone who hated what he was doing.

Almost from the beginning, Glenn understood the importance of preparation. Goalies are notorious for searching out and retaining successful pre-game rituals. Some, such as putting on one's equipment in the same order, or wearing a lucky T-shirt, are based on good luck; others, including having the same pre-game meal or going through the proper stretching routine, are based on physical preparation but all are essential for mental preparedness. For Hall, "getting up" for a game was never a problem. In fact, the opposite was true. From the time Glenn had first put on the pads back in Humboldt, the prospect of playing was so exciting to him that he could barely sleep the night before a game. Now playing at the Junior level, that excitement had multiplied tenfold. "My biggest problem was that I was ready for a 7:00 p.m. game at noon," he said.

It was very early during that first year of Junior that the excitement began to manifest itself in a most unique way. "I was just so excited to go out and play that it made me throw up," he recalled. "I thought of it as a strength." So, just as any other pre-game ritual is established with an athlete, thus did Glenn's vomiting become as natural a part of his pre-game as tightening the straps on his goal pads. Throwing up became nothing more than a sign that he was ready to be at his best. The sickness before most every game was a by-product of his need to gain complete focus and intensity, but was it born out of the sheer excitement and desire to play. It never resulted from fear or dread.

"I just built myself up to an unbelievable peak . . ." claimed Glenn. "I was a little afraid of being hurt badly, but I was scared to death of playing poorly. Five minutes before a game or between periods I didn't hear what a coach was saying because I was in total preparation. All I would be thinking about is what I had to do.

"If I weren't up for a game enough to get sick before it, I felt I wouldn't play well. It was no big deal. I could have a glass of water and throw it up while it was still cool . . . I had to get down for games rather than up. I took the game too seriously. On game day, I ate only because I had to, and then I'd throw up at the rink."

The excitement would not end once Glenn stepped on the ice. The emotion stayed with him after the first drop of the puck, but he could ill afford to leave his crease at every face-off and make a dash to the bathroom. So he learned to choke back the nausea during game time, taking his cue, oddly enough, from a sport in which goaltending is illegal. "I controlled it by deep breathing," he remembered. "I learned that from watching basketball players on the foul line."

When successful play followed the vomiting, the sickness became as essential to his excellence as his gloves and pads. This bears out Hall's contention that the game is 90 percent mental. Says Glenn, "It's about preparation, getting the mind set properly. I don't particularly care for kids coming to the rink and saying, 'I hope I play well.' They should be saying, 'I should play well. I've practiced well, I know the opposition, I'm in good shape, I've looked after myself, I've eaten properly.' It's no guarantee that you will play well, but at least you're prepared."

Glenn's Windsor teammate Glen Skov, whose family Glenn billeted with and who would go on to a distinguished NHL career with three different teams, remembers Hall's demeanor before games well. "We all felt sorry for him," declared Skov, "you know, it wasn't put on. He was genuinely that nervous before games. Of course, we were all nervous. You should be nervous before a game because that helps to keep you stimulated. But Glenn was really affected . . . we felt bad for him."

In an era when there were no goalie coaches, netminders were self-taught. They developed their styles through trial and error, observing how others were stopping pucks and adapting those methods to their own game. Up until that first season in Windsor, Glenn had never seen so much as a single NHL game. But now, just a short drive away from the Red Wings' home arena, the Detroit Olympia, Hall could finally see the big league game firsthand and improve his own game by watching what was bringing the NHLers their success.

The NHL of the late '40s was full of role models for Hall to learn from. Harry "Apple Cheeks" Lumley was in his fifth full season guarding the Red Wing cage at the tender age of 24. In fact, Lumley became the NHL's youngest goalie ever when he made his debut for the Wings in an emergency call-up situation in 1943. Lumley had led the league in games played three of those five years and in shutouts once. But up until this, the 1949–50 season, he'd been frustrated in his bid to lead his team to a Stanley Cup. Bill Durnan, hockey's ambidextrous wonder, was in goal for the Montreal Canadiens and

Turk Broda, in the middle of a Hall of Fame career, played for the Toronto Maple Leafs. A little-remembered goalie for the Boston Bruins, Jack Gelineau, would be the NHL's Calder Rookie of the Year Trophy winner. Gelineau was the first goalie to make it into the league directly out of college, having played for McGill University. Although his career was short-lived (he played the next year for the Bruins before being relegated to the minors, resurfacing to play two games for the Chicago Black Hawks in 1954 in his final NHL appearances), Hall was impressed with him, especially how well he used his blocker to angle shots toward the corners. But none of these goalies would have the influence on Glenn that the goalie for the New York Rangers did.

Chuck Rayner was an immensely popular figure in New York where he'd earned the sobriquet "Bonnie Prince Charlie." Like Hall, Rayner was a native Saskatchewan. At 5 feet 11 inches and 190 pounds, Rayner had a stocky build that gave him an aura of physical strength. His round, expressive face featured thick black eyebrows and was capped with wavy dark hair that was seldom out of place. He'd posted seven shutouts the previous year, with a goals-against average of 2.90 for a Ranger team that finished dead last with a scant 18 wins. He tossed six more shutouts in 1949–50 and was almost singlehandedly responsible for the Rangers' surprising fourth-place finish and return to the playoffs. Rayner's in-season heroics earned him the league's Hart Trophy as the most valuable player, at that time only the second goalie so honored in NHL history. He topped his regular-season play with an incredible playoff performance, as the Rangers upset the Canadiens in the first round and found themselves matched up against Lumley and the Wings in the finals. Because a circus had been booked into Madison Square Garden, the Rangers did not play a single home game in the finals and still pushed the Wings to a seventh contest, the finale a double overtime affair that Detroit eked out. Renowned for his great stickhandling and his very aggressive bent position, Rayner would rightfully be enshrined in Hockey's Hall of Fame.

He first crossed paths with Glenn when Hall and his friend Billy Tibbs, another young goalie, made the trek to a summer resort called "The Hockey Haven," which Rayner owned with NHL goalie "Sugar" Jim Henry. Glenn had been spending the summer after his first Windsor season in Winnipeg, picking up extra money working for Coach Skinner, when he and Tibbs decided to drive across the province to the western Ontario region known as "Lake of the Woods." There, in the town of Kenora, they sought out Rayner to pick his brain about goalkeeping. Glenn doesn't remember much of the conversation that ensued, but he does recall introducing himself to Rayner, who was in the middle of some repair work at the resort. "Many years later Chuck and I were at a function in Saskatchewan and I told him I never saw anyone put a hammer down faster than he did," said a chuckling Hall.

Glenn never forgot that Rayner and Henry, who were busy when the boys arrived unannounced, picked up beers, sat and gave the two wide-eyed youngsters a part of their day, sharing tips about the game. During his playing days and long afterward, Glenn would likewise always welcome inquisitive fans who took the time to seek him out.

But it was from his perch in the standing-room area of the Olympia that Hall learned the most from Rayner. Chuck was extremely adept at passing the puck, as well as deflecting hard shots to the corners with his stick with what appeared to be just a flick of the wrist. Hall couldn't do likewise because he simply wasn't physically strong enough. His desire to achieve those same results soon figured prominently as his own signature style of play evolved.

"I studied them all very carefully," Hall said. "I could get a close look . . . at all the other NHL goalies. I always tried to figure out what made them successful. I used to like the way Broda would cut down the angles. I suppose I would have liked someone to talk hockey with. Lumley and Sawchuk were in goal for Detroit [while Glenn was playing Junior]. If they knew anything about how to stop the puck, they certainly weren't going to tell me because they knew what my intentions were. It was definitely not to their advantage to help me."

Right: Glenn (right) receives the Jack Dent Award as the most valuable player on the Windsor Spitfires. Helping him hold the trophy is Glen Skov of the Detroit Red Wings, the Spitfires' parent team.

Below: Glenn (left) and brother Doug proudly sporting their Toronto Maple Leaf sweaters on the pond at Humboldt.

Facing page: Glenn as an Edmonton Flyer.

Above: Pauline and Glenn's wedding portrait. The beginning of the most important team in Glenn's life.

3

Taking the Next Step

IT WAS THE SUMMER OF 1950, and the Detroit Red Wings had just won the Stanley Cup. As valiant an effort as Chuck Rayner had put in for the New York Rangers, Wing goalie Harry Lumley had found a way to win. For his efforts, he was rewarded by the Detroit organization in a manner that would be repeated five years down the road with the man who would succeed Lumley in goal.

"I played softball that summer [after winning the Cup] and we were leaving the summer cottage . . . to drive to a game . . ." he remembered. "I was just coming to a washout in the road and was about to slow down . . . when all of a sudden, at that precise moment, I heard on the car radio that I'd been traded to Chicago . . . I did not have a clue the trade was coming, I mean, after all, we had just won the Stanley Cup. Plus, it was upsetting going from a first-place club to a last-place club . . . I hated every minute in Chicago. I would sooner have gone to fight in the Korean War!"

What Lumley heard on the airwaves on July 30, 1950, was that general manager Jack Adams had included him in a blockbuster nine-player trade. Black Jack Stewart, Al Dewsbury, Don Morrison, and Pete Babando would accompany Lumley to the Windy City. In return, Adams acquired goalie Jim Henry, Gaye Stewart, Metro Prustai, and shot-blocking defenseman Bob Goldham. Adams did not trade for Henry to replace Lumley. Instead, Adams was positive that the young goalie who had tended goal for Indianapolis the year before, the young man who Red Wing organizational insiders were raving about, one Terry Sawchuk, was ready for the big time. Sawchuk played in seven games for the Wings the previous year, winning four impressively. Henry would move down to Indianapolis to replace Sawchuk, where he and his National Hockey League experience would be close at hand, just in case Sawchuk faltered.

Wing coach Tommy Ivan confirmed that the primary impetus for the trade was Sawchuk's readiness, but also that Ivan and Adams recognized what they had in Glenn Hall. "[Jim] Henry was insurance for Terry, yes," said Ivan, "but he also made less than Harry. So we had a thriftier deal than if we had just brought Terry up and moved Harry down to the farm. But no small part of this whole deal was that we knew Glenn would be ready to step up in a year, so Henry would hold the fort at Indianapolis for a year until Glenn was ready to take over there."

Despite Glenn's first-year Junior success, Doug Hall recalled that people back home still doubted that his brother would reach hockey's pinnacle. "There was definitely a 'nobody makes the NHL' sentiment among the townspeople," the older Hall remembered. "But my parents stayed very encouraging." The town's sentiment was likely bolstered by the experience of another Hall, cousin Harold, who was a highly skilled skater. Harold signed with the Rangers, but the feeling was that he lacked the requisite grit to make it, and he left that organization after only two weeks.

During his second season of junior hockey at Windsor, Hall would get a chance to watch Sawchuk closely. Glenn had already taken note of Sawchuk's unique stance. In an era when goalies stood relatively erect to face a rush, Sawchuk played with a great break in his knees, leaning forward so extremely that it looked as if his chin was scraping the top of his pads. Glenn incorporated this stance, dubbed the "gorilla crouch," into his own style. "I found by looking at Sawchuk that it was impossible to move with the knees straight," said Hall. "His knees were bent, and he could move like nobody else did. I learned a lot from him."

Glenn continued to experiment with the stance. He began to bend his knees even more, but whereas Sawchuk kept his ankles relatively close together, Glenn began to widen his stance a bit both at the knees and the skates. "I found I could get to the posts much quicker," he noted. His balance also improved. This combination of great balance from his evolving stance and the terrific skating ability he'd mastered back in Humboldt were key factors in what would eventually become a revolutionary approach to goalkeeping.

Any lingering doubts about Glenn's destiny began to be erased that second year of Junior in Windsor. Glenn recorded his second consecutive season of over 30 wins and led the Ontario Hockey Association in shutouts with six. His efforts garnered him the Red Tilson Award as the league's most valuable player. Hall is as proud of that award as he is of any individual honor he received in the NHL. "That's quite something you know when you think about it," he said. "There were an awful lot of fine players in the league that year, so that was really quite the special honor."

Exactly how big a splash did Glenn make during those Junior days? "He should have won it [the MVP award] the year before as well," stated Coach Skinner.

When Glenn returned to Humboldt in the off-season, he cut quite a figure. Handsome with his boyish face and thick brown hair, intelligent, and on the cusp of a professional hockey career, he had the young ladies talking. But it was another asset that particularly caught the eye of one of those young ladies, a pretty, petite nursing student named Pauline Patrick. "He had a car," she said, only half kidding.

Pauline Patrick was a pistol. Born in Kelvington, Saskatchewan, she grew up on her family's farm. The daughter of Carl and Margaret Patrick, and sister of Isobelle, Peter, Michael, Patrick, and Gene, Pauline enjoyed playing hockey and listening to it on the radio with her father. If Glenn could be described as equal parts Roy Rogers, for his love of the West as well as the physical resemblance about the eyes, and Will Rogers, for his wit and keen sense of observation, Pauline is equal parts Katharine Hepburn, independent with a stinging sense of humor, and Annie Oakley, strong, determined, and with plenty of fight. "A lot of tough guys came from Kelvington," she would say. "Barry Melrose, Joe Kocur, Wendel Clark . . . and me."

A child of the Depression era, Pauline had a sense of her family's poverty, and on trips to town as a youth, she would ask to be dropped off from her family's horse-drawn wagon a half mile out of town so people wouldn't notice what "we didn't have. But we always had enough to eat."

After graduating from high school, she would leave Kelvington for Humboldt, having decided to become a nurse. "Nurses always seemed to be having such a good time, and they always had boyfriends. That sounded pretty good to me."

Humboldt was home to the closest nursing school, which was run out of the Catholic hospital. She entered the school with great excitement, until she saw the list of rules that the girls had to follow, including a strict curfew. "I saw that and I thought to myself, 'Well, if I stay a month . . .' That month turned into three years. I found that I loved helping people. We had a great feeling of togetherness there. It was kind of like a sorority. If one of us went out on a date, the only thing we'd wear that we owned was our underwear. We'd lend dresses and blouses to each other all the time. Those three years were some of the best of my life."

Pauline had heard about Glenn through some of the nurses in town, and as it happened they had relatives in common. Glenn's uncle had been married to Pauline's aunt. But things kept coming back to that car. "The hospital was a mile out of town and that's a tough walk every day," said Pauline. "So the fact he had a car was important . . . at first."

They dated throughout that spring and summer, but neither thought things were getting serious. When Glenn left for training camp in the fall, they agreed to write to each other. No one would have guessed that a long and rewarding life together would be in their cards.

TOMMY IVAN AND JACK ADAMS had pegged their goalkeeping situation perfectly. Terry Sawchuk was a revelation as a rookie, playing in all 70 games for the Wings, winning 44, posting 11 shutouts, making the First All-Star team, and winning the Calder Trophy as the NHL's rookie of the year. The only blemish on his record was the Wings' upset loss in the first round of the playoffs. Jim Henry had a solid year at Indy and Hall was brilliant in Junior hockey.

Toward the end of training camp in the fall of '51, Adams and Ivan fully committed to developing Glenn by selling off Henry's rights to Boston and installing Hall at the farm club in Indianapolis, then of the American Hockey League. Glenn remembered what it was like to get the news that he would be assigned to that squad. "I was elated to be going to the AHL," he said. "That meant I was going to play professional hockey."

That same year, Detroit began sponsoring another minor-league team in Edmonton, sending many of their top prospects there. Hall, now the number two goalie in the organization, was assigned to Indy because it was closer geographically and it would be easier to get him to an NHL city in case Sawchuk was hurt. The 1951–52 season was an important part of Glenn's athletic education. Indy was a weak squad, finishing dead last in the league in what would turn out to be its last year as a franchise in the AHL. Glenn quickly discovered the difference between facing Junior and professional shooters.

"You figure that about 10 percent of the players you're up against in Junior will become professional . . ." he explained. "In Windsor, when I was facing a rush, whatever shot the player was in the process of was the one I faced. In Indianapolis, the players were skilled enough to alter their shots depending upon what I was doing. I learned very quickly exactly how skilled the pros really were. I got five years of experience in that one year."

Glenn's work in goal for the Indianapolis Capitols was repeatedly singled out with effusive praise from the local press. At year's end, he was given the team's MVP Award. His play had been so impressive that he became the subject of trade rumors. Since everyone knew that Sawchuk had a stranglehold on the Wings' job, conjecture began that Glenn would be moved to the goaltending-needy Boston Bruins or New York Rangers. Although the talk certainly proved to be premature, Glenn created a buzz just as he had done at the initial open camp tryout in Saskatoon with his bare-handed save.

Since the Capitols did not make the playoffs, Glenn was called up to Detroit to practice with the big club during its Stanley Cup playoff run. While there, he witnessed Sawchuk at his very best. That year, the Wings had won the league title running away by 22 points. It was the team's fourth consecutive league title. Sawchuk won the Vezina Trophy with a goals-against average under 2.00, was the First All-Star, and led the league with 12 shutouts. When it looked like there was nothing more he could do, the goalie nicknamed "The Uke" held Wings' opponents to five goals in eight games as they swept their way to a Stanley Cup victory.

With Sawchuk only two years older than Hall, and with only one goalie on an NHL roster, the opportunity for Glenn to take his turn as a Red Wings goalkeeper seemed slim. But the 20-year-old Hall would get his first chance to do so in just a matter of months.

THE INDIANAPOLIS CAPITOLS ceased operations shortly after the 1951–52 season and that, coupled with Terry Sawchuk's dominating playoff performance the previous spring, saw Glenn reporting to Red Wing camp in 1952 somewhat uncertain of what the future would hold. As he did each year at camp, Glenn listened to Jack Adams's perfunctory opening day "All the jobs are open" speech. "Gordie [Howe] must have been shaking in his boots," quipped Hall. "I certainly knew that there was nothing I could do to move Sawchuk out of the job."

"Glenn had a very good camp that year," recalled Tommy Ivan. "We knew we had something special in case Sawchuk faltered. So we were going to keep getting him good pro experience by sending him to Edmonton."

The Edmonton Flyers had become the Red Wings' main affiliate and, like Indianapolis, had come off a dismal season. The team competed in the Western Hockey League in a circuit that included Calgary, New Westminster, Victoria, Vancouver, Seattle, Tacoma, and Saskatoon, and it was led by newly hired player-coach Bud Poile. But before Glenn joined Poile out west, Ivan taught him a nifty trick.

"We used to divide the team in two and play intersquad games," the former coach remembered. "I'd coach one team and Jack Adams would coach the other and Jack hated to lose even those games. So I told Glenn that if we lost a face-off in our end to lean real hard back against the posts and knock the net off so they had to stop play. When that net kept coming loose, I thought Jack would have a heart attack!"

Glenn seldom broke this particular trick out during games, but it was in his arsenal any time he wanted to be a burr under Jolly Jack Adams's saddle.

TO THIS DAY, GLENN BELIEVES that the most unheralded men in the game are the trainers, and when he got to Edmonton, he would meet one of a kind in Tiger Goldstick. One of the most colorful figures in Edmonton sports history, Tiger was known for dispensing valuable wisdom to his troops. Among his most memorable pieces of advice were these words to live by: "Be nice to everybody. You never know who's going to be on the jury."

The team that Glenn would backstop in Edmonton was stronger than the Capitols had been, bolstered by the presence of future NHL stars Johnny Bucyk, Vic Stasiuk, and Norm Ullman. The Flyers started slowly but began improving noticeably near the season's halfway point. Hall quickly made a name for himself in the league, playing spectacular goal while the team was finding itself.

At the 1952 Christmas break, Glenn returned to the family home in Humboldt. It was there that he received a telegram from Coach Poile on Christmas Eve: TRIED TO PHONE YOU. YOU ARE TO CATCH FLIGHT NUMBER TEN OUT OF SASKATOON THREE FORTY FIVE AM TWENTY SIXTH OF DECEMBER FOR MONTREAL. SAWCHUK IS HURT AND DETROIT ARE BRINGING YOU UP. I WILL HAVE YOUR EQUIPMENT ON THE PLANE. PLEASE ACKNOWLEDGE THIS WIRE BY PHONE.

Terry Sawchuk had taken a shot in the skate during a practice, fracturing a small bone in his right instep. The urgency with which Glenn was to join the squad owed to the NHL's one-goalie system. All six teams dressed only one goaltender for a game. If that goalie was injured, the game was stopped until he could make his return. If the man was injured beyond immediate repair, the home team was to supply another goalkeeper to finish the game. The emergency goalie was not a pro, rather, he was a guy who practiced with the team or played local senior hockey and who sat in the stands for every home game. If he was needed to play, he would literally be paged over the PA system and told to report to the locker room. The players would mill around the ice until the substitute suited up and often, frighteningly (for himself and the team that would play in front of him) took his place in the crease. This forced delay in the game was fine with the owners: they not only got a nice spike in beer and peanut sales during the downtime, but they were spared carrying an extra NHL salary in their budgets.

When Glenn got the call-up, he had just enough time to bid his relatives goodbye and head to the airport. "I really wasn't very nervous about it," Glenn recalled. "I just looked at it like a great opportunity. Here I was getting the chance to play against the people I looked up to."

His trip to Montreal was considerably less eventful than the journey his equipment took. His gear never made it to the Forum, lost en route. The Red Wings trainer was Lefty Wilson, himself a goalkeeper who often practiced with the club. Lefty would have to lend his equipment to Glenn who just two and a half months earlier had celebrated his 21st birthday. So Hall was faced with the daunting task of not just making his NHL debut in the Forum against the Montreal Canadiens but doing so in borrowed equipment. Perhaps the true seriousness of this challenge can only be understood by fellow goalkeepers, all of whom are notoriously finicky about their gear.

"The biggest problem was the skates," Glenn remembered. "Luckily they fit okay but the problem was that I was used to very sharp blades and not only were they not sharp, but there was no place to sharpen them. The teams didn't take the sharpener with them on the road in those days . . . I was going to have to make do . . ."

If Glenn's equipment wasn't quite ready for prime time, his new team-mates weren't ready at all for his pre-game ritual. "The guys didn't realize [the vomiting] was part of my routine. So as everyone was getting dressed and taping their sticks, I ran into the bathroom and got sick. I'm sure it was loud enough for all the players to hear. When I came out, I was white as a ghost. They all got a laugh out of that."

Red Wing coach Tommy Ivan remembered the game well. "Like most kids and particularly goaltenders, Glenn was nervous about being in the National Hockey League. The first period was rough and Hall was a bit un-steady [the Wings trailed 1–0]. Gordie Howe got into a fight with a Montreal player just before the period ended. He should have been pretty riled up as we went to the dressing room."

Howe's agitation from the fight should have been compounded by the fact that the Wings were playing an important game against their main rival with-out the NHL's best goalie, who was being substituted for by a kid who'd lost his lunch immediately prior to the opening face-off. But Ivan recalled Howe's actions during the first intermission in the quietly tense locker room.

"The Wings always sipped tea between periods. [It was thought that tea would calm a player's nerves between periods and help settle him down.] I was sitting near Glenn trying to calm him down a bit when I caught something out of the corner of my eye. A baggage trunk separated Howe from Lefty Wilson who was serving the tea. Instead of rising to reach for the paper cup of tea, the Big Guy turned the blade of his stick flat and had Wilson put the cup on it. Nonchalantly as you please, he pulled the stick toward him without spilling a drop. Mind you, Howe wasn't showing off."

Howe's firm hand said to his teammates that he wasn't nervous about facing down the Habs without Terry. It was a silent gesture that intimated Hall was good enough to get the job done. Ivan contends that Howe "was just letting the fellas know they [also] had to show they weren't worried about Sawchuk not being in the nets so that Hall would have that much more confidence in himself. [That gesture] did more to help Glenn than any words I could have said to him. The boys came back and tied the Canadiens 2–2, and Glenn played very well." In a statistic that would portend Glenn's future in the big league, the Wings were outshot 34 to 17 in his NHL debut.

With Sawchuk on the sidelines for two weeks, Glenn was slated to play in five contests. He was in goal for 7–1 and 5–3 wins over Boston and Chicago respectively, before suffering his first NHL loss, a 2–0 game against Montreal. His last game was supposed to be against Boston at the Detroit Olympia. Sawchuk had returned to practice and was to start the next game, which was against Toronto. The Wings were up 2–0 halfway through the contest when Glenn was faced with stopping one of the Bruins' best skaters, Fleming Mackell, one-on-one. Glenn didn't know that he was getting help from above on the shot. In the press box, Sawchuk was jittery. On each rush Glenn was facing, The Uke was twisting his body and moving his arms as if he were in the nets himself. Glenn stopped Mackell, and the Wings went on to win 4–0.

"I told you . . . that Glenn was as good as any goalie in the National League," crowed Sawchuk to the press after the game. "He really showed 'em something out there tonight. That save he made on Mackell was as good as you'll ever see."

The shutout was not only Glenn's first NHL zero, but it was his first professional whitewash. He hadn't had one the year before in Indy and he had yet to post one with Edmonton. As it turned out, Glenn would not return west just yet. Sawchuk said he still felt a twinge when he skated so the Wings kept Hall around for one last game, a 5–2 win over his boyhood favorites, the Leafs.

Despite the professional insecurity with which NHL goalies guarded their precious jobs, Sawchuk had reason to be rooting for Glenn. At the time of his injury, Terry held a six-goal lead in the Vezina Trophy race. The Vezina was awarded to the goalie on the team with the least number of goals scored against, so if Glenn had not done the job during Terry's absence, it might have cost Sawchuk the award and the $1,000 bonus that came with it. Glenn posted a 1.67 goals-against average during his six-game stint, better than Sawchuk's average to that point, and when Terry returned to action he did so with a 13-goal lead in the Vezina race. Glenn's play was so strong that Sawchuk actually fretted about being replaced, just as he had replaced Harry Lumley three years back.

The Red Wings' internal scouting report on Glenn after his initial NHL stint took notice of his style. "He has greatly improved use of his left [catch] hand. Hall has adapted Terry Sawchuk's crouch to get his head low on screen shots, but instead of bending far over like Sawchuk, feet apart, Glenn spreads his legs wide. As a Junior, Hall often went too far out of the nets. In correcting it, he left one weakness . . . he crowds too far back in the crease."

Glenn went back to Edmonton, where the press noted that he played with a sizable boost in his confidence. He led the Flyers to a fourth-place finish in the regular season and would play in his first professional playoff. The first round went a full seven games, the Flyers upsetting Calgary by winning the clincher in overtime. In the second round, Edmonton swept Vancouver and goalie Emile Francis in four games. When this series opened, Glenn displayed the durability that would make him so unique, and help to set him above the rest.

Trainer Goldstick remembered what happened: "The first night we played Vancouver, Hall broke a finger in the warm-ups. But he came into the dressing room and he did not want to be yanked. In those days we didn't have sub goal-keepers and we had a fellow who wasn't dressed. You weren't allowed the two-goalkeeper system, but you could have a man on hand who wasn't dressed and you'd have to change him. We had somebody come down . . . but . . . Glenn still wanted to play. And so he went out and played a terrific hockey game that night. He went on to play the whole series with a broken finger."

The Flyers then took the league title, winning in six games over heavily favored Saskatoon. Glenn was named to the Second All-Star team behind Francis, and he'd played in every game for the farm team except the time he was with the Wings. In Detroit, he played every game available to him, and he made 17 playoff appearances for Edmonton. The 86 games he played that year were the most of any goalie in professional hockey.

Glenn's play was so strong that, for the second consecutive year, the trade rumors popped up. How could you keep such a talent down on the farm? Coach Bud Poile squashed the conjecture: "We won't stand in the way of our players going to an NHL team, except for Hall. We'll keep him here or in Detroit but we can't let him go to another team."

"I never heard any trade rumors at the time," said Hall. "I was quite happy in the Western League and I never gave much thought to moving up. I was thinking, 'I'm playing pro hockey . . . isn't this great!' Besides, in those days, there weren't that many trades, anyway, and I don't think teams were very willing to trade young players they thought might make an impact some day."

Former NHL goalkeeping standout Frank McCool covered the WHL playoffs as a member of the press and wrote, "Detroit will have nothing to worry about in the goaltending department for a great many years."

Meanwhile, the parent Red Wings didn't enjoy their customary playoff success. Sawchuk struggled mightily as Boston eliminated the Wings in the first round. So troubled by Sawchuk's play was GM Adams that, unbeknown to Glenn, Jolly Jack had considered recalling Glenn late in that series. He stayed with Terry instead. Terry's playoff unsteadiness (in the regular season, he had won the Vezina and posted nine shutouts) would set up a potential opening for Glenn to oust Terry from the number-one job in the following 1953–54 season. Adams, who mindful of Terry's fragile confidence rightly handled him with kid gloves, stated publicly for the first time since Lumley's departure that the job was open to whomever earned it. Glenn never believed that.

"There was never any question in my mind that Sawchuk was the number-one goalie," said Hall. "He was just too good. Mr. Adams might have been sounding off, but there was nothing to it. He also might have wanted Terry to feel insecure before negotiating his contract. But there was nothing more to it than that."

If that was Adams's strategy, it worked. Sawchuk returned to form with another strong year. Although he didn't capture the Vezina, Terry had another great playoff run, leading the Wings to the Stanley Cup. He only missed three games that year, and not wanting to remind Terry of the threat to his job lurking in Edmonton, Adams did not recall Glenn to replace him. He inserted journeyman Dave Gatherum instead. Gatherum had subbed in all but one game for Glenn at Edmonton while Hall had stepped in for Sawchuk the previous year. Adams was concerned that another Hall sighting might rattle Terry. So Glenn spent the entire season in Edmonton, earning Second All-Star team honors again, playing in all 70 of his team's regular-season games and all 13 playoff games, and leading the WHL in playoff shutouts with a pair. For the second consecutive year, Glenn made the most professional appearances of any goalkeeper, this time with 83.

Gerry Melnyk, who forged a solid NHL career that reached into the expansion era before spending 30 years as a scout for the Philadelphia Flyers, was a teammate of Glenn's in Edmonton. He recalled one of the traits that made Glenn successful. "There was no one more competitive," said Melnyk. "Glenn hated to lose at anything. When we'd travel, we'd get to the train station and Glenn and our teammate Ray Hannigan would look at each other. There'd be a quick bet over who'd get on board first. It was about 200 yards to the train, and all of a sudden the race was on. Glenn ran like a thousand bucks was at stake. And he'd find a way to win."

Melnyk recalled, too, that Glenn and Pauline had resumed dating during the summers when Glenn returned to Humboldt. The relationship was turning serious and, returning to the automotive theme originally struck by Pauline, Glenn confided to Melnyk that, "I'm either going to get married or buy a car."

Glenn put the new wheels on hold, opting for the ring that he presented to Pauline.

"I remember when Glenn popped the big question," she said, a mischievous twinkle in her deep blue eyes. "But I said, 'No, not until we're married.'"

AT THE NHL, the landscape was beginning to shift, and the winds of change would have a profound effect on Glenn's future. The 1953–54 Red Wings were again the Stanley Cup champions, but uneasy lay the crown on the king. The Montreal Canadiens were coming. It was clear to everyone around the league that Les Habitants were inching closer and closer to a level playing field with the Red Wings. In 1951–52, the Habs finished in second place, 22 points behind Detroit. The next year, they were second again, 15 points off the pace. In 1953–54, they were bridesmaids again, but this time just seven points back. Jack Adams didn't make any significant changes in his lineup for the 1954–55 season, but Coach Tommy Ivan left the Wings for Chicago.

The Wings' owner, James Norris Sr., had passed away the year before, leaving control of the team to his daughter. Norris's son, James Jr., was now president of the Black Hawks, and he was trying to make his team of perennial also-rans more competitive. He wanted Ivan to direct the rebuilding, so brother and sister worked out a deal and Ivan made the move. Adams replaced Ivan with Hall's former junior coach, Jimmy Skinner. The ascension of Skinner, the move of Ivan, and the threat of Montreal on the horizon would all play greatly into Glenn's destiny.

THE 1954–55 SEASON would be Glenn's first as a married man and his last for the Edmonton Flyers. On May 5, 1954, Glenn and Pauline had wed in a small ceremony in front of family and friends in Humboldt.

During the season, he would lead the Western Hockey League in wins with 38, make the First All-Star team, and ratchet his game up a notch in the playoffs, going 11–5 and leading Edmonton to a league playoff title. That year, the winner of the West would play the winner of the East in a best five of nine series. The entire series would be played in the east, split between arenas in Montreal and close-by Shawinigan Falls, Quebec. The Flyers' opponents, the Quebec Aces, won the series thanks in no small part to what Gerry Melnyk recalled in the clinching game to be the "biggest screwing from an official in hockey history. We were in the box the entire night. We were all sure the outcome was predetermined because of the location and because of the referee who was local, George Gravel."

In the NHL, the Red Wings won the regular season once again. But in keeping with the trend over the past four years, Montreal was closer still. The Canadiens finished second again, but this time by a mere two points. Sawchuk won the Vezina and led the league in wins with 40 and in shutouts with 12, but his personal problems were getting tougher to ignore. Terry had started the season sickly thin, and speculation had it that he was either afflicted with mononucleosis or some form of hepatitis, but it was also obvious to all around him that his drinking was becoming a major issue. He'd befriended some hard-partying members of the Detroit Lions football team, and was running with an increasingly boisterous crowd. Still, his barroom habits hadn't affected his on-ice performance until late in the season.

The Wings were stuck in a 1–5, six-game skid in February with the Canadiens breathing down their necks. When Sawchuk was hit for eight goals in a game against Boston, there was major concern in the Wings' front office. In the very next game, he was beaten by a 90-foot shot that tied the game. Jack Adams had seen enough, and Glenn was recalled from Edmonton. Sawchuk was self-destructing, and Adams knew it. But publicly he protected his star goalie.

"We're giving Terry a rest," he said as he announced Glenn's recall for what was intended to be a three-game stint. "We figured this move was both for the best interests of the team and the best interests of Sawchuk. Terry can take some needed rest and come back much sharper. We will get another look at Hall, who has been playing well. And, while Terry is out, some of the other players on the club may appreciate his efforts more than they have part of this season . . . This is in no way a disciplinary move."

But the truth was that Sawchuk was forced to receive team-mandated psychiatric and alcohol counseling. Glenn's play, however, may have been the best therapy for Terry and his teammates. Glenn played in a 2–1 win over Toronto and a 5–1 victory over the Hawks. He was supposed to play the

Wings' next game, but he got word that Pauline had been hospitalized back home. The Halls were expecting their first child and Pauline was at full term. Glenn returned immediately to Edmonton, only to discover that the couple's first child, a 9-pound baby boy, was stillborn. Like so many hockey wives, Pauline had faced the bulk of the crisis alone while Glenn was hundreds of miles away, frantically trying to get back home.

"Of course, it was absolutely devastating," said Glenn, an obvious sadness still in his voice as he recalled the events many years later. "There are times when I still think about him," Pauline shared. "I think about what he would have been like, what he would have grown up to be."

AFTER GLENN RETURNED to Edmonton, Sawchuk went back in the cage, mindful that despite the astounding record he'd amassed over the previous four seasons, he still had something to prove. Terry had seen Glenn play those two games, and knew that in the eyes of management, he was only as good as his last game. The reporters who covered the Wings were privy to Sawchuk's problems, but this was in an era when an athlete's off-ice life never was a matter of public record. In print they were speculating that Hall had actually been recalled as an audition for the playoffs. Detroit went on a roll and made a late-season push that kept the team in first place by the narrowest of margins over Montreal. The Red Wing surge was also abetted by, depending on whether you were a Canadien fan or a Detroit loyalist, either NHL President Clarence Campbell's unchecked power or Maurice Richard's uncontrolled temper.

With just a handful of games remaining in the regular season, Richard, the heart of the Canadiens and at the time the only player to score 50 goals in a single season, had been suspended for attacking a linesman during a game. When Campbell extended the penalty through the playoffs, Montreal fans rioted. Campbell effectively eliminated the Habs' top player, giving the Wings a huge edge, which they would exploit. In the first round of the playoffs, Detroit swept Toronto in four while Montreal bested Boston in five. The Rocket-less Canadiens still pushed the Wings to a seventh game, but the Wings won their fourth Stanley Cup in five years by a 3–1 score.

On the surface, it would seem that another league championship followed by the Stanley Cup victory would have been enough to assuage Jack Adams. Despite the push from the Canadiens, the fact was the Red Wings were the league's crown jewel. But the writing was on the wall, and Adams could read it. Montreal was not going away.

Detroit would have to get stronger. Changes would have to be made.

ESSAY: FOR THE TEAM

OF ALL THE THINGS that can be said about ice hockey, the truest perhaps is that it is the fastest team sport on Earth. The strength of team sport is that the ability to excel is almost totally determined by the capability of its team members to complement one another. The greatest hockey dynasties thrived because the "grinder" understood that his role was as important to the team's success as that of the goal scorer. The playmaker, likewise, recognized his vital role as the link between these two. The great coach made sure they were all appreciated for their unique gifts and he mixed and matched them appropriately on the ice. The physical demands of the sport mandate that skaters' shift time be limited. There are 18 skaters on a team, and when a player takes his turn off the ice, his body recovering and preparing for the next exertion, he knows that he will play again.

Within the world of this ultimate team sport is the ultimate individual sport: goaltending. The demands of this position are wholly separate from those of forwards and defensemen, yet the situations a goalie faces are wholly dependent upon those players. Goalies skate differently. Their skate blades are long and flat, built for side-to-side agility and up-and-down recovery. They must be great skaters, but within a relatively confined space.

Whereas forwards and defensemen try to make opponents react to them, goalkeepers are taught hockey in reverse. Everything a goalie does is based on events over which he has no control. A forward who makes a mistake has two other forwards, two defensemen, and a goalie to cover for him. A goalie's mistakes either rattle off the posts or are counted as goals. This responsibility as the last line of defense brings intense pressure, so the goalie must think differently than forwards and defensemen. He must find a way to make this awesome responsibility fit as comfortably and as naturally as his gloves.

If he cannot, he is doomed.

Unlike the forward or defensemen, the goalie on the bench or in the minors is never guaranteed another minute of playing time. As he sits and observes, his future is usually dictated by another man's misfortune. The goalie ahead of him must establish a certain level of incompetence or suffer an injury, providing an opening through which to step. Once that happens, the new goalie must immediately prove his mettle, because someone else is sitting on the bench or toiling in the minors . . . waiting and watching . . . just as he once did.

And, as the playing goalie stretches to make that big breakaway save, he knows the guy watching him from the bench is torn. The standby is applauding with the rest of his teammates, but inside the heroics tear at him. That unspoken contradiction of individual versus team interest only adds to the mental drain of goalkeeping. Only one goalie can play at a time and every goalie wants to be that one.

That one individual within the team sport.

4

A Career Takes Wing

BY 1955, THE DETROIT RED WINGS had become one of the most dominant teams in the history of sport. They'd won the regular-season title an incredible seven consecutive years, and the Stanley Cup four times during that span. General manager Jack Adams's squad had garnered all that hardware with two different coaches and two different goalkeepers but always with the core of three impact skaters: Gordie Howe, Ted Lindsay, and Alex Delvecchio. The latter-day dynasties followed suit; Montreal ɪ had Maurice Richard, Jean Beliveau, and Doug Harvey; Montreal ɪɪ was built around Guy Lafleur, Steve Shutt, and Larry Robinson; the New York Islanders had Mike Bossy, Bryan Trottier, and Denis Potvin; the Edmonton Oilers had Wayne Gretzky, Mark Messier, and Jari Kurri. Harry Lumley, Terry Sawchuk, Jacques Plante, Ken Dryden, Billy Smith, and Grant Fuhr—all Hall of Fame–level goalies—guarded the cages behind them.

The architects of the National Hockey League's greatest dynasties have always had one belief in common: to stay at the top, you need to change 10 to 15 percent of your roster from season to season. The trick, of course, is to change the right 10 to 15 percent.

Jack Adams could feel Montreal nipping at his backside, and despite the Wings' successes, he decided a shake-up was in order. He'd acquired the nickname "Trader Jack" because of his affinity for making the blockbuster, multi-player deal. Years later, legendary Montreal GM Sam Pollock would say the key to success in any multi-player deal is that no matter how many players are swapped, you have to get the best player. Adams, recalling his nine-player deal after Detroit's Cup win in '50, thought history could be repeated.

His first call went to former underling Tommy Ivan. Ivan had undertaken the burden of rebuilding Chicago, and the Hawks were coming off a dead-last finish with an abysmal 13–40–17 record. On June 3, the two men engineered the first big deal of the off-season as Adams sent Glen Skov, Tony Leswick, Johnny Wilson, and Benny Woit to Chicago for Jerry Toppazzini, John McCormack, Dave Creighton, and Gord Hollingworth. Adams had traded players who scored 38 goals the previous season for players who accounted for 24 for Chicago. He also lost the best player of the group in Glen Skov.

And he was not done.

Montreal was looking for help in goal. Canadien management was not sold on the young man who inherited the job from veteran Gerry McNeil. They were concerned that Jacques Plante didn't have what it would take to put them over the top. Plante was a unique creature, and he had already made a name for himself by becoming the first goalie to leave the comfort of his crease to chase down loose pucks that had been dumped behind his goal. Possessing an enormous ego, he'd publicly ridiculed McNeil during a short-lived but impressive playoff appearance a couple of years earlier, and he told anyone who would listen that he was prepared to become the greatest Canadien goalie of this or any generation. In truth, Plante did have an impressive rookie season and he had played well against Sawchuk in a losing effort in the '55 finals. And despite management's feelings, most of his Canadien teammates had gained confidence in his abilities . . . just not as much as he himself had.

When the '55 finals were extended to a seventh game, Adams told the press purposefully that the Stanley Cup winner would be determined by the better goalie. Adams felt that statement would give Sawchuk confidence and rattle the rookie, Plante. A Stanley Cup cannot be decided in the newspapers, and his comments likely had no effect on either man, but they accentuated the concern felt by Montreal management. The Habs were so serious in pursuit of a quality netminder that they were dangling soon-to-be All-Star defenseman Tom Johnson as trade bait, and word on the street was that for the right deal, even their best defenseman, Doug Harvey, would be made available.

Adams's hands-on approach during training camp and his near-constant presence near the locker room during the season (he had an office adjacent to it) had given him access to the whisperings of the players around the rink. He'd heard firsthand that they were impressed with Glenn's abilities, which confirmed what his scouts were telling him. Perhaps more importantly, he knew that he could trade a player of Sawchuk's stature without disrupting his locker room. There are varying accounts as to whether or not talks between Montreal and Adams about acquiring either Terry or Glenn ever reached a serious stage. None of the principals are alive today, so it is impossible to say with certainty, although one could easily conjecture that there was no way Adams was going to risk trading his All-Star in Sawchuk or his top netminding prospect in Hall to the team that was clearly his biggest rival.

At the same time, Boston Bruin GM Lynn Patrick was in the market for a goalie. The Bruins had made the playoffs the previous season, but were backstopped by a solid but past-his-prime Sugar Jim Henry. Like most of the NHL brass, Patrick knew that Glenn was the top minor-league prospect in the game, and assuming that Sawchuk was untouchable, approached Adams about dealing for Glenn. Like Patrick, Adams knew that Glenn was ready for prime time, but unlike Patrick, Adams knew that Sawchuk was teetering on the edge of professional destruction because of his alcoholism. When Adams turned the conversation with Patrick away from Hall and toward Sawchuk, the Bruin GM was stunned. More names came up in the give-and-take, and shortly after announcing the initial blockbuster trade with Chicago, the two GMs told the hockey world what they'd agreed upon.

Detroit would send Terry Sawchuk, sniper Vic Stasiuk, Marcel Bonin, and Lorne Davis to Boston for Ed Sanford, Real Chevrefils, Norm Corcoran, Warren Godfrey, and goalie prospect Gilles Boisvert. In a few hours, Adams had traded away eight players, or just under 50 percent of his team. Seven of those players had contributed significantly to a league title and Cup championship (Stasiuk spent that year in the minors), and one, the best player of either trade, had been indisputably the best goalie in the NHL for the past five seasons.

Adams explained the trade: "We let Sawchuk go because we found ourselves with two top goalies. Hall is more advanced now than Sawchuk when he joined us, and all the players insist Glenn has been NHL material for the past year. It was a case of trading one of them, and Sawchuk is the established player. Consequently he brought a better offer."

Interestingly the reaction among the Wings' players and the press of the day wasn't anger at trading Sawchuk. Adams's basic reasoning was dead-on. He had a right to be concerned about Sawchuk's future given what he knew about the man's personal demons and, despite the fact that Terry still had outstanding hockey left in him, he never again did equal his accomplishments of the previous five seasons. What outraged the players was that Adams got nothing even approaching equal value in return.

Jimmy Skinner, the Red Wing coach at the time and Glenn's coach in Windsor, recalled the trade. "We didn't want to lose either man. But we knew we couldn't keep them both. Jack told me that for the good of the league as well as for the good of both men we had to trade one. We had to share them. We kept Glenn because he was younger. As far as ability, it really didn't matter. They were both about the same, although Glenn had the better catch hand. But we really didn't want to see either man go."

Red Wing "Terrible" Ted Lindsay was the team's leader on and off the ice. A remarkable competitor, he was a warrior who could beat you just as easily in the alley as with a big goal. He remembered the team's sentiment regarding Adams's wheeling and dealing. "We had Hall coming up so Sawchuk was expendable," he would say years later. "But the only place we had a weakness was on defense. If Adams had traded Sawchuk to Montreal, we could have gotten Doug Harvey or Tom Johnson. With Johnson on defense we would have won five Cups in a row instead of Montreal, and with Harvey we'd have won seven. Instead, Adams deals Sawchuk to Boston."

Wing defenseman Marcel Pronovost put it more succinctly: "We didn't get shit from Boston."

THE DOOR TO THE NHL had now swung wide open for Glenn Henry Hall. When he arrived at Red Wing camp in Sault Ste. Marie that fall, Coach Jimmy Skinner told him the number-one job was his to lose. Skinner's familiar presence eased Glenn's transition from the minors to the NHL, but, when the club broke camp for Detroit, Glenn's first job was to find housing for himself and Pauline, whom they'd recently learned was pregnant again. In those days the team did not help players find housing, but for the Wings, an apartment complex across from the Olympia seemed like the logical place to rent. The units were filthy and dreary, and Glenn set about making it presentable for Pauline, who would be arriving by plane on the first air trip of her life.

"I scrubbed and scrubbed and worked awfully hard to clean that place up," said Glenn. "When Pauline got there though, she took one look at it and started crying. That meant it was time to look for a different place to live." "We fought cockroaches in that place every day," Pauline remembered. "We did find a little house in Windsor to rent and ended up spending the season there."

Pauline found the Red Wing wives to be very welcoming. Pat Lindsay, Ted's wife, had a great sense of humor, and Pauline felt that maybe Pat saw something good in her. Marty Pavelich's wife was another woman Pauline grew close to, and Colleen [Mrs. Gordie] Howe went out of her way to welcome the rookies' wives with parties and get-togethers.

Of the players themselves, Pauline got on the best with Ted Lindsay. "I called him 'Scarface' and got away with it," she recalled. "I admired his approach to life and of course his spirited play. If I had been a hockey player, I would have been like him. His competitiveness and desire to win resemble my own traits. Maybe we were raised to fight for what we wanted."

BY THE TIME THE 1955–56 season began, Glenn knew that he would wear the big number one on the crimson home sweater sported by the Wings. But what he didn't know was that he'd be backstopping a team that had been weakened considerably by Trader Jack's wheeling and dealing.

"Plenty of people looked at Adams like he was some kind of a genius," said Ted Lindsay. "But he was an idiot. Every guy I talked to who played for him in the '30s and early '40s, and I mean every one of them with the exception of [goalie] John Mowers, said he just was not a good hockey man. The trades he made were based on emotion not logic, and we paid the price."

Each year, the NHL season commenced with the All-Star game. In those days, the Stanley Cup winner played at home against the All-Star team. So Glenn's debut as the Red Wing starting goalie would have tested the nerve of any veteran goalie. He would be facing the best players in the league, including Terry Sawchuk, the goalie who had been traded to make room for him.

"Early in the game, I thought my pads would shake off," Glenn said, recalling his state of mind. "But I felt all right after I handled a couple of shots . . . I really didn't get a tough shot until the second period." The timing of that tough shot couldn't have been any better. Harry Lumley had drawn the starting assignment in goal for the All-Stars, and he made 15 saves on 16 shots while Glenn stopped all six he faced in the first period. The home crowd was still reserving judgment on the young new goalie, after having been spoiled by Sawchuk's masterful work during the five previous seasons. But in the second period, the fans would be treated to an example of Glenn's talent.

With the game still 1–0, All-Star Doug Harvey steamed a high shot at the net. The puck made its way through a tangle of bodies, and Glenn picked it up a few feet in front of him, stopping it with his chest. The rebound popped to the far edge of the crease. Harvey's teammate on the All-Stars and the Canadiens, Bernie Geoffrion, stepped out of the crowded slot and snapped the disc toward the open side of the goal. The rookie netminder dived across the goalmouth, extending his catch hand in a desperate reach, and trapped the shot in miraculous fashion. The save earned him a prolonged ovation from the fans at the Detroit Olympia, his first true sign of their acceptance. Just minutes later with the game at the halfway point, Sawchuk replaced Lumley and received a standing ovation from the fans.

"I was glad for him," said Hall afterward. "He's a great goalie and he's always been nice to me . . . I was really glad from a hockey player's standpoint. It showed the fans were warmhearted and didn't regard Terry as an enemy just because he put on another uniform." The Wings won the contest 3–1; the only goal Hall surrendered was a shot that tipped in off his own defenseman.

As the season began, Glenn insisted that he never was preoccupied with living up to Sawchuk's play: "Most of the pressure didn't arise from trying to match Terry," he said. "I didn't want to let the other guys [on the Wings] down. That's what worried me most. Remember, this is a World Championship team I'm playing for."

Ted Lindsay insists that there was no trepidation on the team as Glenn took over, "We knew Glenn was good. I don't think any one of us gave it a thought. We had a lot of confidence in our team. We were still the Red Wings, and despite the bad trades, we were still like a family. Glenn just became part of our family. Right off the bat, we knew he was a great team guy."

But the Wings got off to a rocky start, losing their first three games, going 2–0–2 in the next four, and then going 11 more games without a victory. Hall came under criticism, but not from within his organization.

"Hall's partly to blame," said New York Ranger coach Phil Watson. "He's nowhere near as good as Sawchuk."

"He'll never last," said Chicago goalie Al Rollins, an old-guard stand-up type. "He's down all the time. He does everything a goaltender is not supposed to do. Maybe he got away with that in the minors, but that just won't cut it in the big leagues."

"I wasn't satisfied that we were off to a slow start," Glenn said, reflecting on those opening weeks. "But it never got to me. My teammates and Jimmy Skinner were always supportive. I think we all felt that if we just concentrated on playing well that we'd start winning."

Coach Skinner came to his goalie's defense: "I don't think a goal has passed him that wouldn't have beaten anyone else. He's made some big saves and we're going to start winning for him . . . Wait'll you see him in a few years."

The doubters didn't have to wait that long. Glenn soon caught fire, and by the year's halfway point, he'd recorded a whopping seven shutouts, three of them consecutively in December. Glenn played every minute of the season for the Wings and posted a sparkling 2.11 goals-against average. He led the league in shutouts with an eye-popping 12 (equaling Sawchuk's highest single-year mark), was named to the league's Second All-Star team, and was nosed out of the Vezina Trophy on the last weekend of the season by Montrealer Jacques Plante. That Plante's Canadiens finished 24 points ahead of Glenn's second-place Wings gives you an idea of how good Glenn had to be to stay that close in the Vezina race. For his efforts, Glenn was rewarded with the Calder Trophy as the NHL's rookie of the year. Behind a significantly weaker team, Glenn had virtually matched Sawchuk's first-year numbers and accolades. "I only remember him playing one bad game all year," said Skinner.

Al Rollins's criticism was stinging at the time, but in an odd way it was also insightful. He became the first person to publicly acknowledge that Glenn's puck-stopping style was different. What Rollins saw was his skinny counterpart dropping to the ice more often than was "acceptable." But what he didn't realize was that Hall dropped to the ice with purpose. His wider stance coupled with his excellent skating and agility made him appear at times to be out of control—a "flopper." But nothing was further from the truth. What Rollins was witnessing, along with the rest of the league, was Glenn's continuing stylistic evolution, an evolution that would lead to a goaltending revolution.

The genesis of Glenn's style went back to the days when he so admired Chuck Rayner, and when he was frustrated by his own inability to control rebounds by using his stick as Rayner did. At that time, because he wasn't as physically strong, some shots still overpowered him. So in the minors, he experimented by dropping to the ice with his knees together behind the stick. Instead of relying on his strength to stop a shot with his stick, he now formed a puck-stopping wall behind the stick. If a hard shot made contact with the stick before, it could power its way under the blade or bounce dangerously right back into the slot. With Hall's knees solidly behind the stick, he could stop the shot firmly and at the same time absorb enough of the shot's shock that he could keep the rebound close to him or, with a slight flick of the wrist, deflect the puck harmlessly to the corner. This movement became known as the "V split" because Glenn's skates fanned out toward the posts in a "V" formation. Today it is more popularly known as "the butterfly."

Hall wasn't vulnerable to high shots, because his catch hand was out to his side and ready. He wasn't vulnerable to bad rebounds because he could bounce to his feet much quicker and reset his angle fluidly and more naturally than if he were stopping low shots with the more conventional move of the day, the split or kick save. Still, he didn't use the "V" very often that rookie year. As it would turn out, an opposing forward hastened this style's emergence.

"When I was with Detroit, I had to deal with Jean Beliveau," Hall said of the 6-foot, 4-inch tall Montreal center. A beautiful pure skater gifted with great hands and a quick shot release, "Le Gros Bill" would become one of the greatest players the game has ever known and an elegant diplomat for the Canadiens in particular and hockey in general. But at the time, Glenn was far more concerned with Big Beliveau's place in front of his crease.

"I started using the 'V' to cope with seeing around and through Beliveau. I couldn't move him, so I would drop down to cover as much net as possible while still trying to locate the puck. In order to stop it, you have to see it, and the 'V' gave me a chance to see it."

The "V" was now a weapon in his puck-stopping arsenal, but even without this innovation, Glenn Hall presented a unique form in the goal. Detroit fans were captivated by his acrobatics and his lightning quickness. He brought a flair to the position that was both purposeful and entertaining. If a shot was screaming toward his right, perhaps he'd respond with a flashing skate save. Whereas every other NHL goalie would pull his leg back toward the middle of his body after such a save, recovering to an upright stance and then moving toward the area of the ice the puck had careened to, Glenn would twirl in a dazzling 360-degree turn. But this was no hotdogging. He reasoned that using his body's momentum would move him much more quickly toward the puck than rigidly returning to a stance and then moving.

If a shot knocked him even slightly off-balance, Hall bounced back against the posts, his catch hand gripping the crossbar like a gymnast working a pommel horse. Habitually he tapped the shaft of his stick or swung his catch glove back against the posts to help him set his angles without glancing backward or taking his eyes off the puck. He was the first goalie to use this approach. If a shot was coming at him high toward the middle of his body, he'd leap in the air to get as much of his chest behind the shot as possible, and catch the puck as it fell off his body. It was as if he were in constant motion, and the gusto, creativity, and body language that he played with spoke volumes about just how much he enjoyed the game.

"We never thought anything about Glenn's style," said Ted Lindsay. "All we cared about was the score at the end of a game. Was Glenn getting beaten by bad goals? No. If you beat him, you had to earn the goal. Glenn just never gave up bad goals."

THE DEFENDING STANLEY CUP champion Red Wings defeated fourth place Toronto 4–1 in the 1956 semifinals. Glenn had an impressive series, beaten only ten times and called upon to make clutch saves midway through each game when the scores were close. Montreal, dominant during the regular season and favorites to win the Cup, topped the Rangers in five in the other semifinal series.

This would be the first NHL series to feature a Glenn Hall versus Jacques Plante matchup between the pipes, and the press of the day continued to question whether or not Plante was up to the challenge of winning a Cup despite the dominant team in front of him. Both Montreal and Detroit newspapers portrayed Plante as Montreal's weak link. One paper said that Canadien coach Toe Blake's biggest challenge would be reinforcing Plante's confidence. As tough as it was to envision Jacques Plante having confidence issues, if they were legitimate, he did have the luxury of playing behind Doug Harvey and Tom Johnson. That, in and of itself, could certainly not hurt your confidence.

The Wings were unaccustomed to being underdogs, but Montreal showed why they'd been picked as the favorite very early on. In the opener at the Forum, the Habs came back from a 4–2 deficit, blitzing the Wings with four goals in five minutes in the third as the Wings' holes on defense were exposed. All four goals were scored at point-blank range. Glenn would record his first NHL playoff win in Game 3 to cut the Habs' series lead to 2–1, but Montreal won the next two games and the Stanley Cup.

For his part, Glenn was playing with a major distraction. Pauline was now nine months along in her pregnancy, and the stillbirth of the year before was all too fresh in his mind. To make matters worse, the Wings banned any incoming or outgoing calls from the players' hotel rooms, contending that they were eliminating any potential distractions. In Glenn's case, the prohibition worked with exactly the opposite effect. "I don't see how I could have been playing with the proper focus," Glenn said many years later. "I know going into that last game all I was thinking about was Pauline and the baby."

"My doctor was tremendous," remembered Pauline. "He was a hockey fan so he would come with me to the home games. But when I went into labor, Glenn was on the road in Montreal, so I truthfully tell people I had to walk to the hospital. Of course, the house we were renting was right across the street from the hospital . . ."

There were no complications this time though, and the day after the Wings lost the Cup, on April 11, 1956, Glenn and Pauline welcomed a healthy son, Patrick, into the world.

AFTER THE PLAYOFFS, Glenn's teammates were effusive in their praise for him. Consensus on the team was that Glenn had played as well or better than Sawchuk had in his two previous championship series. So when it came time to point fingers, the public began second-guessing Jack Adams. Ill-suited to accept the goat's horns, Adams singled out Gordie Howe as the reason for the team's inability to defend the Cup. Howe had scored only once in the series, and Adams was very vocal in criticizing him.

But most of the players who'd been around during the Wings' heyday knew the team had been weakened, and they were still seething that Adams hadn't plugged the holes on defense and had gotten so little in his blockbuster trades.

All of that emotion would come to a head the following season.

5

A Season of Changes

———

GLENN HALL'S TEAMMATES describe him as his own man. He was an intelligent, independent athlete in an age when players were treated like cattle. National Hockey League ownership held a legal monopoly over the sport of ice hockey, and each team fostered a plantation mentality over its players.

Salaries in all sports of the '50s were incredibly low, and hockey salaries were the lowest of any. Athletes in the major sports had to hold down off-season jobs to make ends meet. Owners continually cried poor, never opening their books to scrutiny. Hockey players, almost all from small, conservative Canadian towns, counted themselves fortunate to be earning money playing a game they loved so dearly. Seldom did they rock the boat. In a negotiating session, the fact was that they wielded no power. In an era before agents, a player presenting his salary demands too dramatically would be threatened with a trade to a weak sister franchise, and a demanding player on a weak sister franchise could be banished to the minors. With only six teams and therefore six owners (two of whom were blood relatives), blackballing a player took little coordinated effort. Collusion was the way of the world.

One of the hard and fast rules of the day concerned contract negotiations. Players were instructed that no one, under any circumstance, was ever to divulge what was said inside the general manager's office after contract talks were concluded. The players, almost to a man, obeyed that edict, unsure if an eavesdropping member of the training staff or a sportswriter might report such "treason." But some of the athletes were starting to chafe under the system.

When Glenn walked into Jack Adams's office to negotiate his sophomore contract, he went in feeling he deserved a raise from the NHL minimum

$7,500 he'd received in his rookie year. Adams responded that there was just no way the Norris family could afford to pay Glenn anything more. Hall didn't back down, and Adams relented, magnanimously assenting to a $500 bonus "because you came so close to winning the Vezina. Now, son, I don't want you talking to anyone about me giving you this raise."

"Don't worry, Mr. Adams," Glenn replied as he got out of his chair. "I won't. I'm ashamed of it too." Adams, unused to such sarcasm, was taken aback. He didn't like the backtalk, and his relationship with Glenn began to turn sour.

Hall opened the season with another appearance in the All-Star game, this time in an All-Star jersey. He played the first half of the match and stopped all 13 shots he faced before handing the game over to Terry Sawchuk who was beaten once by Maurice Richard in the 1–1 tie with the Canadiens. Although the game itself was always a tremendous affair, this particular All-Star game was significant not so much for what happened on the ice as for what happened off it. Ted Lindsay had observed the unfair treatment of teammates by management for years. He saw the younger players manipulated, he saw the older players abandoned as well. It would have been easy to sit back and accept how things were, but what made him such a special talent also made him stand up for what was right. Lindsay recalled, "I was interested in fairness. I'm sure some owners were honest, but I'm also sure some were crooked," he said. "Something had to be done."

The season before, Lindsay had begun gathering information with an eye toward putting together a players' association. He was looking to create an avenue through which players could have some sort of voice. He was not seeking to create a monster, and he was not trying to break management's bank. Informally and quietly, he began spreading his idea to selected teammates and opponents. Secrecy was a must. He understood it was crucial that no one in management find out what he was trying to do, as they had the power to smash his efforts before they'd got off the ground. Approval among the leaders of the five other teams was nearly unanimous.

The lone holdout was Toronto's Teeder Kennedy, with whom Lindsay had a particularly intense on-ice rivalry. But Kennedy earned Ted's eternal respect by not going to Toronto management, in the person of Conn Smythe, and revealing what was going on. When Smythe did eventually find out after the movement became public, he ostracized Kennedy for not sharing the information with Toronto management. The five other team leaders agreed to hold a meeting about the proposed association at the All-Star game, as it was the one time all of the league's elite gathered in one place.

Under Lindsay's guidance, the team leaders agreed to the need for player solidarity and they went back to their teams to determine whether or not to go forward with an "association" (as opposed to a "union," which had a largely negative connotation among the generally conservative players). After some months of wrangling, the teams reached a consensus and they announced their intentions to organize at a New York press conference in January. And, as Lindsay put it, "That's when the shit hit the fan."

Although most teams withstood the pressure that was brought to bear by management immediately afterward, they were eventually forced to crack. In the bowels of the Detroit Olympia, a dramatic locker-room scene unfolded, and Lindsay and his teammates witnessed ownership win the war firsthand.

Soon after the New York press conference, Adams assembled his players in their dressing room and began to harangue them. Epithets echoed from wall to ceiling to floor. He confronted each player in full view of the entire team, alternately cowing, intimidating, and cajoling them all as he asked them if they were for or against the association. Adams's craggy face was flushed with indignation, his pudgy hands balled into fists as he jabbed the air, extolling the virtues of the Wings' organization and how well it compensated its players. Most players in the room cast their eyes downward, mumbling responses, deferring to the show of power.

When Adams came to Gordie Howe, who considered him to be a second father, a look of near shame crossed number nine's face. The fact is Howe didn't want the business side of things to interfere with the game, but he was the league's top star and had the most clout. Adams asked Gordie directly if he felt management had been unfair. Seated, Howe tilted his head downward, his arms resting on his thighs, his enormous hands dangling in front of his knees. "Um, no. I mean . . . you've been good to me and my family. I don't know. I just want to play hockey."

And with that, Lindsay could feel the association slipping away.

"The Big Guy let us down," Lindsay said. Glenn was more forgiving of Howe, "Gordie wasn't totally to blame. He took too much heat for it."

The repercussions for the Wings would be dramatic. Adams actively tried to engineer a split in the locker room by portraying Lindsay as a troublemaker. Glenn was one of the first people targeted by Adams. The GM had Jimmy Skinner tell Hall he was not to speak with Lindsay anymore, that "Terrible Ted" was a bad example of a team player. Adams had picked the wrong target.

Glenn had an abiding respect for Lindsay that dated back to Hall's junior career. Ted had made a point of going to the Windsor Spitfire games to support the next generation of Wings. After a hotly contested Junior game, the Spitfire locker room would be filled with jubilant 18-year-olds all sharing the dream of playing big-time hockey. As they'd begin to peel their sweat-soaked gear away, all the while trading good-natured jabs and making post-game plans, the door would open and in would walk the captain of the team they all want to play for. "When I was in Windsor," Glenn remembered, "Ted was starring with the Wings and he'd come to watch our games. Afterward, he'd come into the locker room to speak with us and encourage us, and I never forgot that."

Couple Hall's undying respect for Lindsay with his independent nature and his distaste for being treated like a child, and he responded to Adams's admonitions by telling him that when he wanted to talk to Lindsay, he *would* talk to Lindsay. He embellished his response by making a very particular physical suggestion to Adams—one that would have necessitated a great deal of flexibility on Jolly Jack's part. It is unlikely Jack Adams had ever heard anyone tell him to go fuck himself. It was a comment Adams wouldn't forget.

Despite the internal turmoil, Glenn followed his freshman successes with a strong sophomore campaign. He led the league in wins with 38 and finished second in the Vezina race behind Plante once again, with a 2.24 goals-against average. More important, he led the Wings back to the top of the standings, as Detroit finished with 88 points, six better than Montreal. They clinched the regular-season title with a 2–1 win over the Canadiens, in which Glenn snuffed two breakaways. Their first-place finish saw them open the playoffs against third-place Boston, the team to which Adams had traded Terry Sawchuk. But Sawchuk was not in goal for this series.

At the season's halfway point, Sawchuk was recovering from a bout of mononucleosis. He came back from his illness too quickly, his play slipped, and with it his mood. Dark and brooding by nature, Sawchuk had been separated during the season from his wife and family who stayed back in Detroit after he was traded. Feeling lonely, exhausted from the mono, discouraged because of what he felt was ineffective play, Terry suddenly and unexpectedly walked away from the team, convinced he was washed up. He was hit with a hail of negative publicity generated largely by Bruin management who publicly branded him a quitter. Efforts by teammates and others to talk him back into the nets failed, and Terry took the train back to Detroit. He'd played 34 games to that point and posted a 2.38 average, hardly the numbers of an ineffective goalie.

Boston, now backstopped by goalie Don Simmons, had finished the season in third place, two points behind Montreal and only eight points off

Detroit's finish. One of the rare NHLers to catch with his right hand, Simmons had proved to be more than an able replacement for Sawchuk, playing 26 games with a 2.42 average.

In many hockey books, this is the place where the author writes about how a team is licking its chops at the prospect of facing a team's number two goalie. But professional athletes, particularly of that era, never presumed that anything less than their best efforts would earn them a championship. That would certainly be the case with the Wings as they entered the semifinals, and it would certainly be the case for Jack Adams who saw the series and the possibility of capturing another Stanley Cup as a chance to show the world just how shrewd he had been in making the big trades two seasons previous.

Simmons was very good in Game 1 at the Olympia, and the Bruins upset the Wings 3–1.

Buoyed by their first-game success, the Bruins pressed the Wings hard in Game 2 from the first drop of the puck. Just three minutes into the game, ex-Wing Vic Stasiuk found himself in the Detroit slot, the puck on his stick. He'd scored 24 goals for the Bruins, the second most on the team, and was known for his "heavy" shot; not only was the puck a threat in terms of velocity, but when it hit you, it had significant extra sting. He let the puck fly. Crouching low, Glenn was prepared for the shot to make its way through the crowd of legs in the slot. He sensed one of his defenseman moving, but did not pick up the puck until it was too late. Screaming through the scrum of players in front of the goalie, the bullet smashed into the right side of Hall's mouth, opening a ghastly wound and leaving him writhing on the ice. One reporter said that it looked as if someone "had run a hacksaw across the goalie's lips. He looked dead."

Trainer Lefty Wilson ran to the ice and pressed a towel to Glenn's face, and Hall, haltingly, started to get back to his feet. Years later, recalling the injury, he spoke about the unwritten code of honor among goalkeepers, the sense of history that made the men who played without the masks such incredibly unique athletes. He remembered, "I got up, not because I was tough or anything, but because Charlie Rayner and Turk Broda and Frank Brimsek and all of those guys prior to me, that's what they did. The goalkeeper considered himself tough. That was foremost in my mind: 'Don't let the tradition down.' Boy, you go in the closet and cry. Don't cry on center ice. I think that you didn't get up for yourself, you got up because of all the old goalkeepers."

Hall was led from the ice through the dimly lit hallway to the corridor beneath the stands and then directly to the locker room. By the time Wilson and the team doctor managed to get Glenn propped on the training table near the back of the locker room, the concussive power of the shot had started to show its full effect. His eyes had already blackened, a ripple effect from the blow to the mouth. His lips had ballooned, and blood continued to spill down his chin, forming dark blotches on the crimson of the home sweater. The team doctor surveyed the damage and shook his head.

Hall asked through the left side of his mouth, "How many'll it take, Doc?"

"A few I'm afraid," came the response. "You really caught one."

"Well," Glenn whispered, "let's get it over with."

It took nearly 30 minutes for the doctor to clean the injury and embroider Glenn's mouth with 18 stitches. His lips were little more than distended lumps, his eyes blue and purple. With images of Rayner, Broda, and Brimsek still dancing in his head, Glenn swung his legs over the end of the table, put his gloves back on, and started to walk back out of the locker room through the shadowy hallway and back toward the ice. The game had been held up, as was the custom, while the team was determinating whether or not Glenn would return or if the emergency backup, Norm Defelice, would have to get dressed. (Defelice had actually been in line to replace Sawchuk earlier that year when he was Boston property. But the sheer prospect of playing in the NHL tore at his nerves so badly that he was ineffective even in practice with the big club. Bruin coach Lynn Patrick was mortified as shot after shot baffled Defelice in practice. Seeing that the rookie wasn't equipped to handle the pressures of the NHL, Patrick released him in favor of Simmons.)

"I was afraid Stasiuk's shot hit him between the eyes and that one of them might swell shut," said Wing coach Jimmy Skinner. "When I saw where he was cut, I wasn't worried. Glenn was cut for ten stitches over the right eye in our 8–3 win over Montreal early in the season. Another time, he had eight stitches over his left eye. Both times he went right back in the nets without losing any of his effectiveness . . . When he got hit in the mouth, they did a bad job on the stitches. He had a lot of guts though. Back in Windsor, he took a skate to the cheek that tore right through it, but he insisted on finishing the game. He could have put his tongue clean through that cut. There were times this year when I didn't want to play him [because he was hurt]. But he never complained."

It was a disbelieving Olympia crowd that witnessed the man with the white number one on the back of his sweater step from the shadows of the runway and back out onto the ice. Players on the Bruin bench wondered aloud at what it would take to keep this guy out of a game. That particular question, as it turned out, would not be answered for many years. Glenn was greeted with a standing ovation, just recognition for his old-world courage, and the din continued as he assumed his place in the crease and shifted from side to side to make sure the ice in the crease was to his liking. The noise continued on until play finally resumed. Glenn's valiant effort paid off as he made 30 saves in the 7–2, series-evening victory.

But when the scene switched to Boston, the Bruins would not be denied. Simmons continued with the hot hand, and the Bruins went back to Detroit up three games to one after 4–3 and 2–0 victories. With their backs against the wall, the Wings returned home only to lose the fifth game 4–3, losing a lead going into the third period. Glenn, whose face was still swollen and discolored, had not been sharp in that last encounter.

Trainer Wilson recalled the post-game scene, "The old man [Adams] followed Hall into the dressing room and said to Glenn, 'I've done a lot for you.' Glenn gave it right back to him and said, 'Mr. Adams, I've done a lot for you.'"

If Adams said anything after that, Hall didn't hear it. Frustrated, Adams left the locker room to speak with the press. "I don't mean to criticize," he began, preparing to criticize, "but Hall looked bad on Doug Mohns's goal and worse on Cal Gardner's. We should have had a two-goal lead after the second period."

The public criticism gnawed at Glenn, who was at the end of his rope with his GM. At the same time, Adams was preparing the end of his own rope, readying it as a noose for his insubordinate goalkeeper. Jack Adams was ready to make sure that when the battered goalie skated off the Olympia's ice that night, he had done so for the last time as a Detroit Red Wing.

ESSAY: THE GAME IN THE '50S

B<small>LACK AND WHITE.</small>

Wasn't everything black and white in the '50s? Lucy, automobiles, men's suits. Everything.

Hockey certainly was. All the highlight film is recorded without color and in eight or 16 millimeter, and those facts alone jaundice the eye of the 21st century as it peers back to evaluate the game through the primitive technology of the time. Fancying myself an objective historian of the game, even I find it impossible to watch the grainy, skipping footage without first noting how different everything looks.

Start with the rink itself. The ice and boards are not polluted with sponsors' logos. The crease is a clearly defined red rectangle. Most of the rinks have wire fencing to protect the fans from errant pucks, the only exception the Montreal Forum, of course, where the sparkling new Plexiglas is firmly in place. Whether it's chain link or Plexiglas, you notice the barrier's borders end at about where the corners become the sideboards. Fans are leaning on top of the dashers along both sides of the rink, craning their necks for a better view of the action in the corners by stretching out over the actual ice surface. It's easy to spot those heads by the way, because almost all of them are topped by fedoras. The men are all in suits and ties, the ladies in dresses and formal wraps.

Above the rink looms the large, four-sided scoreboard. There's an enormous round clock in the middle of the board with two smaller replicas on each side. A large black arm on the clock face moves slowly, ticking off each minute of play, while a smaller arm sweeps underneath, tracking the seconds. This technology is incredibly approximate in nature, and fudging a second or two here and there had to be an irresistible temptation to home-team timekeepers. Determining accurate release time from the sin bin on multiple penalties was a true act of faith.

They might as well have been using a sundial.

When watching the actual play, it's impossible to miss the referee because he's so often right in the middle of the rink. He edges precariously out of the

way of rushes, often finding himself clogged in the middle of an attack, and
when he makes a call, he's often literally on top of the play. His signals look
like the ravings of a lunatic.

The pace of the play itself seems slower, more deliberate, than the pinball
we see in today's game. But that's an optical illusion, owing to the speed of
the film itself. Soon, as you watch enough of the action, your mind begins
to adjust and you appreciate the speed of the day, the toughness of the game.
Factoring in the primitive blades, the leather boots and the lack of skate-
sharpening technology, you appreciate those attributes all the more. You also
learn that the memories of reduced stick fouls in the day before helmets and
masks are decidedly selective. In almost every game, you can pick out a cruel
slash, high stick, or spear that, today, would be the subject of legal action.

What is inarguable is that the shots do not attack the goalies with the
fierce velocity that is today's norm. There doesn't seem to be the "shoot from
any angle" mentality that pervades the game now. There are more patterned
attacks, fewer deflections and screens, and infinitely more backhands. The
number of backhands taken in the '50s corresponds almost exactly with the
number of slap shots taken today. You can count slap shots on one hand
throughout playoff films of the '50s, and on those that were taken, the back
swing seldom goes higher than the knees.

All of those facts spring from the other thing that catches your eye immediately—the sticks themselves. The blades are long, very long and very
straight. They remind you of steel-table hockey games, where the figurines
sport blades that look as long as goalie sticks. With no curves on the blades,
the backhand was a better shot than the slap shot, more unpredictable and
faster from close in. Understanding this, and seeing that most of the shooting
takes place from closer in because there are so few slap shots, you understand
that the challenges goalies faced then isn't so different from the challenges
goalies face today.

You notice that the equipment itself, or the lack thereof, is distinctive.
Helmetless players attack maskless goalies, and you cringe and wince at the
pileups in the crease, assuming a fatality must be near at hand. Goalie gloves
are first-basemen mitts with a thin, attached cuff. The leg pads look somewhat familiar, distant cousins to today's weightless wonders. The blockers
look huge and heavy, as do the sticks. Each goalie looks painfully thin, a
mirage enhanced by the slight arm protection under tight sweaters that failed
miserably to protect their bodies from the ravages of the puck that was every
bit as hard then as it is today. The nets look much bigger, because the equipment is so much smaller. Goalies of the '50s were, in fact, protecting bigger

nets than their modern counterparts because their pads and gloves were smaller, and because, without masks, they couldn't use their faces to stop shots as well.

There are also smaller, more nuanced differences in the hockey of these old films. Defensemen take the face-offs in their own end, strength taking precedence over quickness and guile. The game moves more quickly without the infernal TV timeouts or the overt line jockeying by coaches. Dump-ins are rare; they're often used to take advantage of quirks in the boards of a particular rink. Goalies use their skates regularly to save shots toward the posts, and while they sometimes pounce on pucks to get face-offs, you see them sweeping rebounds off to the corners more in an effort to keep their faces out of danger. Front-of-the-net scrums and goalmouth jam-ups force skates-first defenses, their maskless faces tucked back in the net, safely away from flashing skate blades and whacking stick blades that raid the crease.

Was the game harder without all of today's equipment? Is the game better today because of the speed and technology? Were the players tougher back in the day? Are today's athletes better by nature?

Old-timers and young turks can argue these points, but in so doing they lose the big picture. Hockey was black and white then, purposeful and deliberate, brought to its widest audience through words over the airwaves. Today it is a swirl of colors, controlled mayhem accessible to millions pointing remote controls.

It was great in black and white; it is great in color. The passion in hockey can never be defined by limiting it to the technology of a particular era.

We still laugh at Lucy, and we still love the game.

6

The Trade

THE ILL WILL BETWEEN the owners and the players who were active in trying to form a National Hockey League players' association reached its peak by the end of the 1956–57 season. Ted Lindsay remained the most visible proponent of the plan, which was now openly endorsed by the Montreal Canadiens' Doug Harvey and the Toronto Maple Leafs' captain Jim Thomson. The players had clearly gained a sense of solidarity in the cause for better wages and working conditions, and the owners knew that despite their stalled momentum, something needed to be done to put down finally and absolutely what they interpreted to be a burgeoning rebellion.

Jack Adams was the owners' chief shill. He was pressured from league management above to help quash the movement, and he felt the heat from below, remaining wildly resentful of Lindsay for spearheading the movement and Glenn Hall for refusing to bow to his bullying dictates. For the past few years, the owners had been dumping their "problem children" on the league's weakest franchise, Chicago. It was not unusual for a player haggling over a contract with a general manager to hear, "Well, if you don't like what we're paying you here, maybe you can ask the Black Hawks for a raise." With the Hawks seemingly trapped in the NHL's cellar, drawing only 5,000 or 6,000 fans a game, the threat was enough to induce a player to sign on the dotted line. With the Wings' upset loss at the hands of the Bruins, Adams was handed the perfect opportunity to punish both Lindsay and Hall, quash the proposed association, and steer the fingers that were pointing accusingly at him for the Wings' downfall in another direction.

Tommy Ivan, the longtime Red Wing coach, piloted the Hawk franchise as their GM and coach, having replaced Dick Irvin in the latter capacity. Ivan was convinced of one truism in building a hockey team: you build from the goal out. He'd seen firsthand what Terry Sawchuk meant to the Detroit dynasty, and he was convinced that Chicago's road to respectability would have to be paved with a franchise goaltender. Ivan inherited the reliable Al Rollins (who had been openly skeptical of Hall and his new style of goalkeeping) in net, and the Hawks also owned the rights to former Red Wing prodigy Harry Lumley as well as to the young prospect Hank Bassen. But Ivan knew that none of the three could give him what he wanted.

Knowing that Sawchuk's mid-season meltdown had spelled the end for Terry in Boston, Ivan called Bruin GM Lynn Patrick to ask about The Uke's availability. The conversation was casual, and Patrick mentioned in passing that Adams had already called about reacquiring Sawchuk. Ivan deduced that Adams was willing to part with Hall and could barely contain himself. He knew Glenn well from his Detroit days and felt he was the perfect centerpiece around which a championship could be built. Ivan called Adams, and the two men struck a deal, contingent upon two factors: Adams getting Sawchuk from Boston, and Ivan taking Lindsay off Adams's hands as part of the trade.

From the time Sawchuk first called it quits in Boston, Adams was looking for a way to bring his "good son" home to the Wings. Sawchuk had been the loyal Adams foot soldier, viewing Jack as a second father. Although Jack certainly had a paternal feel for Terry, that emotion didn't prevent him from trading Sawchuk when it was clear Hall didn't have the injury baggage, was every bit as good as The Uke, and would come at a cheaper price. When Hall did not turn out to be a complacent son, and was indeed ready, willing, and able to treat Adams's condescensions with pointed sarcasm, Trader Jack viewed the heresy much as a slave owner would view a backtalking field hand. Since giving 40 lashes was no longer a legal option, a trade was the next best thing.

Adams called Patrick and offered him a forward he was convinced had limited potential, one Johnny Bucyk, for Sawchuk. Patrick agreed, and Bucyk would go on to be one of the Bruins' best forwards of all-time, a leader, and an eventual Stanley Cup champion. Adams then turned his attention to Ivan, agreeing to ship Hall and Lindsay to the Hawks for goalie Bassen, Forbes Kennedy, Bill Preston, and Johnny Wilson. That transaction would go down as one of the biggest steals in Chicago sports history.

"Lindsay was on his way down by then," Ivan would recall (erroneously as Lindsay was coming off one of his best seasons). "The man we were after was Hall."

"Glenn changed after the Stasiuk shot," Adams had said. "He was puck-shy and just wasn't effective after that."

Hall first heard of the trade when Lindsay called him with the news. For his part, Glenn did not seem surprised by the turn of events: "I felt sure I wouldn't be back in Detroit when I was so severely criticized in public print for my play against Boston. I can suggest a couple of reasons why I was traded. Number one is that they didn't think I would play well enough to be good over the long haul. The other is that you should never tell your general manager to go fuck himself. The combination of the two made it easy to trade me. Jack Adams felt he was always right . . . and he might have been once or twice. When we were together, I never looked at him . . . There are not many people in hockey I didn't like. Jack Adams was at the top of that list. It made it great for me in Chicago to try and prove him wrong."

Ted Lindsay, ever thoughtful and always opinionated, put the trade in perspective: "Adams was trading out of spite. He wanted to hurt us, but he only hurt the Red Wings. Glenn ended up being the best goalie in the NHL for the next 14 years."

Pauline Hall was not sorry to leave Detroit, although the prospect of moving to Chicago was intimidating at first. She recalls, "I thought, Chicago . . . Al Capone . . . we're all going to be wiped out!"

The situation Glenn was about to step into looked bleak. It had been four years since a Hawk goalie had allowed less than three goals a game. It had also been four years since the Hawks had made the playoffs. Each of those four, the team had finished dead last. In fact, they'd finished last 11 of the last 12 seasons. The team had gone 16–39–15 in 1956–57 with goalie Al Rollins posting a 3.21 average. Glenn would be going from the penthouse to the outhouse.

"So many players are hesitant to go to a team that isn't doing well," he said. "But we got a chance to lead a team out of the wilderness."

To add to the challenge, Chicago's fans had a well-deserved reputation for treating their goalies savagely. Glenn understood this to be part of the game: "All cities are rough on goaltenders. It's like this. Your play either pleases the fans or they get on you. Of course, it's easier to please them when you've got a good team in front of you."

And now Glenn didn't.

The Hawks held their training camp in St. Catharines, Ontario, where they also sponsored the local Junior team. Coming to camp, Hall assumed he would be in a three-way battle for the top job with the returning Rollins and Hawk property Harry Lumley. But Tommy Ivan had a surprise in store. He didn't even bring Rollins to camp and immediately assigned Lumley to the farm club in Buffalo.

"It gives you a bit of a lift when your boss shows obvious confidence in you," said Glenn. "We all are always out to win. But when a fellow has other capable men and still entrusts the job to you, you just want to do that much better in appreciation."

When camp ended, the club moved south to prepare for the season. Home games were played in the massive Chicago Stadium. The impressive gray edifice was located on Madison Street in the deteriorating west side of Chicago, surrounded by one of the worst slums in the United States. The drive to the arena necessitated a trip past skid row and the disoriented denizens who inhabited the neighborhood. Glenn called the drive "an education."

As poor as the Hawk record was, there were a few positives on hand before Glenn arrived. One of those positives was the leadership of Ed Litzenberger. "Litz" came to the Hawks from Montreal and deserved credit, according to teammate Glen Skov, for bringing a winning attitude to the locker room. "When I got traded to Chicago from Detroit in '55, I went from a first-place team to a last-place team," Skov recalled. "The team had a defeatest attitude. Some guys were happy with a tie game. Litz stood up to them by telling them when you tie a game . . . that's not a win. That's nothing to celebrate."

"When Glenn came to Chicago, we knew things were going to be better," said Litzenberger. "Glenn and Bobby and then Stan would be the nucleus of the family." The "Stan" he was referring to was Stan Mikita who would join the Hawks a year from then, and "Bobby," of course, was none other than the man who would come to be known as "The Golden Jet," Robert Marvin Hull.

Bobby Hull would carve a singular niche in the franchise's, and indeed the sport's, history. In his first year for Chicago, he scored an impressive 13 times, showing brief flashes of the charismatic play that would elevate him to super-star status. Powerfully built with a muscular frame and a thick mat of curly blond hair, Hull shot the puck with precision and intimidating velocity. From a goalkeeper's perspective, Hull's most dramatic effect on the sport was his eventual popularization of the slap shot. But that was a few years down the road.

Despite Pauline's trepidation about gangsters, the Halls found a home to rent in west suburban Berwyn. Pauline made the trek from Edmonton alone with baby Patrick, going the entire way via rail. Many of the players had settled in the general vicinity, and Pauline became fast friends with Doreen Litzenberger and Ann (Mrs. Pierre) Pilote. The Halls were especially fortunate to have a wonderful neighbor family, the Bortzes, who took Pauline under their wings and became lifelong friends.

Before the season started, Glenn met up with a couple of his teammates at a local establishment. Chicago is a town where politics is the main competitive sport, and a local judge happened upon the small group of hockey players.

In Canada, John Diefenbaker had just been elected prime minister. A westerner like Glenn, Diefenbaker earned Glenn's eternal admiration for giving voice to the concerns of the true backbone of the country, the farmers. The judge, who was already well liquored, began spewing his political opinions loud enough for all to hear. He caught Glenn's attention when his diatribe turned to the subject of politics north of the border.

"Tell me how in the hell a country could elect a guy like Diefenbaker?" he asked Glenn.

"Well, to tell you the truth, I would have voted for Diefenbaker myself," Glenn replied.

The judge let a look of disdain cross his face and replied, "When I think that there's a country that could elect a guy like that, I will get down on my knees tonight and thank my God I'm an American."

Without missing a beat, Glenn said, "Judge, I'll get down on my knees tonight and thank my God you're an American too."

THE SEASON STARTED just after Glenn's 26th birthday, and he opened it in dramatic fashion with a 1–0, 26-save shutout over the Leafs. Appropriately Lindsay scored the game's only goal. A minuscule crowd of just over 6,000 witnessed Glenn's play. Used to the sellout crowds at the Detroit Olympia, Glenn found himself playing in a building that was so sparsely populated that it could have qualified as the world's largest echo chamber. "If the parking attendant brought his wife to the game," Hall observed, "attendance was doubled."

The adversity of playing on a team that paled in comparison to the Wings was challenging for Glenn. He got good advice from Lindsay on how to handle the toughest times. Said Hall, "Ted told me to take it one shot at a time. I've always remembered that, especially when things got rough."

There were plenty of rough times that first year, but the team was growing closer under the influence of Litzenberger and Lindsay. "We had home games almost every Sunday night," remembered Litzenberger. "And we said that after every second Sunday, the whole team would go out to one place. It didn't matter if it was the north or south side. We'd be together. That's how we started to become a family."

"The camaraderie was easier to establish back in those days because of the train travel," said Lindsay. "But we wanted to bring a sense of togetherness to the team like we'd had back in Detroit."

"Even if we were on the road, if one guy said, 'I'm going to this place to have a beer,' the whole team would go," said Litzenberger. "When the bill came, we'd divide it equally whether you had one beer or you had a few."

Some athletes saw post-game dalliances as a natural by-product of the boys'-night-out mentality. It was an occupational hazard that Pauline Hall was well aware of. "Our second year in Detroit, I had a terrible case of the mumps," she recounted. "I'd just gotten over it and had finally recovered enough to go to one of the team parties. They were playing some game . . . passing an orange with your neck. I felt I might still be a little contagious so I declined to participate, but Glenn sure as hell didn't decline, and I remember this one bimbo who I felt had her eye on Glenn joined the game with great exuberance. Let me tell you, the orange didn't have a chance of falling to the floor when she had it. Did you wonder about infidelity? You heard rumors of it. I dispelled it, but the seeds were planted and you wondered . . ."

Ed Litzenberger, who became a very close friend of Hall's, said that Pauline never had anything to worry about: "Glenn was a one-woman man. I never saw him stray." In truth, both Litzenberger and Hall were devoted family men, and like teammates Lindsay and Glen Skov, weren't averse to a couple of post-game cold ones, but they never went on the post-game prowl.

The boys also enjoyed pre-game afternoon barbecues, initially at Glenn's house. The cook for the day was the loser of that day's last hand of cards. With all this time together the players developed a certain familiarity, and the familiarity begat the gallows humor that is crucial to a harmonious locker room. Litzenberger tagged Hall with the nickname that only teammates would call him, a nickname that his former mates use affectionately to this day.

"I started calling him 'Ghoulie,'" said Litzenberger. The twist on "goalie" came from Glenn's pre-game, white-as-a-sheet complexion. When Litzenberger, whose locker was directly across from Glenn's, first saw Glenn streak for the bathroom prior to a game, he gave his teammate a warning, "You ever get any of that on me and you'll never make it to the ice."

Glenn's aim must have been good because he made it to the ice for all 70 games once again, the third consecutive NHL season in which he played every one of his team's games. Although the quantity was impressive, it was the quality that everyone in the league noticed. The Hawks were outshot in 55 of the 70 games they played, but Glenn's play was principally responsible for lifting the team out of the league's cellar for the first time in four years. The team finished fifth. Hall posted a respectable 2.89 average, better than Sawchuk's 2.96 for third-place Detroit. He notched seven shutouts, second only to Plante's nine for first-place Montreal, a team that finished 41 points ahead of the Hawks in the standings. His efforts earned him First All-Star status for the second consecutive year ahead of Plante. Glenn had been a First All-Star the year before with a first-place team and he repeated the honor with a fifth-place finisher. He also became one of only a handful of athletes in any sport to be named a First All-Star for two separate teams. He also became the first Hawk goalie to make an All-Star team since Lorne Chabot in 1934–35.

Most significantly, though, Glenn employed his V split more and more regularly that year. It was not a conscious decision; it had just become a natural reaction, a natural part of his game. Playing on a weaker team that exposed him to more potential rebounds and screens, the V gave him better maneuverability and rebound control. The fans in Chicago noticed the team's improvement, and as the crowds grew, they realized that Hall, with his acrobatic heroics, was reason for that improvement. The locals picked up on how different their goalie was: Glenn's style was almost completely inverted from what was considered the norm. He thought nothing of leaping into the air to trap a rising shot against his chest pad then spinning into dazzling 360-degree pirouettes after low shots that caromed off his padding and into the corner.

Typical of the fans who took notice was Jack Fitzsimmons. "Fitzy" had been a regular at Chicago's home games since the early '30s. His lengthy and loyal history as a fan gave him a unique perspective on every athlete who wore the Indian Head crest. When he first witnessed Glenn's play, he couldn't quite believe what he saw. "I watched him when he first came here, and here was this guy hopping around and dropping to his knees and doing everything different from every other goalie in the league," he recalled. "I couldn't figure out how he got away with it, but I knew immediately that we now had the best goalie in the NHL. What you couldn't miss was the quickness. There wasn't a game he played where he didn't just flat out steal a goal because he was so darned quick. Eventually I got a seat right behind his net because I wanted to get as close to him as possible. I just couldn't believe how much talent I was seeing."

Glenn quickly became a fan favorite, and he regularly received rousing ovations for his work.

"Frankly the trade to Chicago was the greatest thing he [Adams] ever did for me," declared Hall. "I found that I really was a goaltender that year. I didn't have the defense I had in Detroit, but I soon discovered that I could play just as well with a weak team as a strong one."

Lindsay got the last word on Glenn's season: "The guy has kept us close all season. And no matter how tough the going, he never squawks. Most goalies put on a show and blame others for their mistakes. But I've never yet in three years heard Glenn say anything after a goal has been scored against him except to tell the guys on the ice that the goal was his fault. He's really astounding."

7

Building a Champion

THE YOUNG TEAM that Tommy Ivan was molding in Chicago was beginning to take shape. Glenn Hall was the team's cornerstone, and Ivan continued to tweak and add to the lineup. He revamped the defense, keeping young standouts Pierre Pilote and Elmer "Moose" Vasko and purchasing Dollard St. Laurent from the Montreal Canadiens, drafting Jack Evans from the New York Rangers, and also drafting Glenn's former Windsor, Edmonton, and Detroit teammate, Al Arbour, from the Red Wings.

Ivan reinforced the offense by calling up speedy Ken Wharram from the American Hockey League's Buffalo Bisons, and purchasing forward Tod Sloan for cash from the Toronto Maple Leafs. That the Chicago Black Hawks only gave up cash for Sloan would come back to haunt him. Once he was comfortable around his new teammates, Sloan was subjected to the black humor of the locker room, and halfway through the season it was accepted that Sloan was not bought by the Hawks, but actually brought in by barter for a horse.

It was that same no-sacred-cows-here locker-room humor that Glenn was occasionally the butt of. Still getting grief for his lisp, Glenn would be seated quietly on the team bus as it made its way from the training camp site in St. Catharines, Ontario, to an exhibition game in Toronto when a voice from the back would shout, "Hey, Ghoulie, how far are we from Toronto?"

The boys on the bus would titter at the "Thikthy thikth miles" reply.

Catching on immediately, Glenn was ready when he was next asked the question. "Fifty-eight and eight," he responded, a satisfied grin crossing his face.

GLENN'S SEASON STARTED with yet another All-Star game. It was his fourth consecutive appearance at the event, and for the first time he was on the losing end, finishing with 33 saves in the 6–3 Montreal win. It was his second consecutive full-game performance as an All-Star, a feat accomplished only once before—by Terry Sawchuk. Rudy Pilous, who'd taken over the coaching duties from Ivan halfway through the previous year, spent his first full season behind the bench in 1958–59. Ten thousand fans showed up for the home opener, a 1–1 tie with the Rangers. The crowds continued to grow as the Hawks kept improving throughout the year. Though the team still lost more than it won, the fans grew increasingly loud and fiercely loyal.

Although the hockey landscape was improving in Chicago at that time, there was little real change in the relationship between players and management. Despite the efforts of Ted Lindsay, Doug Harvey, and some others, the owners' stranglehold was not loosening. Early in the season, when Montreal thumped the Hawks 9–2, GM Ivan was livid, stalked into the locker room, and fined each player $100 for "indifferent play." "If you don't like it, you can quit," he said, turning on his heel.

Glenn remembered the moment well: "Howie Glover was up with the team for that game and he dressed but he didn't even play. But he had to pay the fine too. I seriously considered quitting because of the fine. It was such an insult. Montreal was so talented ... When you think about it and you take a look at who was on that team. [Maurice] Richard, [Jean] Beliveau, [Dickie] Moore, [Doug] Harvey, [Tom] Johnson. They were so powerful. They just beat us that night, but it was because they were better than us. There certainly was nothing indifferent about anything we did. I was angry enough to quit. But there was nothing we could do about it."

Not all management-player feuds were as dark. The year before, Canadien Bert Olmstead sent GM Frank Selke a letter prior to the start of the season asking for a raise. Selke's written reply was priceless:

Dear Bert:

It is a good thing I have a stout heart. Like many other men my age or even more so, I have many things wrong with me, but the doctors always tell me my heart is good. Consequently, I was able to withstand the shock when I read that you expected a $2,000 increase.

Since the training camp is not far away and as you are not much of a letter writer, I am going to say let's skip it until you come to training camp to conclude our contractual obligations for the coming year as one farmer to another ...

IT MUST JUST HAVE BEEN a coincidence that at the end of that year, Olmstead found himself unprotected and was drafted by the then out-of-the-playoff Maple Leafs.

As the season wound down, it looked as if the Hawks had a chance to make the playoffs. Although Montreal held its customary lead in the regular-season standings, spots two through six were wide open. That year, playoff order wasn't determined until the last week of the season. When the dust settled, the Hawks had squeaked into third place. They leapfrogged Jack Adams's Wings who finished dead last, and ended the year only four points behind second-place Boston, four points in front of fourth-place Toronto, and five points in front of fifth-place New York. Chicago made its first playoff appearance in six years.

Hall was the only goalie in the league to play every game of the season, and it was the fourth consecutive year he'd played every minute. His 2.97 goals-against mark was the first time since 1939 that a Hawk goalie had back-to-back seasons with a goals-against average under 3. But, for the first time in his career, Glenn did not make the All-Star team. He was nosed out of the second-team spot by Sawchuk, who finished the year with a 3.12 goals-against mark for the last-place Wings. In the two years after Hall and Lindsay left Detroit, the Wings went from league winners to third place (and were swept in the first round of the playoffs by Montreal) and then dropped into the NHL cellar.

With Montreal first and Chicago third, goalkeeping purists were treated to another Hall versus Plante playoff showdown. On paper, the series was a complete mismatch: Jacques Plante and his powerful Hab teammates had won the first meeting in 1956, and the Canadiens, who were peaking as a dynasty, finished 19 points better than the Hawks in the regular season. But the playoff appearance certainly helped to further hockey interest in Chicago.

The opening game of the series in Montreal was tied 1–1 after the first, but the Habs were just warming up. They ended up outshooting the Hawks 42–13, winning 4–2. Afterward, Montreal coach Toe Blake acknowledged Hall, who was heroic in defeat: "Games like that can go either way. I thought we should have had more goals in the second period when we outshot them 18–4. But their goaltender was real hot."

Hawk coach Rudy Pilous, who fancied himself to be quite the motivator, handed out miniature Stanley Cups to his team between Games 1 and 2 in an effort to help the players visualize what they were playing for. It didn't help. Montreal won Game 2 5–1, sending Pilous back to the drawing board. There was one light moment in that game when Plante and hulking Hawk defense-man "Moose" Vasko got tied up outside the crease, both losing their sticks. Vasko accidentally picked up Plante's and played with it briefly before notic-ing that something wasn't right. At mid-play, he went to the Hab cage and exchanged sticks with the goaltender.

Hawk owner Jim Norris took over the Department of Psychology when the series moved to Chicago for Games 3 and 4. Norris handed unsigned checks of $3,350 to each player on the team, telling them he'd sign them once the Hawks won the Cup. This incentive probably didn't hurt, but playing for the Stanley Cup requires emotion, which cannot be measured in dollars and cents. In front of a crowd of 14,723 fans, the Hawks won their first game of the series 4–2. Defensive defenseman Al Arbour, the only player in the NHL who wore glasses on the ice, scored the Hawks' first goal.

The win was headline news in Chicago, and playoff fever swept the Windy City. For the next game, over 17,000 filled the Stadium. Hall was brilliant throughout. Outshot 31–21, the Hawks tied the series with a 3–1 win. Not since 1952 had the Habs been pushed past five games in the semifinals. After the game, The Ghoulie flashed a big smile.

"One of the Montreal writers was just asking why I happened to become a goalie . . . and I'll be darned if I know," he said. When asked if the game was his best ever, he said, "It was a good game . . . I think I've had better nights. Yeah, I've had better. You can't kid yourself. This was a good one . . . Some nights a goalie might make only ten saves and still it's a great night because maybe three or four of those were tough ones."

When asked about the crowd's great enthusiasm, Hall responded, "The fans always give you a lift. But it shouldn't be that way. A good athlete should be able to ignore the crowd so he isn't bothered when playing away from home . . ."

As with any team bursting with magnificent ability and unparalleled pride, the Habs would exact their revenge. In Game 5, Montreal scored four times in the first period, and held on for a 4–2 win. Back in Chicago, a record crowd of 18,521 witnessed the sixth game, a wild affair from start to dramatic finish. Montreal dominated most of the game and held a 4–3 lead with six minutes left to play. When Lindsay beat Plante to tie the game, the din in the Stadium was ear-shattering, and the fans littered the ice with a joyous shower of debris. Moments later, referee Red Storey signaled a penalty against the Hawks, who narrowly escaped the kill against the high-powered Hab power play. With less than two minutes to go in regulation play, Bobby Hull sped toward the Canadiens' end of the ice. He was tripped and lost possession of the puck.

All 18,521 fans looked at Storey, who kept his arm at his side. As boos filtered down from the rafters, the Habs took the turnover and attacked Hall, with Claude Provost piercing the goal line. Now the 18,521 fans wanted blood. Two people jumped the boards and tried to attack Storey on the ice immediately after the play, and it took several minutes to get the Stadium under control. So dire was the situation that, for a few minutes, officials thought about calling the game and awarding a forfeit to Montreal. Play did resume, and with Hall on the bench for an extra attacker, the Hawks came close. Plante made a diving poke check to prevent fleet Hawk defenseman Pierre Pilote from getting a shot, and the Habs advanced.

Pilous and the team were livid, and the colorful Hawk mentor told the press after the game that the fans were right to attack Storey. NHL President Clarence Campbell huddled with Storey in the officials' room before meeting the press, and his public defense of the embattled official was tepid at best. "I thought it was a well-officiated game until the last calls," Campbell said.

Storey, one of the game's most veteran and respected referees, was livid. He couldn't believe that Campbell wouldn't back him completely, and he was so affected by what he saw as a total betrayal that he turned in his whistle and resigned from the game.

"We would have won the Cup that year," maintained Ed Litzenberger. "I was convinced of that and I felt Storey stole the game from us. But I spoke with him much later about it, and he told me, 'I wouldn't have called a penalty unless someone pulled a gun out. Let the boys decide it you know. It wasn't up to me to win or lose the game.' I understand that, and now I consider Red a good friend."

Montreal had a tougher challenge from the Hawks than they did from the Leafs, who'd upset Boston in the semis. The Habs won the series 4–1, winning the Cup a record fourth consecutive year, topping the previous best of three in a row by the 1947–49 Maple Leafs and earning the right to be called the greatest dynasty in hockey history.

FOR NHL HOCKEY PLAYERS, summers have long been a time to get away from the game, pursue promotions, take a vacation, and then attack a conditioning program. But in the days before free agency and multimillion dollar salaries, summer also meant work. Glenn got involved with former Edmonton Flyer teammate Ray Hannigan in fast-food restaurants in the Edmonton area. He always had it in the back of his mind that he'd be farming some day, but purchasing farmland was still beyond his reach.

Fall saw a return to camp at St. Catharines for the Hawks, who'd been buoyed by their close encounter with Montreal in the playoffs the year before. It looked as if the offense was in better shape. Young Czech émigré Stan Mikita was going to make the team this year, and there was a feeling that Bobby Hull was on the cusp of greatness. The tall rookie, Bill "Red" Hay, had an outstanding camp. Ted Lindsay was coming off a tremendous year, Ed Litzenberger had scored 33 goals the season previous, and Tod Sloan had scored 27 more goals than the imaginary horse he'd been acquired for. The defensive unit was exactly the same, and Glenn was ready to anchor the squad.

Only Rudy Pilous experienced problems in training camp. Pat Walker, who'd known Glenn since his days at Windsor when she was the secretary of the Spitfire booster club and who'd befriended Pauline when Glenn was a Red Wing, remembered the coach was very concerned that some of the boys had been breaking curfew. Pilous took to staking out the lobby of the team hotel, the Queen's Way. He'd settle into a strategically placed easy chair that, even if he fell asleep, required truants to step over him to get to their rooms.

"What Rudy didn't know," Walker related, "was that one of the players would always place a matchbook on the hinge of the back door of the hotel so they could sneak in without Rudy ever catching on."

The start of the 1959–60 season was difficult for Glenn. He struggled early on, and the enthusiasm that the team had come out of camp with evaporated quickly. In a career marked by incredibly effective consistency, Glenn battled through the first, and what remarkably would be the only, prolonged slump of his career. He was hit for 35 goals in the season's first ten games, and Hawk brass actually began looking into trade possibilities. Hall did not ask for a break to clear his mind, instead he played his way out of the slump. He recovered brilliantly, and by mid-season the Hawks were in the thick of the playoff hunt.

Pat Walker remembered visiting the team in Toronto when they played the Leafs: "After the games, the team would have to catch the train out of town. Sometimes the train would leave at midnight, sometimes later. Well, the team would go to an establishment right by the train station and have a few beers. I wasn't a drinker, but I'd go to see the boys off. Glenn would always carry his suitcase into the bar, which I thought was a little odd, and he'd hand it to the bartender to keep behind the bar. It was always very light when he gave it to the bartender. But when they had to leave to catch the train, Glenn would get the suitcase back and all of a sudden it was very heavy. It took me a while to figure out that the bartender would fill it with beer so the boys could have a few on the train."

Walker also recalled how different things were then from the world we live in today: "Last call would be 11:30 p.m., but if the train was leaving real late the boys would have nowhere to go. The owner would close the bar, tell the boys to leave the cash for what they drank on the bar, and be sure to lock up when they left."

Coming into the season, Glenn had already become a true fan favorite. His work during the season only reinforced his status and built on it, and that popularity got a big boost from Johnny Gottselig, a former Hawk player and then the team's public-relations director. Gottselig was an unabashed admirer of Hall's, and when he christened Glenn as "Mr. Goalie" the moniker stuck.

The Chicago Stadium's public announcer soon picked up on the name. When the starting lineup was being announced one day, he decided to open it with: "In goal, Number One . . . Mr. Goalie . . . Glenn Hall!" The words whipped the Chicago crowd into a frenzy.

Chicago fans were gaining a reputation as the most boisterous in the league. The Hawks were a physical team, an improved team, and combining those factors with the Stadium's smaller ice surface (about 190 feet in length versus the standard 200, and slightly smaller in width) and the building's acoustics made Chicago an increasingly difficult place to play. The strong bonds the team were forging provided the purpose and direction, the togetherness that is so crucial to the success of any team. The foundation had been laid, the first story of team-building was taking shape.

Into the second half of the 1959–60 season, the Hawks continued to flirt with the .500 winning percentage level. Bobby Hull was fulfilling the prophecies of excellence, en route to a league-leading goal total of 39 and a point total of 81. Red Hay made a splash and earned rookie-of-the-year honors. But Lindsay's production fell off dramatically, as did Litzenberger's. The hard miles of Ted's career caught up to him, while Litz endured a terrible family tragedy, losing his wife, Doreen, in a car accident.

"I had to go and pick up the Litzenbergers' son," Pauline remembered. "He stayed with us for a week before going off to live with his grandparents. It was so terribly sad. I remember thinking, 'Why isn't the world stopping?' Around me, I saw life going on, people going about their everyday business, and here we'd lost this wonderful lady in the prime of her life. There's no understanding it."

BY THE LAST WEEKEND of the season, the standings were all but set. Montreal had clinched the league by 13 points over second-place Toronto, which was ten points ahead of third-place Chicago, which was two points ahead of Detroit. Only two issues had not been settled going into the season's last regular-season game: the Vezina Trophy and the league scoring title. History repeated itself as Jacques Plante was being given another tough run for the award by Glenn whose Hawks finished 23 points behind the Canadiens. Going into that last game, Plante had played 68 games and allowed 172 goals. Charlie Hodge had played one game for Montreal and allowed three. The Ghoulie had played 69 games and allowed 175 goals. The teams were exactly tied. Hall and the Hawks were playing in Boston; Plante and the Habs were in New York. Jacques was going for his fifth consecutive Vezina, which would eclipse the previous best of four consecutive achieved by former Canadien goalie, Bill Durnan. Hall was gunning for his first.

Another unsettled race that night was for the scoring title, and the two combatants were Chicago's Bobby Hull and Boston's Bronco Horvath. Both the Hawks and Bruins went all-out that night to win the scoring title for their respective players. In so doing, they left Hall marooned in a way that Plante never had been by his defensive-proud Montreal mates. Hull outscored Horvath by a point in the 5–5 tie to win the Art Ross Trophy for scoring, which left Hall two goals shy of his first Vezina. It was the second time that Hall had lost the Vezina on the last weekend of the season.

There are some interesting factors to consider about the Vezina at the time. First, Plante's Montreal defensemen were rumored to have Vezina bonuses written into their contracts. After all, the award truly was a team defense award. Plante was always the first to say that the team with the best goals-against average usually wins the league title, and that was the Canadiens' philosophy. When Tommy Ivan ran things on the ice for the Hawks, they too had a defense-first policy, but as the team progressed under Pilous and acquired more skill, they moved away from that.

Statistically no adjustments were made in the Vezina award to take into consideration empty-net goals. Research shows that the Hawks gave up five empty-netters in 1959–60, very likely more than the Canadiens who usually protected a lead late in games. That was more than the margin of victory in the Vezina race. Glenn, remaining the consummate team player, never voiced any disappointment that his teammates didn't set winning the Vezina as a team priority. But he certainly had a right to.

The league still recognized Hall's remarkable season. That the Hawks finished 23 points behind the Canadiens, yet Hall was so close to the Vezina, was nearly miraculous. He led the league in shutouts for the second time in his career, notching six. He became the first Hawk goalie to post three consecutive years with a goals-against average under 3. Most significantly, for the third time in his five-year career, Hall was named to the First All-Star team, matching Sawchuk's honors during the same time span.

For the second time, Montreal coach Toe Blake blasted the voters: "We win first place, Plante wins the Vezina for the fourth time, and he's not the All-Star?"

"My guy was the best," shot back Pilous. "And he played without a mask."

Pilous's comment was a direct shot at Plante that must have registered with Blake. On November 1, 1959, Jacques had been bloodied by an Andy Bathgate shot in New York. After getting the requisite stitches, he informed Blake that he wanted to wear the mask for the remainder of the game. Blake had battled Plante's experiments with facial protection over the previous years, sure that the contraptions would limit vision at his feet, and convinced that such equipment was a sign of cowardice.

"Does jumping out of a plane without a parachute make you a coward?" retorted Plante.

As it turned out, there was much more drama in the Vezina race than in the contest for the Stanley Cup. Montreal continued to assert itself as one of hockey's most dominant dynasties. The team swept past Hall and the Hawks in the semis in four games, Plante whitewashing Chicago in the last two games of the series by 4–0 and 2–0 scores, and then topped Toronto in the finals in four games. The Habs' fifth consecutive Stanley Cup victory is a hockey record that has never been equaled. It seemed that the Canadiens could go on winning indefinitely. Even with Maurice Richard's imminent retirement, the Habs would be left with an amazing array of talent in front of Plante. No one would have predicted that on the night of April 14, 1960, when Plante threw his hands in the air after the final buzzer sounded to give the Cup to the Canadiens, he'd won it for the last time in his career.

8

The Changing of the Guard

FROM THE VERY BEGINNING of the 1960–61 season, it was clear this would be a milestone year for Hall and the Hawks. Glenn made the usual trip to camp, leaving Pauline, son Pat, four, and daughter Leslie, two, to join him after the team moved back to Chicago.

Glenn arrived at camp knowing he would not be getting a substantial raise in pay. In late July, he received a letter from Tommy Ivan whose secretary was apparently unfamiliar with the name of the team's only goalie:

Mr. Glen Howell [sic]
15806 94-A Ave.,
Edmonton, Alberta, Canada

Dear Glen [sic]:
   In answer to your letter with your request for your basic salary ...
   No. 1. Your request is too high.
   No. 2. I have been reviewing your previous contracts since you joined the Chicago hockey club and I find that regardless of the results, attendance, etc. of the Chicago hockey club, you have had a raise in your salary every year.
   I think we have been more than fair in our dealings, and as training camp is rapidly approaching, I would like to hear from you as soon as possible.
   Very truly yours,
   Thomas N. Ivan

Despite his tendency to squeeze the players at contract time, Ivan had his strong points. Glenn remembered that when he was being criticized for his unorthodox style, Tommy related a story: "He told me once that when he was a Midget coach, he had a goalie who made him very nervous. It seemed like he was doing a lot wrong, and he spoke to another coach. He told that coach that every time the other team took a shot, he [Tommy] would cringe, fearing the worst was going to happen. The coach looked at Tommy and said, 'But is he stopping the puck?' The answer was 'Yes.' I think that was Tommy's way of telling me to ignore the critics."

Before Pauline's arrival, Glenn had opened his rented bungalow in Berwyn to teammates Stan Mikita and Ed Litzenberger. Two close members of this circle of friends were missing now. Ted Lindsay had retired, and Glen Skov had been traded to Montreal over the summer for Ab McDonald. "You cannot overestimate what Ted meant to our team," said Glenn. "He instilled the value of perseverance. He taught us all so much and we continued to feel the importance of those lessons even after he'd left."

By the time Skov was dealt, he'd played four years in front of Sawchuk and four years in front of Hall and was in a good position to evaluate both men. "They were virtually indistinguishable in the '50s," he reflected, "although Glenn had the better catch hand."

PAULINE HALL HAD WILLINGLY played mother hen to Mikita the year before as the magical Czech adjusted to life in the United States, but when she arrived with the kids early in the 1960–61 season, she found him firmly ensconced in her home. She remembered: "Stan and I had so much fun. I laughed at everything he said or did. Glenn would admonish me and say you're only encouraging him to act sillier. But I had a hard time dislodging Stan and Litz from our house. When they were at practice, I'd put their suitcases on the lawn, and they'd come home and just bring them back into the house. Stan had a penchant for sleepwalking, talking, and doing various things in his sleep which I can't mention. This old house we lived in had an attic that could only be reached by a ladder of sorts, and you had to be very agile to master the ascent. One night I heard this terrible ruckus upstairs, so I had to get up and climb the ladder and find the one light bulb to see what the heck was going on. There, in a corner covered in dust and dirt from the old attic, sat Stan. I asked him what in hell he was doing up here. He looked at me blankly and only said, 'Ed isn't coming home tonight.' I thought, 'Thank God.' So I convinced him he should come downstairs and I put him to bed."

"Pauline could see I'd just come from a small farm town in Canada," recalled Mikita. "It started when [the Halls] invited me for dinner and they treated me like one of their own. I couldn't have made it without them."

Litzenberger eventually rented a house nearby, which he shared with the night-wandering Czech. But game-day pre-game meals were still barbecued in the Hall yard. "Stan would pass his steak over the barbecue for a minute, and if you gave the steak a little encouragement it would have come to life and made for the pasture," recalled Pauline.

Not everyone was thrilled with the pre-game tradition. The Halls had a next-door neighbor who Pat and Leslie had nicknamed "The Mean Lady." If any of the smoke from the cooking wafted her way, she stomped out to her backyard, pulled her laundry off the line, then harrumphed her way back into her home, shut the windows, and drew the drapes. After enough of these protestations, the barbecues were moved to Ed and Stan's place.

Glenn's pre-game meal included the steak—rare—and a baked potato. Glenn remembered: "They used to have the marathon seven-day bicycle races [events held at the Chicago Stadium]. I met Torchy Pedein, who was a terrific racer and had these huge legs. He told me that when he ate a baked potato, he could ride two hours longer."

Pauline never minded not cooking: "How would you like to cook for a guy who's going to throw up what you just made in a matter of hours?"

After the meal, it was time for the afternoon nap. Long before it was "discovered" by sports medicine, Glenn and most athletes of the day practiced visualization. "Like, I'd always picture plays in my mind that might occur in the game that night," said Glenn. "I didn't know there was anything scientific to it. I just did it as a natural part of my preparation."

ON THE ICE, Glenn celebrated his return to the First All-Star team by back-stopping a 2–1 win over the Stanley Cup champion Canadiens, making 26 saves in a victory that was a sign of things to come. The Ghoulie was nosed out of the Vezina again in the season's last week, this time by four goals to defense-oriented Toronto and its goalie, the ancient marvel Johnny Bower. Glenn made the Second All-Star team, also behind Bower. For the second year in a row, Glenn's six whitewashes led the league. More significant, his Hawks broke the .500 winning percentage mark for the first time in over a decade, making the playoffs for their third consecutive year with their third consecutive third-place finish. Their record had improved each year with Glenn in goal, but they still finished 17 points behind front-running Montreal.

The Hawk wives became as close off the ice as their husbands were in the locker room. "We were a 'forced group,'" states Pauline. "We found ourselves brought together by circumstance, and perhaps at the beginning our relationship to one another was coincidence. But we supported each other and we made our own fun. We did become genuinely close after a time. [Daughter] Leslie's first birthday party was a gathering of the wives. We'd go out to buy new hats, and we'd keep wearing the lucky ones. Of course, they were lucky if we'd won the game we wore them to."

Chicago embraced their Hawks too. The Stadium that was once three-quarters empty regularly hosted full houses. And the Chicago fans were easily the rowdiest and most indescribably partisan in the game. A home-team goal was saluted not only with a thunderstorm of noise, but a shower of paper cups, toilet paper, and almost anything that wasn't nailed to the floor would rain down from the upper reaches of the second balcony. Delays to clear the ice were routine after each home score, as many of the fans gave themselves and their belongings totally to the ebb and flow of the game. They were unlike fans in Montreal and Toronto who, while rabid, viewed each game as if they were critiquing a play. The noise, the clapping, and the enthusiasm accentuated the Hawks' already tangible home-ice advantage, and all throughout the season, that advantage grew as the team climbed above the .500 mark.

"Chicago was a Midwestern, blue-collar town," said sophomore center Bill Hay. "The people were solid. I think they responded to our blue-collar work ethic. They looked at us as players and felt we were their kind of people. I think that's why they responded so well to us."

The Canadiens had won the league title four years in a row and the Stanley Cup five years in a row. They'd also won their last ten playoff games. In 1960–61, they won the league by a scant two points over Toronto. Montreal coach Toe Blake continued to trumpet his goalie's virtues to the press, but the tone had changed. Jacques Plante's eccentricities and his physical unreliability continued to wear at Blake. The complaints about asthma (which seemed to affect him only in Toronto), the whining about injuries that other goalies shrugged off as normal, and the open criticism of his teammates were driving Blake mad. Toe had been confiding to Canadien insiders that he was fed up with coming to the rink and not knowing whether or not his goalie was going to play. Jacques had recorded his career-low third shutout in the Canadiens' last regular-season game of the year. Although Plante had never played a full 70-game season, he made only 40 appearances due to a legitimate knee injury, and recorded a career-high 2.80 goals-against average. Blake was uncharacteristically silent when Plante was not voted to the All-Star team.

The Hawks could easily have felt frustrated at facing the Habs for the third consecutive playoff semifinal. Montreal held an 8–2 edge in the win-loss column over the previous two series. But despite the disparity in points accumulated during the year, the Habs and Hawks split their 14-game season series right down the middle in 1960–61, each club posting five wins with four ties. Neither team had exploited any home-ice advantage head-to-head. Both teams actually had better success away, each fashioning three road wins. The Hawks won their last meeting of the year between the teams just a week before the playoffs opened, 4–1 at the Forum, despite being outshot 38–20. Each team scored 80 goals, 40 at home and 40 on the road.

Chicago entered the series relatively injury-free. Montreal's Bernie Geoffrion incurred a leg injury that required a cast, but even he made an appearance in the series by removing the cast (against doctor's orders) with some help from Doug Harvey. Dickie Moore was the Habs top scorer against the Hawks; meanwhile the Canadiens had held Bobby Hull to two goals throughout the season. Plante entered the series with 11 career playoff shutouts, two shy of Turk Broda's all-time best of 13. Hall had yet to record a single one.

The series opener in Montreal was tight until the third period. Plante was excellent in the first period as Chicago dominated play, outshooting the Habs 12–4, but only coming away even at 1. The teams exchanged goals in the second period, but the Habs were absorbing Chicago's physical play and looked to have more energy. In the third the Hawks looked gassed, and goals less than a minute apart by Moore and Phil Goyette broke the game open. The Habs coasted to a 6–2 win. The one positive for the Hawks was that head coach Rudy Pilous abandoned the hideous "lucky" green suit.

Game 2 started out close as well. Plante stopped nine shots in the first period and Hall eight. Neither man was beaten. In the second, Chicago took a 2–0 lead behind goals from Stan Mikita and Ken Wharram. On the second goal, Wharram blocked a shot, and the rebound skipped harmlessly toward the Canadien blue line. Plante took a step out of his cage slowly and then committed to chase the puck down. His hesitation cost him. Wharram, one of the fastest players in the league and the fastest on the Hawks, outraced him to the puck and slipped it into the open net. That incident would have destroyed a lesser team, but the Canadiens were the Canadiens, and they stormed back. Before the period was over, Bernie Geoffrion and Henri "Pocket Rocket" Richard had tied the game and the Canadiens had outshot the Hawks 13–6. Hull gave the Hawks a third-period lead, but Goyette answered before Ed Litzenberger notched the game winner on a point-blank chip shot over Plante's left shoulder. The Hawks had tied the series with a 4–3 win.

That win seemed to bond all of Chicago. The Hawks' young team had now fully captured the town's imagination. Hall's magical consistency, Hull's charisma, Mikita's feisty temperament and creative puck work turned Chicago into a full-fledged hockey town. "When I first got there," Hall said, "there would have been a traffic jam if you saw a kid carrying a hockey stick down the street because people would be stopping their cars to look."

When the series shifted to Chicago's West Side on March 26, there was a palpable buzz throughout the city. With the tickets sold out for the game, the line for standing room formed early. Published attendance figures said that 16,666 people attended the games, but that figure was a fictional understatement manufactured to satisfy Chicago's fire code. In truth, upward of 20,000 jammed inside the Stadium for the home opener. What they saw was a classic.

Montreal hit the ice ready to make a statement. They pelted Hall with 19 shots while the Hawks could only muster seven. The first period ended scoreless. The second stanza was more even. For every strong save Hall made, Plante answered in kind at his end of the ice. With a minute and a half to play in the second, Hull intercepted a Doug Harvey clearing pass and moved the puck to center Red Hay. Hay's shot was stopped, but Murray Balfour poked home the rebound to make it 1–0. The home loyalists went wild. The third period was all Montreal. They strafed Hall with shot after shot, each of which he turned away acrobatically. Coach Blake tried desperately to solve Hall, uncharacteristically juggling his lines hoping to create a break. With less than four minutes to play, it looked as if Montreal's fate was sealed when Jean-Guy Talbot was sent to the box by referee Dalton MacArthur. The crowd roared its approval as it watched the clock tick down.

Just seconds before Talbot stepped out of the box, MacArthur's hand shot up in the air and he whistled the Hawks' Hay for tripping. A pall of apprehension descended over the crowd. Talbot jumped back onto the ice with less than a minute to go and headed to the Canadien bench. Racing there next to him was Plante, lifted for an extra attacker and providing the Habs with a 6–4 manpower edge. With 42 seconds to play, the Hawks couldn't get the zone cleared and settled for a face-off. Phil Goyette won the draw for Montreal and pushed the puck back to Henri Richard. On the choreographed play, Richard stepped through a seam, made a deft head fake, and caught Hall leaning. His against-the-grain shot found the back of the net. The crowd was silenced; there were 36 seconds left in regulation play, the goal pushing the contest into overtime and depriving Hall of his first-ever playoff shutout.

The best seats in the Stadium were in the first row of the balconies. You had an incredible view of the entire ice surface, and the lip of each balcony hung almost directly over the action. That night, those in the first row were treated to a pressure goaltending clinic featuring two of the greatest who ever played at the height of their powers. It was Hall versus Plante in overtime, proving why their styles and innovations would be staples of the trade forever.

As you looked down from the balcony, the masked one was to the left. He was wearing an updated version of the hideous facial protection he'd worn initially. His features were covered by a pretzel-like configuration of fiberglass that protected him from pucks and sticks, and also hid a scowl of intensity. You could see it in his body language. Every time a Hawk got possession of the puck, the mask twisted back as he glanced at his posts, calling upon that intuitive radar that told him exactly where to plant himself so the shooter could see almost nothing of the target. He pushed hard off his skates in an "I dare you" challenge to set his stance and angle in preparation for the rush. His catch glove habitually pushed down at the top of his left pad, exposing a slash of white fleece at the top hem as he dipped that knee lower than the right. He dangled his glove inches from the ice, the big red *C* with the little blue *H* inside at the center of his white sweater.

To the right was the cherub-faced warrior, his hairline starting to push back. His sweater was blood red, the proud Indian crest in the front-middle, a sleek number one halving the back, black-and-white piping at the elbows and along the bottom hem. As the Canadiens pushed the puck up the ice toward him in a coordinated attack that was as deadly as it was dazzling, he sprinted forward, almost to the hash marks. He pushed his weight to the front of his skates, his catch glove hovering low toward the ice, knees slightly touching, skates more than shoulder length apart. As the onslaught neared, he squinted his eyes as if aiming two lasers, his arms swinging slightly, readying for a strike. Then he began a retreat, shifting his weight slightly from side to side in a dance that gave him his puck-stopping rhythm. The closer he got to the goal line, the wider base he formed with his skates, his body folded almost in half crunching his 5-foot, 11-inch frame below the 4-foot height of the crossbar.

The first overtime was defensive in tone, the teams posturing like two prize fighters feeling each other out. Hall snared a Beliveau wrister with his glove and slammed the door on a partial breakaway from Richard: Plante made a stretching skate save against Hay. The only goal-line violation came when Harvey tipped a puck past Hall with a high stick. It wasn't a close call, and referee MacArthur immediately waved his hands. Neither goalie faltered, neither team stepped up with the game breaker after that, and the period ended scorelessly.

The second overtime was the polar opposite. A livid Toe Blake watched as MacArthur whistled Talbot to the penalty box again. Plante stopped a Hull shot with his chest and whipped the rebound into the corner. The penalty kill accomplished, the Habs set about to end the game. They mounted several rushes, displaying the "fire wagon" system of moving the puck up the ice quickly with short passes to whomever was the lead man. Hall shut everything down. Halfway through the period, Hawk defender Dollard St. Laurent took a turn in the box. Beliveau led the feared Hab power play onto the ice but came up empty. Two minutes after the kill, the Habs took another penalty, to the delight of the crowd. Blake was incredulous that his team faced a second kill in overtime, but they faced it and killed it. Period 5 ended without a decision.

The first ten minutes of the third overtime cemented the Hall legend in Chicago. Only eight seconds into the period, Hawk Ron Murphy was penalized. Thirty seconds later, Beliveau found himself alone in front of the net against Hall and he fired low right. Hall's pad save brought the fans out of their seats. The penalty was over, but the Canadiens threw wave after wave at the Hawk net. At the other end of the ice, Plante cut his angle on a rare Hawk incursion. He forced a shot wide, but wing Tod Sloan went uncovered on the weak side. He had the puck and six by four staring at him . . . and missed the net. Hall stopped Marcel Bonin and Junior Langlois from close in. Later in the period he robbed Bonin again. But the saves anyone present that night remembers came near the seven-minute mark. Richard stripped a Hawk defender of the puck and broke in alone. He deked twice and Hall stayed with him, sprawling aggressively to take the lower half of the net away, stoning the Pocket Rocket. Two minutes later, Claude Provost found himself on a breakaway. He dropped a shoulder, trying to get Hall to commit. Displaying nerves of steel, Hall didn't budge so Provost shot. The puck was stabbed out of its flight inches from the goal by Glenn's trapper. The assemblage responded with an ovation that sounded like the home team had finally scored.

"We had it practically sewn up at least twice in overtime," recalled Hab defender Doug Harvey. "When Richard broke in the clear, I thought it was over. After that, they had us." Said another Hab of Hall: "I wished to hell he'd been a forward." By the halfway mark of the third overtime, Hall had made 53 saves to Plante's 43.

At 11:44 of the sixth period, MacArthur's hand went up again, and he signaled Canadien sharpshooter Moore off the ice. Blake was inconsolable. He screamed and gestured wildly, protesting to no avail. Seconds into the power play, Pilote passed to Mikita at the point. The diminutive center sent a shot toward the goal. Murray Balfour was facing the shot in front of Plante. He caught the puck with his stick, stopped, and slithered a slow shot toward the goal, his back still to the net. Balfour never saw the puck cross the goal line, but he heard the detonation of joy as 20,000 spectators did.

"That was the greatest moment of my life," he would say after the game. Balfour lived only a few years longer before succumbing to cancer at age 29.

Toe Blake had other thoughts, mostly centered on wrapping his hands around MacArthur's throat. With the Stadium exploding all around him, Blake made a beeline toward MacArthur and took a swing at the referee. The story was that his attempt didn't make contact with the embattled ref. But league Presdient Clarence Campbell connected with a whopping $2,000 fine. Blake had expected to divvy out $500 (after all, he said, he missed), but he accepted the punishment without appeal. "A suspension would have hurt me more," he said. But the truth was that Blake actually did strike the referee, a fact that Campbell, perhaps fearing a replay of the Richard riots if he had to eject Blake from the playoffs, likely wanted to cover up.

The Black Hawk post-win euphoria lasted exactly 48 hours. With Blake having regained his composure, the Canadiens showed up at the Stadium ready to administer a thrashing. They fired 60 shots at Hall (52 in the first two periods alone!), while the Hawks mustered a measly 21 at Plante en route to a 5–2 loss that evened the series at two games each.

The first four games of the series were a microcosm of the worlds that these two goalies lived in. Hall had been beaten for 15 goals in the first four games to Plante's ten, but the series was tied. The Hawks were being dramatically outshot. Glenn *was* the Black Hawk defense, Jacques had to be there when his defense broke down. Glenn's job was to keep his team afloat and close. Jacques was needed only to put a nail in the coffin. Hall's challenge was to stay on top of his game while battling fatigue from overwork. Jacques faced the task of staying focused past long periods of inaction. That Plante played behind the more talented team was never in dispute.

The series moved back to the Forum, and the Hawks tested Plante early and often, firing 14 shots his way. Hulking defenseman "Moose" Vasko solved him on a power-play shot from the point that Blake felt Jacques should have handled. The Hawks held a 1–0 lead through two periods—Les Canadiens had managed only 15 shots on Hall in 40 minutes. The home team responded in the third period, firing away. Dickie Moore, Phil Goyette, and Jean Beliveau all had good chances for Montreal, but the first goal of the period was scored by Chicago's Ab McDonald, staking the Hawks to a 2–0 lead. Panic set in on the Hab bench, and the Canadiens shot more and from all angles, but with less than five minutes to go, Mikita sniped one from 15 feet away to give the Hawks an insurmountable 3–0 lead. That margin stood, as Hall turned aside all 17 third-period shots and 32 on the game to record his first career playoff shutout and move the Hawks to within a game of a stunning upset. A Montreal reporter said this about Hall: "Glenn Hall was so good he could have stopped the Johnstown Flood for 60 minutes."

Another maniacal crowd filled the Stadium for the sixth game of the set. Roars went up every time the Hawks neared the Canadien zone. Hall turned aside all 12 shots in the first, including four on a two-minute, two-man advantage the Canadiens enjoyed. Just a minute into the second period, Hay scored for the Hawks. Four minutes later, linemate Hull buried a shot past Plante from the left side, and ten minutes after that Balfour scored, staking the Hawks to a 3–0 lead. When the siren ended the second period, the Hawk faithful leaped to their feet in a deafening salute. The blood was in the water, and the sharks were circling the Canadien dynasty. In the third period, the Habs went out with a whimper as the Hawks finally outshot them, 12–5. With four minutes to go, the crowd rose to their feet pleading for a second consecutive shutout for their beloved Mr. Goalie. When it was over, firecrackers popped and paper and debris poured down on the ice in a salute to the home team and to Hall. He had gone 137 minutes without allowing a goal over the last three games and had made 200 saves in the six-game series.

After the game, the Hawk locker room was flooded with press who recorded the accolades Hall's teammates laid at his feet. But the biggest tribute came from the enemy camp. Hab general manager Frank Selke entered the room and went right to Hall. Extending his hand, he quipped, "Let me shake hands with a thief. You killed us."

Hall shook his hand and answered, "Thanks, but that's only part of the story. Seventeen other guys played just as well as I did to make this victory possible." Hall reminded reporters that the Hawks felt they could win the series going into it because of the regular season. "In other years, they outplayed us all during the regular season. This year was different. We played them even. I think we all realized we were in the same class with them. And we did it with a team performance. Everybody contributed his share."

In the other semifinal, Detroit pulled an upset of their own, ousting the second-place Leafs in five games behind stellar work from Gordie Howe and Terry Sawchuk. Sawchuk earned game-star honors in all five games and was hailed as "the Sawchuk of old." The Wings had not been to the finals in five years, when Hall backstopped them there in his rookie campaign. Their victory set up the first U.S.-only final series in 11 years.

The Stanley Cup finals opened at the Chicago Stadium on April 8. The town was consumed with all things Black Hawk. The team had not won a Cup since 1938 and had not been in the finals since 1944, and the city had not hosted a professional sports championship in 14 years. That had been a Chicago Cardinal football title. Chicago was ready to be the Second City no more.

With Game 1 about to begin, Jack Adams was perched high above the action, watching Hall clear the ice shavings from his crease. Across the rink was Sawchuk. Glenn was totally focused on the game. He was never the type of athlete who needed extra motivation to excel, but it was there for him in this series. He was pitted against the goalie he'd replaced who, in turn, came back to replace him. On the highest stage of the hockey world, the man who earned the nickname Mr. Goalie could now earn the last laugh on Adams.

The Hawks raced off to a 3–0 first period lead on eight shots and drove Sawchuk from the nets. The oft-injured veteran was fighting off shoulder pain that was aggravated when he was hit while trying to clear a loose puck behind the net. Taking his place was the goalie involved in the Hall trade, Hank Bassen. Bassen, who shared net duties all year with Sawchuk, performed admirably in relief stopping all 21 shots he faced. Hall held the fort until late in the second period, when a Wing goal cut the Chicago lead to 3–1. It was the first shot to beat him in 173 minutes. Detroit scored in the game's last minute to make the final 3–2, Hall finishing with 34 saves.

The second game was played in Detroit's Olympia with the Wings reversing the scoring trend. They bested Hall twice in the first period and limited the Hawks to two shots on goal in that frame. The Wings rallied to protect Bassen, who gave up a soft goal in the second period to Pilote. Detroit scored into an empty net, with Hall pulled in the last minute, to carve a 3–1 final.

Game 3 was back at the Stadium. Hall was brilliant in the first, stopping 14 shots, and his mates netted three behind Bassen in the second period to give them a 3–1 win and a 2–1 series lead. Game 4 was back in Detroit, and Sawchuk returned to the nets in good form. With seven minutes left in a 1–1 tie, rookie Bruce MacGregor drove one at Hall that the goalie seemed to have smothered, but the puck leaked through his pads and across the goal line. The Hawks protested that Wing Howie Glover was in the crease but to no avail. Photos of the play show Glover clearly in the crease. Coach Pilous and GM Ivan complained vociferously to the press, and they were rewarded with $200 and $300 fines from the league respectively.

Back in Chicago for Game 5, the Wings doubled the Hawks shots in the first period but came away tied at two. The teams exchanged goals late in the second, setting up a third period that would put one team within a game of the Cup. Having been outshot 22–17 at that point, the Hawks rallied for their best period of the playoffs. Chicago lost their leading clutch goal-getter Murray Balfour early in the period and for the rest of the series with a broken arm, but to the delight of the partisan crowd Mikita scored three minutes into the stanza. Five minutes later, Pilote extended the lead to two goals, and six minutes after that Mikita nailed it shut. The Hawks threw 24 shots at the beleaguered Sawchuk in the third, while Glenn handled 11 flawlessly. Each team had defended its home ice in each contest, and the 6–3 spanking sent the series back to Detroit.

"Before that sixth game, we knew we were 'this close' to the Cup," said Glenn. "We didn't want to go back to Chicago and have it come down to one game. We knew we had to have this game."

A total of 14,328 Wing fans watched the Hawks start the sixth game feebly. Bassen was back in goal as Sawchuk's shoulder was ailing yet again, and he watched his Wings get to the first intermission with a 1–0 lead. Bassen faced only four shots. In the second period, Detroit was looking to expand its lead on an early power play. During these two minutes, two momentum-changing events inspired Chicago. While killing the penalty, little-used Reg Fleming intercepted a pass and surprised Bassen with the tying goal, his only score of the playoffs. The Wings were stunned, but came right back on the attack. Defenseman Pete Goegan was set up in the slot with a shot. His drive tipped off a stick and hit the crossbar behind Hall. Reacting to the initial shot, Glenn was on his way down and then with the tip, he jerked his upper body backward. After the puck struck the crossbar, it shot straight down. Hall never lost sight of it, somersaulting backward to catch it before it hit the ice or crossed the goal line for a near-miraculous stop. The Hawks started to feel as if it was meant to be. A few minutes later, the Wings were on another power play, and Howe fired one from 25 feet away. Hall blocked the blast with his right arm, only to see the puck pop over and behind him. He twirled instantly to trap the puck before it could cross the line. National Hockey League President Clarence Campbell said later that Hall "broke Detroit's back with those saves."

With less than two minutes in the period, Hull's bullet drive from the wing produced a rebound that McDonald powered home, and the Hawks went to the dressing room with a lead, 20 minutes away from the Cup. The combination of standout saves and this late goal left Detroit deflated. The Hawks punched three more past Bassen in the third to reach the end of the rainbow.

When the final buzzer sounded, the Hawks raced toward Hall, smothering him with a cloud of gloves and hugs. As the Stanley Cup was brought to center ice, the team lifted The Ghoulie on its shoulders and gave him a ride around the rink, prompting one newspaperman to note, "It's about time they carried Hall. He's been carrying them for the past four years."

Hall had made 386 saves in the 12-game playoff. He threw a wall up against Montreal, almost singlehandedly putting an end to the Canadien dynasty and rebutting Toe Blake's insistence that Jacques Plante was the game's premier goalie. He beat the team who traded him, beat the goalie he was traded for and the goalie he replaced. The Hawks became the first team that finished lower than second place in the regular season to win a Cup since 1948. Those facts could not have been lost on Glenn. And they must have added to the incredible satisfaction of having his name on the Cup. But staying totally in character, Mr. Goalie had this to say immediately after the win: "I was mighty happy after it was over. I was a member of a Stanley Cup team, and there's no doubt that's the ambition of every hockey player. It was the final result of what you had been looking for all of your life. It was an 18-man effort. Everyone contributed and worked as hard as they could have."

Years later, Glenn remembered the post-game scene in the locker room, "Only one of us had won a Cup before. The rest of us really didn't know how to celebrate. So we looked at Ab McDonald [who'd come to the team from Montreal] and he was just sitting there smiling and happy to be a part of it."

A blizzard prevented the Hawks from returning home to celebrate, so Hawk brass set up a party in Detroit. The Hawk wives who'd stayed back home celebrated on their own. "A bunch of us girls decided we would make sure 'The Mean Lady' knew we'd won the Cup, so we tossed an awful lot of snowballs at the side of her house," Pauline noted proudly.

When the snow cleared, a second celebration was arranged at a swank downtown hotel with loads of food and champagne for the conquering heroes. The legendary "Boss," Chicago's mayor Richard J. Daley, proclaimed that the Hawks were "the best team of any sport at any time."

NHL President Clarence Campbell was present that night, and Pauline lobbied for a cause dear to her heart. "I hated that the boys always had a game on Christmas," she recalled. "Would it have been so hard to leave Christmas open for them to spend with their families? Well, I gave Campbell complete hell about it that night and I don't know if that conversation was the reason but soon thereafter the games on Christmas were dropped."

When the last of the champagne was poured, Mr. Goalie headed back home to western Canada and his summer job at the fast-food restaurant. The image of Hall behind a counter flipping burgers just weeks after killing the Montreal dynasty seems incongruous. Here was the acrobat who'd just elevated one of the world's largest cities onto the world's hockey stage, turning it into a hockey hotbed in the process. But when that acrobat pulled in all of $11,500 in salary for his efforts, that's how you spent your summer vacation.

9

The Streak

FOR THE SECOND TIME in his career, Glenn Hall opened the season playing against the National Hockey League All-Stars. It was his first return to Chicago Stadium after the Stanley Cup win, and the Chicago Black Hawk loyalists were ready to show their appreciation. The Hawk public announcer introduced Hall with his customary flair: "Ladies and gentleman, Number One, Mr. Goalie . . ." By the time he'd belted out the last syllable of *Goalie*, the 14,000 plus had drowned him out, honoring Hall with a standing ovation that reporters described as not only the loudest and longest in Black Hawk history, but in the history of the game—greater than for Gordie Howe in Detroit or Maurice Richard in Montreal. The standing ovation lasted over three minutes, leaving Glenn's eyes damp, overcome with emotion.

"I was afraid I was going to burst out crying," he said. "It was marvelous considering that there were so many truly great players on the ice tonight. If that kind of greeting doesn't make me play better, I doubt if anything ever will."

Although it was true that Hall had already earned great admiration as a pro, reflected chiefly in his selection as an All-Star, winning the Cup led observers of the game to become more public in their appraisals of his work. New York GM Muzz Patrick had long held that Terry Sawchuk was the best in the business, but after the Hawks won the Cup he told *The Hockey News* that he considered Hall the league's best. Stan Fischler, a beat writer for the New York Rangers who continues in his legendary career as an opinionated scribe and has been one of hockey's most prolific authors, proved his prescience in November 1961 when he commented almost as an aside that Hall "may have invented modern goalkeeping."

President Ken McKenzie's "Passing the Puck" column was the first thing most fans turned to when they picked up their weekly copy of *The Hockey News*. McKenzie was the Walter Winchell of the hockey world, a gifted observer, influential, and informed. If it was in his column, it was good as gospel. He chimed in with the choir praising Hall: "The acquisition of Glenn Hall from Detroit to Chicago seemed to herald the advent of the Black Hawks future successes . . . The Hawk fortunes started to rise from the time Glenn played his first game as a Black Hawk on October 8, 1957 . . . The Hawks had finished last in the four previous seasons and had amassed a total of 60 wins during this time . . . They didn't make the playoffs during Hall's first season but they did escape the cellar . . . Then began a series of third-place finishes and the peak was reached last spring when Chicago won the Stanley Cup . . . During all that time Glenn Hall was the class performer of the team . . ."

The Hawks started the 1961–62 season in wretched form and struggled through the first two months, but they began to get their game back together by late December. On December 28, Hall battled Johnny Bower to the first 0–0 tie in the NHL in four years, each goalie making 30 saves. Hall sealed the tie with less than two minutes to play in the game, when Dave Keon broke in alone. Keon held the puck and deked. Hall refused to commit, forcing Keon wide and into a shot he didn't want to take. Hall answered the shot with a stack save. "I figured he was going to try and thread the puck through my legs when his deke failed," said Hall. "I threw my legs straight across and took it on the side of the pads."

Glenn Hall's durability was adding to the respect he'd been earning as a premier NHL netminder, and was setting him above the rest. Coming into the 1961–62 season, he'd played every game, regular season and playoffs, for his teams for all six seasons of his NHL career. To put that into perspective, 35 goalies had played in the NHL since Hall's rookie year. Of those 35, only four had played *one* entire season without a break. By the halfway point of the season, Glenn was nearing a milestone for endurance. On January 17, he started his 500th consecutive NHL game: 463 in the regular season and 37 in the playoffs. While the NHL record book wouldn't reflect the combined regular-season/playoff game totals, hockey publications and Hawk fans would.

In a game against the Rangers on January 15, Hall's streak nearly came to an end when his own defenseman was driven into the net off a rush, twisting Glenn's knee around the post. But, like so many other nicks, scrapes, stitches, and worse he endured over the years, Hall shook it off. The other time the streak was in serious jeopardy was two years earlier, when Glenn had an adverse reaction to penicillin that caused his eyes to swell nearly shut. But he recovered in time for the next game.

What was the key to his durability? Hall explained: "They say there are players who would play this game for nothing. And I think it's true. I make my living at this game, so the money's important. But if I happened to be in some other line of business I'd be out playing the game for nothing, just for the fun of it. Actually [playing all the time] it was easier for me. Playing every night, I didn't have time to think. It was when I had time to think that I was in trouble. Tired? Certainly I was tired. But if I'd have worked in a smelter, I'd have been tired too. I wouldn't be tired after a good night's sleep. Sure, there have been times in the last years when perhaps I wasn't in condition to play, but making that decision is not my job. My job is to stop the puck. If someone wants to bench you, okay, but you don't bench yourself. You don't give your job to somebody else.

"There's one thing I want to make clear. Playing 500 straight games is something I am proud of. But in this league you don't make a living on your past reputation. My one ambition is to stick in the NHL a few more years, and I know I'm not going to do it because I played 500 games in a row but only if I can do a goaltending job in the future that's up to NHL standards. That's my aim."

Hall had more incentive at work than pride. The Hawk organization recognized that someday someone would have to replace Mr. Goalie. The heir apparent was one Denis DeJordy. A St. Hyacinthe, Quebec, native, DeJordy had amassed impressive minor-league credentials. A typical stand-up type goalie, minor-league scouts used superlatives to describe his play and his potential.

"There was no doubt that DeJordy was being groomed to replace Hall," said veteran New York sportscaster Bill Mazur. "You had to see DeJordy to believe him. He was every bit as good as Sawchuk in his prime and every bit as good as Glenn when Glenn played in the minors. It was simply a matter of Hall faltering. The moment that happened, and [Hawk GM] Ivan would become convinced that Glenn was permanently losing it, Hall would be traded just as Sawchuk had been before him and DeJordy would become the Hawks' number-one goalie." But that was a long time coming.

The 500th game itself was played at Chicago Stadium. Glenn wasn't told beforehand that there would be an on-ice pre-game presentation to mark the occasion. After the players took to the ice, Hawk fan club president Gene Metz served as master of ceremonies. He called Mr. Goalie to center ice and the Hawk faithful honored their netminder with a thundering standing ovation, the intensity of which rivaled the salute they gave him before the All-Star game at the start of the season. Metz presented Hall with an inscribed gold goalie stick, and then The Ghoulie got the surprise of the night, as a brand-new Chevrolet was driven onto the ice next to where he was standing. Owners Arthur Wirtz and Jim Norris had arranged to have Glenn go to a Chevy dealer and pick out any model of car he wanted. An overwhelmed Hall was handed the microphone, and he declared, "It's ridiculous for a hockey player to get all this. I just wish I had the education to make a speech."

After the presentation was over, Hall took his spot in the crease and proceeded to play one of the worst games of his career, losing 7–3 to Montreal. "I guess I was kind of stunned . . . Anyway, I don't know when I've fought the puck so hard before in my life," he said.

The day after the landmark game, Pauline Hall answered her doorbell. Standing outside holding a congratulatory cake intended as a gift for Glenn was Jack "Fitzy" Fitzsimmons, the Hawk fan since the '30s who'd been so captivated by Glenn's play that he'd arranged to have his seats moved behind the Black Hawk goal so he could get a better view of him. Glenn wasn't home, so Pauline told the man to come back in a few hours, when Glenn would be there to appreciate the gesture. Fitzy returned, and a lifelong friendship was struck.

"Can you imagine an athlete today, and Glenn wasn't just an athlete, he was a superstar, accepting some stranger into his home like that?" asked Fitzy. "That's what makes Glenn so special. He was not just the best goalie. He's the best person you can possibly imagine."

THE HAWKS ENDED the season on a high note after a near-disastrous start. They'd won only ten games by January 1 and were clearly wearing the title of Cup champions heavily. After his 500th game jitters, Hall returned to form with wins over Boston and Detroit in Chicago before playing a return match against the Detroit Red Wings on February 1 in Detroit. The Hawks won the game 7–4 in a match that was another snapshot of the Black Hawks of the '60s. Bobby Hull lit up Terry Sawchuk four times for the Hawks who mustered 27 shots, while Hall butterflied, dived, sprawled, and smothered 51 of 55 Red Wing shots. That same week, he became a father for the third time, Pauline gave birth to his second daughter, Tammy.

Sports Illustrated, which had picked the Hawks to win the league in a preseason poll, did a feature article on the team in February, as they were heating up and looking as if they were getting ready to make another run at the Cup. In the article, Glenn talked about his pre-game nerves, "You wouldn't think after all this time that I'd still be so afraid of a bad game I'd get sick about it. I used to be able to fight off the nausea, but this year it's worse than ever." Hall also came out publicly for the first time with his disdain for practice, saying, "I really don't believe in practice. It's all right for the players who aren't getting much playing time on the ice. But when you're playing three or four games a week you don't have much chance to get out of shape."

Hall recorded a whopping nine shutouts, easily leading the league in that category for the third straight year, but the Hawks still finished a distant third, 23 points behind Montreal. With the hopes that history would repeat itself, the two teams faced off in the semifinals for the fourth consecutive year. For the fifth time, Hall met Jacques Plante in the playoffs.

Plante was coming off of one of his best seasons. He won the Vezina for the sixth time as well as the Hart Trophy as the league's most valuable player, and he was the First All-Star to Glenn's second-team nod.

"He was the reason we ran away with the league," Canadien coach Toe Blake told the press.

"If Plante should have won it [the Hart] this year, my man should have won it the last three," responded Rudy Pilous, the Hawk's coach.

The series opened in Montreal. The Canadiens had been waiting a full year for revenge, and they took the first game by an uncomfortably close 2–1 score, Hall and Plante both playing strong games. In Game 2, the Habs hit Hall for four goals, but the Hawks did score three of their own. The 4–3 win was another close shave, but unlike the year before, the Habs left Montreal with a two-games-to-none lead. All they had to do was equal what they did a year ago, win one of the next two on Stadium ice to have a chance to close the Hawks out in five games. But the Hawks didn't cooperate. The third game was played on April Fools' Day, and the joke was on the Canadiens, who lost 4–1. The Hawks' encore effort two nights later tied the series as they scored a 5–3 win. Back on Forum ice, the Habs looked like a team feeling the pressure. Plante looked particularly jittery on the Hawks' second goal in the 4–3 Chicago win, and he and the Canadiens skated off the ice to merciless booing. Jacques's regular-season brilliance had been all but forgotten by the fickle Montreal fandom.

The atmosphere at the Stadium for Game 6 was as charged as it had been the year before. Chicago fans sensed that history was about to repeat itself— the Hawks would upset Montreal and then go on to win a Stanley Cup. They were half right.

The locker rooms at the Stadium were located well below ice level. Fans who were sitting high in the mezzanine or at just the right angles in the balconies could look down the deep stairwell behind either goal judge and see the teams start the long climb up the stairs toward the ice surface, always led by the starting goalies. That night, Hall and Plante started up those steps at nearly the same time. There was a constant din in the building as the game progressed, the buzz growing every time the Hawks brought the puck anywhere near Plante. Ab McDonald solved him just four minutes into the game, completing a perfect passing play.

By the second period, the game turned into a classic Hall versus Plante tilt. In the early going, Hall sprawled to stop a tricky drive from the top of the circle. Gilles Tremblay ended up with the rebound and a wide-open net and shot, yet somehow Hall scrambled back into position to smother the puck.

Then came *the* save. Nine minutes into the second period, Dickie Moore raced behind Hawk defenseman "Moose" Vasko and bore down on Glenn. The shifty Hab tried three fakes but finally shot from point-blank range. Hall responded with seeming superhuman quickness and did a full split to make the save with his catch glove. *Chicago Tribune* sports columnist Dave Condon described it this way: "To picture it, you must imagine a baseball player stopping one of Mickey Mantle's line drives . . . about four feet in front of home plate." The home fans stood and accorded Hall a 60-second standing ovation.

"Hall's save was the turning point," said Hawk coach Pilous. "That gave us a big lift."

Montreal's Toe Blake concurred: "Hall was very good in the last two periods. His save on Moore's breakaway was the turning point. If Moore had scored, we would have been tied and things might have gone differently."

Kenny Wharram added a goal, and the Hawks eliminated Montreal 2–0. For the second straight year, Glenn sent the Habs home via the shutout.

The second-place Toronto Maple Leafs had eliminated New York in six games and hosted the finals. Toronto held serve in the first two games of the series at the Gardens, 4–1 and 3–2. Back at the Stadium, Hall tossed a relatively easy 19-save shutout as the Hawks played their best game of the play-offs, dominating Toronto in a 3–0 win. By this time, of course, the Hawks had some well-established home histrionics. Public announcer Bob Foster whipped the crowd into a frenzy when he introduced Hall as "Mr. Goalie" before every game. With each goal, the fans continued the tradition of littering the ice with toilet paper, eggs, and empty cups. Foster iced that cake by announcing the home-goal scorer complete with nickname, the number of goals he had in the playoffs, and any other information that would keep the cauldron of emotions boiling on West Madison Street.

But Foster pushed the envelope at the end of that 3–0 win. With ten seconds to go, he grabbed his mike and, referring to the shutout, announced, "Mr.

Goalie has done it again!" NHL President Clarence Campbell was not amused and put a stop to the announcer's methods. "He's free to give out the necessary information," said Campbell, "but we can't tolerate the cheerleading."

Chicago tied the series the next game 4–1, driving Johnny Bower from the net when the goalie made a great split-glove save on Hull, pulling a groin in the process. Don Simmons took over for Bower, just as he had replaced Sawchuk for Boston halfway through Hall's last year with Detroit. Hawk coach Rudy Pilous warned anyone who would listen that Toronto would play better now because they would tighten up in front of Simmons. He was right. The Leafs crushed the Hawks 8–4 in Toronto in Game 5.

When the series shifted back to Chicago for Game 6, the Hawks tried to play it physical but in doing so, they forgot to play hockey. Hall gave the team a chance to win, making 27 saves in the first two periods while Simmons saw only 12 shots as the third period started tied at zero. Hull gave the 20,000 home loyal some hope when he broke the scoreless tie nine minutes into the third, but it took less than two minutes for Bob Nevin to answer and four minutes after that Dick Duff scored the winner. One writer described Hall's work as "almost impossible."

That Hall had earned a permanent place in the hearts of Chicago sports fans could not be questioned. In the baseball and football crazy town, he'd won a berth among the best and most popular. *Chicago Tribune* columnist Dave Condon expressed it best: "Chicago's professional sports teams have some gifted athletes. Ernie Banks of the Cubs, Bill George [the precursor of Dick Butkus] of the Bears, Luis Aparicio of the White Sox. Each is a standout in his own game, in his own time. But we submit that of all of the great athletes not performing in Chicago, Glenn Hall is the most skilled. He is great."

THE SUMMER OF 1962 passed quietly enough for the five members of the Hall family, and too quickly for the clan's head of the household. Glenn never looked forward to training camp, largely because he was an athlete who took good enough care of himself in the off-season that he didn't need much work to get into game shape. He and his teammates knew that much of the conditioning that they'd face in camp would come down to how quickly the weight of some of their teammates, who were less vigilant over the summer months and annually spent the beginning of camp huffing and puffing up a storm, would meet the team requirements. Elmer "Moose" Vasko was usually the center of attention at the daily weigh-ins.

As Moose approached the scale each day, his teammates would be busy tying their skates and taping sticks. But when the big defender stepped on the scale, all eyes stole glances at the dial which, depending on which side of 220 it landed, determined how hard that day's practice would be. According to Glenn, Moose, a man unfamiliar with diet and off-ice exercise, had a unique approach to conditioning: "He *hoped* he'd weigh in properly."

Prior to practice on November 6, 1962, Glenn was bending over in his locker stall to fasten a toe strap on his leg pads. He felt a pop in his lower back, but righted himself and practiced through the discomfort as he'd done so many times before. But by the next night, his back was aching and he sensed he was in trouble. He took his spot in front of the Hawk cage anyway for the game against Boston, hoping the usual pre-game competitive adrenaline rush would mask the pain. Early in the game, a shot from the slot skipped through his pads. When he was "on," he would have handled that puck, but he simply couldn't bend enough to work out of his normal stance. So it was, on that night, that Mr. Goalie removed himself from the goal, replaced by the much-ballyhooed Denis DeJordy.

When DeJordy started for the Hawks in their next game on November 10 against Montreal, Hall's regular-season consecutive game streak was officially concluded at 502. The injury was diagnosed as a ligament strain. At least, that was what the official press release said. But that diagnosis was never given the chance to be confirmed.

"When I went to the doctor's office, he told the nurse to get an inch-and-a-half needle," Glenn recalled. "She could only find one an inch and a quarter. So he stuck it into my back extra hard and wiggled it around until I about fainted. I hated needles and I hated pain. So I said, 'I'm cured, Doc.'" As he relates the story, Glenn re-creates the posture he left the doctor's office with by doubling over and staggering. "I walked out and never went back."

Despite the rigors of being an NHL goalkeeper, sitting on the sidelines was tougher. "It broke my heart when I had to be replaced," said Glenn. "I didn't want to give anyone a chance to take my job. And they were building up DeJordy so much that I had to play, even when hurt. Fear of losing your job is a tremendous motivator, but you can't overlook the other aspect, which was the most important thing . . . the love of the game. Despite all the tension, the injuries, the hassle, I loved playing goal and I hated it when I played badly. Knowing that the record was there also helped me to go on . . ."

Hawk coach Rudy Pilous felt the end of the streak helped Hall. "I think all of us would have to agree that the business of going in game after game finally got to him," he said. "Maybe he was playing at times when he should have been resting an injury. Let's just say he needed a rest, and his injury finally forced him to take one. He missed all of three games."

Sportswriter Bill Mazur noted, "Even then, Hall refused to wilt. DeJordy only played in five games total in 1962–63 and six the following year."

"[At first] I was afraid I'd suffer by comparison [to DeJordy]," Hall said. "But that changed. I decided it would be better to have Denny with me. There was satisfaction in the thought that if I began to go bad, Denny would be in our net."

The streak had lasted over seven full NHL seasons and encompassed 31,195 minutes and 33 seconds of regulation play. But even those incredible numbers do not tell the full story. During that span, Hall played in 50 consecutive playoff games, lifting the actual total to 552. He'd been eligible to play in seven All-Star contests during that time (either through vote or Stanley Cup victory) and did play in those, raising the total to 559. That does not count the pre-season exhibition games he played in (the records for which are too sketchy to reliably add here). But the full picture still does not emerge. Glenn did not miss a game he was eligible to play during his four years of minor league. When he did miss games for the minor-league team, it was because he was playing for the big club.

So during the first half of his professional hockey career, which spanned from the fall of 1951 through November of 1962, Glenn played all 881 games in which he was eligible to play.

Without a mask.

The official NHL record of 502 is indeed the one record in sport that will certainly never be broken.

"If you don't think I was familiar with that puck [after 502 games]," quipped The Ghoulie, "then let me tell you exactly what was written on it— 'Art Ross patent no. 22656.'"

Of course, he was right.

THE NHL THAT HALL was playing in when the streak ended was a decidedly different league from the NHL he'd played in when it began. Bobby Hull's weapon of choice, the curved stick, was an unregulated monstrosity that added power and dips and curves to shots. It made the puck increasingly dangerous. The slap shot was adopted by a myriad of forwards, and the game began an evolution from artistry to sheer power. As forwards warmed to the curved stick, the backhand became a dinosaur, both as a shot and as a passing option.

At the same time, another change took place at the end of the bench. No longer was the goalie's job a strictly one-man show. Most teams began rostering two goalkeepers—not because the owners were ready to willingly add another salary to their payroll or to lighten the load on their workhorse netminders, but because of the demands of television. With more games being televised across Canada and even in the United States, networks did not want to face a long pause in the action if a goalie went down with an injury that required extensive repairs. The powers-that-were in the league wisely created an extra roster spot, and the backup goalie came into being.

The old-school goalies had a difficult time with this change at first, seeing the newcomer as a potential threat to their territory. There was just more pressure to perform better every night because a potential successor watched every move, ready to step in. It would take time for the system to become a success.

By the halfway point in the 1962–63 season, Hall had played 21 games, weighing in with a miserly 1.95 goals-against mark. He was named to the first-half First All-Star team, and the Hawks were a real threat to win the league championship, which would have been their first in franchise history. Although they'd won a couple of Stanley Cups in the '30s, the team had never won the league title. Perhaps they simply never had very good personnel, or perhaps the real reason was more ethereal.

In its maiden year, the Chicago franchise was coached by one Peter Muldoon. He steered the club to a decidedly unremarkable sub-.500 season and was fired upon its completion. As the story goes, Muldoon felt that this was more than unfair, and so he told an eager press that the Black Hawks would *never* win the league championship. A full 35 years later that prediction held true, and Chicago ascribed the drought to "The Curse of Muldoon." As the Hawks built an eight-point lead over second-place Detroit and a nine-point lead over third-place Toronto with just 11 games left to go, the club was ready to bury the curse.

But out of nowhere the club was seemingly hit with a lethargy that defied explanation—outside of the curse. Toronto went on a tear. Typical of the malaise, the Hawks had two games in which they could have clinched a portion of first. They had a showdown with the Leafs at home on March 10, settling for a 1–1 tie as Hall made 39 saves while the Hawks took a total of 18 shots at Don Simmons. Detroit stuffed Chicago at home in the last game of the season while Toronto won on the road at Boston to take the league title by a single point.

If you believed the story, you just knew that somewhere Pete Muldoon was smiling.

For his part, Hall continued to perform at a high level, winning his first Vezina with a 2.55 goals-against average. His five shutouts led the league for the fourth time in a row, and he was named to the First All-Star team for the fourth time in his eight-year NHL career. Despite these results, Rudy Pilous had a troubling exchange with Glenn in the middle of the season.

Recalled Glenn: "After this one game, Rudy says to me, 'I think you should have stopped that last one.' I asked Rudy if he knew what happened on the goal, and he said 'Yes.' I asked him if he was sure, and he insisted that he was. So Rudy and Tommy Ivan suggest that I should go get my eyes checked. Well, I did go and get them checked and the optometrist told me that my eyesight was so good that he'd only heard of one other pair of eyes that could pick up what I could. Those eyes belonged to Ted Williams [baseball's greatest hitter]. I knew there was nothing wrong with my eyes, because neither Rudy or Tommy really saw what happened on the shot they were talking about. That puck got deflected. They really didn't know what happened on that goal. So I had to get my eyes checked out because they couldn't see!"

To this day, Glenn attributes a large percentage of his success to his eyesight, especially his peripheral vision. He notes: "I'd practice looking all around me all the time. When I was driving, when I was sitting at home. I tell goalkeepers today that they should practice it too. The more you are capable of seeing off to the side and back behind you, the more you can concentrate not only on where the puck is, but where the puck is going. "I also believe that it's part of a coach's job to know how every goal happened."

The playoffs that year proved the Hawks' late-season collapse was not a fluke. Drawing fourth place Detroit, a team that had finished only four points behind the Hawks in the tightest regular-season race in years, the Hawks won their opening games at home 5–4 and 5–2. But coach Pilous's demanding practices, which some blamed for the Hawks' late-season woes, clearly caught up with the team. Pilous became one of, if not *the* very first coach, to institute game-day skates. The tradition started when the players gathered at the rink around noon on game day to tinker with sticks and sharpen skates, or maybe to take a turn on the ice to make sure the blades were just so. Not leaving well enough alone, the game-day appearances deteriorated into organized skates, the benefits of which are dubious.

The press began referring to Chicago's poor play as the "Pilous Plague," noting that the team looked like "zombies on skates." The Wings outshot the Hawks 48–21 in Game 3 in a 4–2 win and won the next three in a row. The total collapse cost Pilous his job.

ESSAY: MAGIC

WE ALL HAVE MOMENTS of magic in our lives, moments that we need to keep close so we don't totally lose touch with our youth. There is a uniqueness in those moments: the feeling that you are the only one in the world who is feeling what you're feeling. It is a moment of total exhilaration, in which your eyes literally widen in wonder, and suppressing a smile is a physical impossibility.

I was eight years old when I felt the magic. My father owned a Henry's Drive-In hamburger stand on Madison Street on Chicago's West Side. In those days, two franchises competed for fast-food dominance, McDonald's and Henry's. That you have probably never heard of Henry's or at least cannot remember its existence, and that you cannot drive more than two blocks anywhere in the civilized world without passing a McDonald's, tells you a bit about the business acumen and foresight of my father. Cash flow aside, the one positive of that location was that the Henry's was located directly across the street from the hulking monolith known as Chicago Stadium.

Chicago's West Side had been a bustling, prosperous, largely Italian neighborhood when the Stadium was constructed in the 1920s. Al Capone was nearing the height of his powers, and Chicago's politicos were already deeply entrenched in the practices of graft and corruption that would be handed down from one generation to the next. The Stadium was a state-of-the-art arena, its imposing gray outer shell topped with richly detailed frescoes depicting Olympic contests of strength and skill. With a seating capacity of nearly 16,000, the complex took up an entire city block, framed on the east by Wood Street and on the west by Wolcott, on the north by Warren Boulevard and on the south by Madison Street. The doors that led into the building were painted bright red and they were numbered Gates 1, 2, and 3 along Madison, Gates 4, 5, and 6 along Warren. There was one other gate along the side street on the west—Gate 3½.

Gate 3½ was where the privileged entered. The athletes themselves came into the building there after parking their cars in the small fenced-in lot that was directly adjacent. Certain select box-holders also gained admittance through this portal: to get into the Stadium through Gate 3½ was a sign that you were somebody.

Through the years, the Stadium hosted football games, political conventions, prize fights, the Ice Capades, basketball games, and concerts, but first and foremost it was the home of the Chicago National Hockey League franchise. That there was something very special about this place was evident from its surroundings. The Stadium held on to its imposing beauty and its vitality as the neighborhood around it succumbed to age, erosion, and horrid poverty.

Over time thriving businesses moved to the city's north side, slowly at first, almost imperceptibly. But then the flight picked up its pace, leaving behind a vacuum of empty storefronts and abandoned walk-ups. As property values plummeted, the once immaculately kept Victorian apartment houses that lined Madison became disheveled and rat-infested. To the east of the Stadium, where once was a block filled with laundries, barber shops, saloons, and shoe stores, the poor moved in and the area became known as Skid Row.

In the middle of this, we sold burgers for 15 cents, cheeseburgers for 18. The customers were all local, the employees were all local. But any night there was an event at the Stadium, the faces of our customers were less local, and our business picked up tremendously. The small parking lot that circled our drive-in became a Stadium parking lot, and we'd wedge as many cars as possible into the lot at $3 apiece. We were always full because we were so close to the Stadium, and people coming to the games didn't want to have to walk for very long through the neighborhood.

On the nights that our lot was filled with cars, I knew that a hockey game was going on in the Stadium, but I really had no idea what hockey was. I was a chubby kid, picked last in gym class for whatever game we were playing, and I wasn't remotely interested in sports. But there was a mystery to that great old building across the street, and I was incredibly and uncharacteristically curious about the events inside. While the games were going on, Don, one of my father's car-parkers, sat in his car and listened to the game on the radio. He waved me into the car one night to listen along. I could hear the excitement in the announcer's voice, but he might as well have been speaking a foreign language with all the goofy terms he was using. An odd thing happened, though, when he shouted, "Here's a shot aaaand a goal!" As the cheers exploded over the radio, the great gray building on my right literally began to shake.

What could possibly have happened that was exciting enough to make that colossal structure shake to its very foundation?

I decided I needed to wage a campaign of terror against my father until he got me into that building. Not a conversation passed without my mentioning that I wanted to see what a hockey game was. I'd find printed Hawk schedules, circle certain games, and leave the programs lying around the house, in his car, on his desk at the drive-in. Since my father worked a lot, we did not share a lot of time together. There were no games of catch in the backyard, and I learned how to ride a bike from a neighbor. We never felt comfortable around each other, but somehow I instinctively knew I could guilt him into getting me into that building.

The day finally came. We were driving to the restaurant to work the parking lot, and on the way there he broke the news. "One of our good customers is a writer for the *Chicago Tribune*. He gave me two tickets to the game tonight so, if you're good and work hard, we'll go to the game. The Hawks are playing the Bruins, and they're good seats, so you better appreciate this."

I don't believe another word that was spoken to me the rest of that evening ever registered any meaning. The minutes were ridiculously long. I knew the game started at 7:30 p.m., and I was hoping my father wasn't going to wait until the lot was totally full because that usually didn't happen until just after 7:30. By 6:55, I was nervously looking his way, hoping to make enough eye contact that he would sense my anguish and leave the lot to the workers and head across the street. By 7:10 I was in a state of full panic. "Come on. Come on. Come on. Come on."

At 7:20 I saw him slip his bundle of money to Don and walk toward me. "Let's go."

We waded into the crowd of people outside Gate 2, and at times I felt as if I were being swallowed by the mass of adults. My father held on to my sleeve and kept pulling me forward. We stepped through a turnstile, our ticket stubs returned to us by an Andy Frain usher costumed in a blue uniform and a police-style hat. There was so much to look at in the corridor that it seemed as if I were being bombarded by flashes of color and noise. Snippets of conversation drifted my way: "Programs, get your programs here. Twenty-five cents for tonight's lineups . . ." "I just hope Bobby gets one tonight . . ." "Well, we should win tonight. The Bruins are the worst team . . ."

The ladies all wore nice dresses and had fancy hairdos, and a lot of the men wore ties. Dense cigarette smoke filled the halls. After walking a few more feet, we went up one short stairway, and my father gave the ticket stubs to another uniformed usher. He told us to follow him, and I took my first step inside the building that would become my cathedral.

Magic.

I still remember the brightness. It felt as if I were being washed in light. There was a dull undertone of noise, a low rumble, anticipatory in nature. Over that swept the sounds of organ music mixing perfectly with the muffled noises of the crowd. As I took another step, I looked straight up at the ceiling, which seemed to be miles and miles above my head. There was a crisscrossing network of gold catwalks, and suspended from the ceiling hung a huge contraption with a large round clock in the middle and two smaller clocks in the lower corners. Above one of the smaller clocks was written HOME and above the other was written VISITOR. Above and behind the clock and in the background two separate sections of seats seemed to extend out over the ice. They were balconies, cheaper places to sit I would learn, and they were packed with people. Behind those seated were rows and rows of people standing, leaning against long red restraining bars.

Finally I looked out onto the ice at all those strange blue and red markings over the glare-white of the surface. I expected it to be cold in the building, but it wasn't. Why wasn't the ice melting? What if it melted during the game? There were so many mysteries.

Our seats were at one end of the rink, directly behind one of the nets, about ten rows from the back of the building. Just as we sat down, a loud roar crackled throughout the building and the players emerged from a hidden staircase. Their jerseys were sharp red with big white numbers on the back and an Indian Head logo on the front. The socks they wore looked like candy canes to me—red with black and white stripes all the way down to their skates. I watched, hypnotized, as they circled the end of the ice closest to us. "Number 9 there, that's Bobby Hull," my father said. "And 21, there's Mikita. He's good, but he's in the penalty box too much."

I had no idea what a penalty box was, but I guessed you weren't supposed to be there. As my father was speaking, one of the players caught my attention and I couldn't stop looking at him. The big white number he wore was one. He had different equipment than the other players. Their gloves were small. He had what looked like a big rectangular box that was decorated with little white holes on one hand, and on the other what looked like a baseball glove, only cooler. His stick was wider and looked heavier than the ones the other guys were carrying. But what was really special were those pads on his legs. They looked like little couches, brown, soft, and comfortable, with puffy rolls in them.

As my father tried to tell me who all the other players were, I paid less and less attention to his words. The guy with the number one stitched into his jersey was standing sideways in the net, and he started to move side to side, herky-jerky, as his skates tore away at the ice inside the red lines that framed his net. It was like he was trying to make snow there, and every time some would collect, he took that big stick and pushed and piled the snow against the outside of the bottom of the net. What was that all about?

A disembodied voice asked the crowd not to throw anything on the ice and to stand for the national anthem. An opera singer bellowed out the song right along with the organ, and as the song ended, another rush of noise pounded at my ears and continued to swell. Some guys from the red team met some guys from the white team in the middle of the ice, and a man with a black-and-white jersey stood right there between them. He threw something on the ice (didn't that voice just tell us not to throw anything on the ice?), and all the players started moving around. Not too long afterward a whistle blew and everybody slowed down. But that whole time, the guy wearing the number one stayed right where he started the game. The other players went off the ice, but he stayed on. I thought that must mean he was very important because he was the only one to play the whole game.

The guy wearing black and white threw the little black "puck" on the ice again, and after a while a guy in a white jersey skated really fast toward the guy wearing number one. The guy in white knocked the puck at the guy with the number one on, and that puck went so fast I could barely see it. The guy with the number one must have slipped—he fell, but his hand with the baseball mitt flew out and he caught the puck. All of a sudden everyone around clapped and yelled, and the guy next to me said to his wife, "That Glenn Hall's gonna save us again. He's the best."

I turned to my father and asked, "Is that number-one guy Glenn Hall?"

"Yeah. Hey, now pay attention, here comes Bobby Hull. There he is, Number 9. See him? Hey, I said do you see him?"

But it was already too late. In the time it took that guy in the white to shoot the puck to the time it settled into what I thought was a baseball glove, I'd felt it. I felt it inside.

Magic.

"Dad, Glenn Hall's my favorite."

The Two-Goalie System

TRADE RUMORS RAN RAMPANT during the summer of 1963. The mighty Montreal Canadiens had suffered the embarrassment of a five-game semifinal series loss to the Toronto Maple Leafs. It marked the third consecutive year they'd been eliminated in the first round. The well-known friction between Jacques Plante and management had already strained to the breaking point, and the Habs' quick exodus from the playoffs allowed them to peddle the petulant puck-stopper. At one point coach Toe Blake stated publicly that if Plante was back with the team, he [Blake] wouldn't be. One of the first rumors to surface was of a straight-up exchange of Plante for Glenn Hall. Glenn was especially attractive to Montreal because of his steady demeanor and his record for showing up to work, both attributes that Plante sorely lacked. Such a trade would have had an incredible effect on hockey history in the '60s. But, of course, it never happened. When Plante heard about that one, he (*quelle surprise!*) had an opinion: "My own goals-against average was the best in the league. Hall has just won the Vezina Trophy for the first time. For that, both of us must go?"

The Canadiens did move Plante in a blockbuster deal, but Glenn wasn't involved. Jacques found himself in New York Ranger blue as part of a multi-player deal that saw Lorne "Gump" Worsley land in Montreal. Worsley had toiled brilliantly in the relative obscurity of the also-ran Rangers, but even he had a teammate willing to criticize him publicly.

"Look at the pictures," said Ranger star Andy Bathgate. "Gump is always down on the first shot and dead for the second. But the other goalies like Glenn Hall get up in time for the rebounds."

When Glenn arrived at training camp, head coach Rudy Pilous had been replaced by Billy Reay. Reay had coached the Maple Leafs for two years in the late '50s, and it was under his watch that Hall of Fame goaltender Johnny Bower made the NHL to stay. Reay had spent the last two seasons behind the bench for the Chicago Black Hawk farm club at Buffalo, where his main goalie was Denis DeJordy, the same DeJordy who was being touted as the "next Sawchuk" and the goalie who'd served as Hall's very occasional backup. DeJordy's minor-league credentials were terrific and he played a stand-up style that comforted the old-world coaching mentality.

DeJordy vied for the backup role that year with Dave Dryden, a rare college-educated player who'd interrupted his pursuit of pro hockey for two years to begin a teaching career. Tall and rangy at 6 feet 2 inches with size 13 skates, Dryden cut a memorable figure between the pipes. He eventually teamed with Hall and went on to a solid NHL career before becoming a mover and shaker with the league's players' association.

Reay was eager to establish himself as the boss early on, and perhaps he feared a lack of respect from his new team since the Toronto teams he'd coached in the late '50s were losers, which earned him the sack. Reay immediately noticed that Hall took his time getting into the net behind the youngsters, and that he exited the net at the first sight of a high shot or after fielding just enough pucks to get a sense of timing.

"Billy was one of those coaches who felt that if you were over 30 you needed to work even harder than the younger guys to stay in shape," said Glenn.

Reay expressed his displeasure with what he perceived to be Glenn's poor work ethic. Hall established some territory of his own: "I remember telling Reay, 'I can play in the games or I can play in practice. I can't do both, so take your pick.'"

Wisely Reay let Hall choose his spots in practice. At 32 years of age, Glenn understood what he needed to accomplish in practice. If he was having a hard time with a particular player or a particular move, he'd re-create that scenario during practice so he could figure out the right defense. But beyond that, he knew he was wasting his energy and exposing himself to injury, especially as the league became more and more accepting of the slap shot.

When Dave Dryden became a teammate of Hall's, he saw firsthand Glenn's struggles with practice sessions. "One of the frustrations Glenn had was that he actually liked to work hard, practice hard," recalled Dryden. "But the way things were set up in Chicago when he was there, and the way the game was going with the curved stick and everything else, it simply wasn't safe for a goaltender to practice hard. He got into that fix of: 'Shoot, I want to practice hard, but I can't so I don't feel good about that.' He did things like standing over in the corner of the rink while guys were on line rushes, and then the guys would drill shots at him in the corner. He'd get so bloody upset, and they'd say, 'Come on, Glenn, work hard.' And he'd say, 'I want to work hard but the drills are going to kill me.' And he was exactly right."

Teammate Bill Hay became a good friend of Glenn's. A fellow native of Saskatchewan and one of, if not *the* very first, skater to make it to the NHL after graduating from college, he and Glenn shared a love of the open spaces of the West. After a very successful playing career, Hay enjoyed further success in geology and became a member of the Hockey Hall of Fame Selection Committee. He understood Glenn's growing reticence toward health-threatening practices.

"Glenn didn't have to practice to be effective," he recalls. "He was so much better than everyone else, so quick. He didn't think he was that good, and he always tried to be better. In his own quiet way he never wanted to let anyone down. But he knew the game, he knew the opponents, and he was our stabilizing force. He was the ultimate team player. The truth is, Glenn was our meal ticket."

Glenn was wearying of the dangers of practice, which included the unique peril of facing Bobby Hull's bullets every day. By this time in his career, Glenn had been experimenting with various face masks during practice, including a clear contraption and a white fiberglass one like the model Sawchuk wore. Still, those devices didn't offer much protection against the 100-plus-mile-per-hour bullets Hull served up and, of course, they didn't lessen the pounding to his poorly padded arms, chest, and shoulders. But Glenn wasn't the only one in danger.

"During practice," Glenn recalled, "the cleaning ladies would be working in the stands and when one would bend over, Bobby would shoot a puck at a seat next to where they'd be working." The *thwack* of the rubber cannonball ripping into the wooden seat would transform the working woman into an Olympic sprinter, a wash cloth and bucket left in her wake. "It got to the point where they refused to work while we were practicing."

But he made it clear as he got older that he saw too much overcoaching. "I feel quite fortunate to have played in a time when the goalkeepers and players could think for themselves," he said. "Whenever I took less time practicing, it put more pressure on me to play well. If I was going to say I didn't need that much practice time, I'd better back it up," said Hall.

Despite the increased dangers of the game, Glenn maintained his dry sense of humor, a side of the him the public seldom saw. "He kept his humor in the locker room," said teammate Al MacNeil. "But he's a very sharp-witted guy. You don't want to start trading barbs with him."

The low-scoring defenseman had discovered that firsthand. During the season, Glenn outscored MacNeil, two points to one. Glenn, who got both of his assists before January, did give credit where it was due after Al tallied a helper in February. Said Hall: "He did have a better second half than I did."

THE GHOULIE PUT TOGETHER another tremendous year, playing in 65 of the team's 70 games in the 1963–64 season. Glenn led the league in wins with 34 and was second in shutouts with seven. Jacques Plante was gone from Montreal, but the Canadiens still won the Vezina with Charlie Hodge, who'd beaten Worsley for the job, in the Montreal cage. Plante and his Rangers finished out of the playoffs, and Jacques ended the year with a 3.44 average. DeJordy had topped Dryden for the backup role, and the right to work very hard in practice. Denis didn't see his first game action until the second month of the season, when Glenn was felled by the stomach flu. The backup man played his last game of the year in a 5–1 New Year's Day loss to New York. Glenn's goals-against average was 2.31, DeJordy's 3.17.

The two-goalie system was still new to Glenn, but he came to appreciate DeJordy's presence. Commenting on the system, he said, "If the two goalies are mature, understand each other, and are friends the way Denis and I are, the system is much better. Denis is younger than I am by some seven years, and I realize that someday he'll be taking my place. I realize that with the game being as wild as it is now, it's the best thing in the world for me to have a competent replacement around in case I get hurt.

"Last season, I wouldn't have won the Vezina if it hadn't been for the fine job Denis did when I was hurt. His average and mine combined in rating the various averages for the trophy. Denis had an average of 2.40, mine was 2.51; our combined was 2.54, which was just enough to beat out Johnny Bower and Don Simmons, who had a 2.57. So you see, if Denis's average was much higher, I'd have lost out to Toronto and also out of the $2,000 that goes to the winner." Glenn rewarded Denis with a portion of the winnings.

Forward Johnny "Pie" McKenzie was recalled to the team for the 1963–64 season. He ended up rooming with Glenn and Stan Mikita on the road, a combination that could have been intimidating for a younger player. McKenzie remembered: "Glenn is a real guy's guy. He was terrific to the younger players. When the three of us roomed together on the road, there'd be two beds in a room plus a cot, and Glenn always insisted that Stan and I take the beds.

"Stan had a great way of repaying Glenn. Glenn was very shy in public, very humble. When we were on the road in Montreal, he'd duck out of the locker room real quick after a game and we'd go eat at this great little Chinese restaurant. Well, we'd order the food and just as they were putting it on the table, into the restaurant walks Mikita. 'Why look, ladies and gentleman,' Mikita would say, 'sitting right there is the great goaltender for the Chicago Black Hawks, Glenn Hall!' Glenn would turn all red and then he'd say to me, 'Come on, Pie, let's get out of here.' The food was untouched when we left, but I'm sure Stan ate very well."

THE END OF THE CHICAGO season was another crushing disappointment, and Pilous was no longer around to be the scapegoat. For the second year in a row, the Hawks collapsed just when it seemed they might capture that elusive league championship. Once again, Glenn lost his Vezina bid by two goals on the last day of the season. Scotty Bowman, who would coach Glenn during the last four years of Hall's career, shared a story that he'd been told by one of Glenn's teammates. It was a telling example of why Glenn's name wasn't on the Vezina more.

"Glenn was leading the [Vezina] race by six goals with two games left in the season," Bowman recounted, "and on the plane trip to Toronto all the Black Hawks were talking about was how many goals they needed to score to make their bonuses. Glenn never said a thing, which he wouldn't, knowing him. So Chicago ends up in a couple of shootouts, and Glenn lost the Vezina on the last day of the season. It tells you how well Glenn had to have played all season to have been even close."

"Bobby and Stan were developing into true superstars," observed teammate Bill Hay. "And I think some of the emphasis on individual numbers hurt our team game." But Mr. Goalie polled second in the Hart MVP Trophy voting for the year, beaten out by Montreal's Jean Beliveau.

Pauline Hall had noticed Beliveau as well: "Jean Beliveau stood out as one player you could run away with," she said. "He never asked though. He exuded such sex appeal. Carol [wife of Glenn's teammate Ron] Murphy and I both thought he was something. So one night after a game we stuttered and stammered and giggled and asked him for his autograph. I hope he didn't know who we were."

For the fifth time in his nine-year NHL career, Glenn was named as the league's First All-Star goalkeeper. The Black Hawk Standbys, the team's fan club, gave Hall its MVP award for the fifth time, and longtime Hawk beat writer Ted Damata of the *Chicago Tribune* felt that the 1963–64 season was

Hall's best. Billy Reay was quoted all year as saying that Glenn was his key player. "The biggest surprise in training camp was Glenn Hall," said the Hawks' first-year pilot. "I had heard Hall was good, but you never really appreciate him until you see him in action for your side. He kept it up all season."

"Glenn was one of a kind," said John McKenzie. "His angles, his quickness. If you hadn't seen him, you wouldn't have believed it."

The Hawks couldn't thwart their late-season loss of momentum going into the playoffs, and they lost their semifinal playoffs to fourth-place Detroit in seven games. The failure led to a distinct sense of restlessness among the Hawk brass, and a storm of post-playoff trade winds threatened.

WHEN THE BLACK HAWKS broke camp in Chicago to open the 1964–65 season, Billy Reay once again announced his intention to spell Hall more often with DeJordy. This year, he meant it. The expected purge of the roster didn't happen: the Hawks only added solid Boston Bruin defender Doug Mohns and brought several rookie forwards to camp. Although Mohns helped offset the Hawks notoriously poor commitment to defense, the season started with Hall facing the now-usual onslaught with minimal support.

Glenn made his customary appearance in the NHL All-Star game, shutting down the Maple Leafs in his half of the 3–2 All-Star win. He opened the regular season in spectacular form, making 32 saves to shut out Boston 3–0 and, in the second game of the season, backstopping the Tribe to a 4–2 win over the Detroit Red Wings. That game, like so many during Hall's Hawk tenure, was yet another perfect example of why he continued to earn All-Star nods over goalies with better goals-against stats. The Hawks were outshot 42–24 in the game, Hall's 16 first-period saves coming while his mates tallied three times at the other end of the ice.

A month later, the Hawks beat Montreal 3–1 despite being outshot 47–25. Later in the season, Hall topped the Rangers 4–1 as his team was outshot 45–21, and his last shutout of the season was a 7–0 plastering of the Canadiens. You look at the score and assume it was a romp. The Hawks were outshot in that game 34–29.

One of the rookies who made the 1964–65 Hawks squad was another Hull. Like his older brother, Bobby, Dennis could shoot the puck a ton. Many thought Dennis's slap shot was harder than Bobby's. He was certainly far less accurate, which made him even more of a threat, especially to his own goalie at whom he was shooting every day in practice. With two Hulls on the team, Glenn grew more reticent to fielding practice shots, and he gave the brothers a wide berth on the far side of the goal, as they came down the left wing, sending life-threatening bullets his way. Even when Glenn stood out of the way, Dennis's misses often went right at him. That prompted Hall to leave the net entirely any time Dennis wound up for a shot. Even Coach Reay understood Glenn's life-saving retreats.

In the dressing room, Hull's rookie status and his erratic shooting made him a natural target for Hall's sarcastic wit. Hull was not familiar with Glenn's pre-game ritual, and he was stunned to hear Mr. Goalie vomiting. When Hall walked back to his cubicle next to Hull, Dennis asked the goalie if he always got sick before a game. "Only since you joined the team," replied Hall.

Early in the season, the Hawks played in New York and carried a 6–0 lead late into the game. Dennis Hull, like the rest of his family, was not exactly a stalwart defensive player. (While showering after a game, Hall would see the brothers and say, "Hey, how you guys doing? I haven't seen you since warm-ups.") He was on the bench late in the game so as not to jeopardize the shutout. When the Rangers broke through to make it 6–1 with just over a minute to go in the game, Coach Reay sent Hull out onto the ice to mop up the garbage time. Hall saw his chance.

Remembered Hull: "The face-off was in the New York end. As we were lining up, Glenn began banging his stick on the ice and the referee, Art Skov, skated down the ice to see what was going on. Art came back and came over to me and said, 'You're Dennis Hull, right? Well, Glenn wants to see you.' I skated all the way down the ice, and the New York fans were going nuts, screaming and carrying on. I was concerned that I'd done something wrong and Glenn was angry. But I'd just got on the ice and couldn't figure out what I could possibly have done in such a short period of time. I asked him what was up. 'Listen, kid,' he said to me, gesturing toward the scoreboard, 'don't screw this game up.' I'd been had."

WHILE THE PLAYERS TOILED on the ice, their wives kept things going behind the scenes. Ted Lindsay once said, "The wives are the most instrumental part of team harmony." Glenn couldn't agree more. "That's who a book should be written about—the wives."

The wives of Glenn's era could easily be depicted as the last of the great frontierswomen. And Pauline Hall would qualify as one of the greatest. When Glenn left for camp, Pauline would move the rest of the family to Chicago, a move that was accomplished in segments. First they went from the summer home in Edmonton to Pauline's hometown of Kelvington, Saskatchewan, where Pat and Leslie went to school for a month. From there they traveled the 1,200-plus miles to Chicago, Pauline shepherding her two school-age kids and baby Tammy without any help.

Once in Chicago, Pauline became the family's traffic director. To keep Glenn free from as much worry as possible, she paid the bills, oversaw the kids' schoolwork, and responded to fan mail. Recalled son Pat: "When I think back to everything Mom had to do, I'm amazed. She was the glue. She allowed Dad to do what he needed to do. She was very pragmatic, and while she knew her limitations she was one of the most motivated of the wives. She thrived on all of the activity going on around her. They say that opposites attract and that's the case with Mom and Dad. There is a great balance between them."

On game days, she made sure the kids were quiet so Glenn was properly rested. Going to the games only added to the burden. "It was awful to watch," she said. "It was no fun because of the injury factor. Whenever the fans booed, it was hard to take. Some fans seated near you were even worse if they found out you were married to one of the players."

"I don't know how she could have done it," admitted daughter Leslie. "But that was just our way of life. It all seemed normal."

When the season ended, Pauline moved the group back west, where the kids finished the school year in Edmonton. That also made for an interesting existence for the Hall children. "I counted up all the moves we made and it totaled 36 by the time I was 14," said Pat Hall.

But Pat and his siblings never thought that their Dad was anything so special: "He was just 'Dad.' I think it was around second or third grade when kids would ask me about my dad being on the Black Hawks when I started to figure out that something was going on. Of course, when you looked into a cooler of Coca-Cola and saw a picture of your dad there, you knew he was a little different than other fathers."

One of Pat's favorite players was Boston goalie Eddie Johnston. "It was Eddie's hair," said Pat. "I was a huge Beatles fan, and when Eddie used to make saves, his hair would flop over onto his forehead like it was in a Beatles cut. I thought, 'That guy's gotta be cool!'"

IF ONE STATISTIC COULD properly quantify Glenn Hall's true value to the Hawks, it would be save percentage. Unfortunately even save percentage falls short of reflecting a goalie's effectiveness: what constitutes a shot on goal varies from rink to rink. Scorekeepers often miss shots in traffic, giving credit to saves made on shots that would have gone well wide and, in general, not recording the proper stats accurately. During the 1964–65 season, save percentages were published for the first time. The stat would not gain real acceptance in the league until a decade later, but Hall lead the league, finishing with a .921 (92.1 saves made out of every hundred shots taken) efficiency. This season was also the first time that he truly experienced sharing the net. Coach Reay got DeJordy into 29 games. Hall played 41 times, finishing second in shutouts with four and carving a 2.43 goals-against average.

But he went an alarming 18–18–5 in his win-loss-tie numbers, a stat that some say shook his confidence. For the first time in his career, he was quoted talking about retirement. It was also the first time since 1959 that he wasn't an All-Star and only the second time in his ten-year career that he was not so recognized. Hall was a true perfectionist: he expected a great deal from himself and was often quoted as saying that he didn't just love the game, he loved playing to his best abilities. Halfway through the year, fatigue hit him hard, and he asked management for a break. DeJordy filled in for four games while the weeklong respite allowed Glenn to refocus. It appeared as if the pressure of the game was starting to get to the 33-year-old. To the public and to reporters, he took on more of a surly, unapproachable facade. Where he had once been a reliable source for a good post-game quote, he started to shun the press and was routinely the first player dressed and gone from the locker room.

"It's a lonely position," he said. "And it was worse for us [back in the one-goalie days] because we had no other goaltender to talk to. We were always considered loners. I was a loner because I couldn't relate to anybody. I'd go for walks by myself to get ready for a game, going over the other team and its players . . . I liked it best when nobody recognized me. Before a game, I kept to myself because I was so miserable I didn't think anyone would want me around. I didn't especially like people, and I couldn't force myself to be a nice guy when I didn't want to be."

"DAD WOULD NEVER BE the first one at the rink for practice," remembered son Pat. "He'd always be there in an acceptably professional time frame, of course, but never real early. On Saturdays before the team would practice, the players' kids would all go skate at the Stadium. I remember those mornings because we'd have toast with peanut butter and then I'd grab my stick and gloves and I'd ride to the Stadium with my Dad and Leslie. I'd get real antsy the closer we got to the rink. We'd go in through Gate 3½ and we'd get to skate until the first player came up the steps and got out onto the ice. Then we had to leave.

"The players always made us feel so good. They made eight-, nine-, and ten-year-old kids feel important. If Bobby Hull was the first one on the ice for practice, we didn't have to get off the ice. He'd pass the puck back and forth with me. To me, he wasn't 'Bobby Hull, the superstar.' He was just a real nice guy."

Pat and Leslie sat in the small box-seat area between the benches at the Stadium. Like Pauline, they sometimes found watching the games difficult. "Dad was so consistent, so good all the time. If he'd get scored on, I'd think, 'Oh, that's okay, Dad.' If the fans were booing, I'd think, 'Why are you saying that about my dad?'" Pat recalled.

"I was a daddy's girl," said Leslie. "It would break my heart if the fans were mean. I'd get nervous for my dad to the point where it made me nauseous."

But there were also some other terrific perks. "In '66, Bobby Hull became the first player to break the 50-goal barrier," said Pat. "After he scored it, there was this huge ovation and the game stopped, and Bobby went to the bench and shook all the players' hands, and when he got to the end of the bench, he came over and shook my hand too."

Later in his career, when Hull was on the verge of becoming the first player to break the 50-goal mark twice, he made a promise to Pat. "He'd promised that he would give me the puck he scored that goal with. Well, time passes, of course, and after Dad had moved on to St. Louis almost a year after Bobby scored that goal, I was outside the locker room and here comes Bobby toward me. He reaches into his pocket and pulls out this wad of tissue paper, and wrapped inside is that puck with a gold-plated inscription commemorating the goal! I've never forgotten that moment."

THE HAWKS FINISHED the season in third place, drawing first-place Detroit in the Stanley Cup semifinals. Hall took the 4–3 loss in the opener, and Billy Reay started DeJordy in the second game. It was the first time that a goalie other than Hall started a playoff game for Chicago since the '40s. DeJordy fumbled his opportunity, making only 22 saves in a 6–3 loss. Hall returned to the crease and shook off any distractions that his brief displacement might have caused. When the series shifted to Chicago, the Hawks won 5–2 and then 2–1, despite being outshot in both games. In the latter, Hall put on an incredible display in the second period while the Hawks were on the kill that must have brought back memories of '61 to Gordie Howe and company. The Wings won the fifth game at the Olympia, but Hall pitched a Hawk-typical 4–0 shutout to even the series at three. Chicago was outshot 33–28. Game 7 in Detroit saw the Wings race out to a 2–0 lead in the first period in which they outshot the Hawks yet again, but Chicago scored four unanswered for the upset, avenging its loss of the year before.

The Ghoulie was back at the top of his game.

The Hawks then faced Montreal, which had topped Toronto in six games. The Habs' goalies were the 5-foot, 8-inch Worsley and the 5-foot, 6-inch Hodge, and while Gump got most of the work that year, Hodge was just a year removed from winning the Vezina Trophy. This was the first time in Worsley's nearly 15-year pro career that he had a chance to play for the Stanley Cup. He started the first three games of the series for Montreal, winning the first two at home and getting his first career playoff shutout in the process. He lost 3–1 when the scene moved to Chicago, and coach Toe Blake was forced to put Hodge into the net for Game 4 after Worsley pulled a muscle in the pre-game warm-ups. The game was a tense 1–1 affair going into the third period. After the opening draw of the third, Bobby Hull took the puck at center and lofted a floater at Hodge. He fanned at the easy drive with his glove, and the goal ignited the Hawks as they poured three more past him in the third to turn the nailbiter into a rout at 5–1.

The fifth game followed the same script with the Habs leading 2–0 going into the third. They notched four in the third (three against DeJordy, who Reay put in net when the outcome was no longer in doubt) for a 6–0 win which, besides giving the Canadiens a series lead, helped restore Hodge's confidence. For his part, Hall came back with his best hockey, as he did throughout his career after a good shellacking. The first period of the sixth game was marred by an ugly brawl, Stan Mikita and Terry Harper being the principal combatants. The rough stuff helped the Hawks slow down the Habs, but they still went into the third period down 1–0. Just two minutes into play, Jean Beliveau got around a Hawk defender and drove from the right side of the ice to the middle. Hall challenged him, staying with him on a deke. Beliveau tried to flip the puck high against the grain, but Hall snapped his trapper shut, the puck tucked safely inside. The Hawks fed off that save and scored two goals quickly to force a seventh game.

Blake stunned everyone by returning Worsley to the net. Gump's solid play and Montreal's home ice were too much, and the Habs raced to a 4–0 first-period lead. All four goals were point-blank as Glenn was left virtually alone. The Hawk defense did not improve when the game resumed, and in the second period Glenn made a glove save for the ages. A quick shot from inside the circle to his right caught a piece of Glenn's pad and then the short-side post, caroming out to the other side. A Hab forward shot immediately into the seemingly open net, only to have his low shot smothered by Glenn's trapper right on the goal line.

Montreal, however, outshot the Hawks 32–21 in the finale, winning 4–0.

After the final round, Glenn and Bobby Hull were the Black Hawk final-ists for the Conn Smythe Trophy, the new award designated to reward the playoff MVP. It was given deservedly to Beliveau, but coach Reay was having none of it: "I think Hall should have won that award. He gave us great goal-tending all the way. I think he deserved it more."

Having completed his tenth NHL season, The Ghoulie headed back to the Edmonton area to ponder his future. Was it time to leave the game? Pub-lished reports claimed he was contemplating retirement, but Hall was not showing his cards. He certainly put pressure on himself to play at absolutely the highest level possible. And, in Glenn's case, the mental pressure a goalie typically faces was compounded by the ceaseless rigors of his consecu-tive game streak (no physical or mental vacation in-season over a span of 881 games), and further by the particular demands of playing behind a high-powered but defensively ineffectual team. On top of that, he never really adjusted to living in a big city. According to friends, Glenn longed for the open plains of Alberta more than ever.

If Pauline had any say in the decision, Glenn would not be retiring. She enjoyed the buzz and camaraderie of the pro hockey lifestyle, and "Whenever it came up," recalled Pauline, "I said, 'No, you're not!'"

Painting the Barn

———

FOR GLENN HALL, the summer of 1965 provided the calm he needed after another hectic year tending goal. He and Pauline purchased a small grain farm 20 miles west of Edmonton, in the speck of a town called Stony Plain. The pastoral setting couldn't have been a more dramatic contrast from the urban environment of Chicago. Long stretches of two-lane roads cut through the magnificent green, gold, and brown fields. Solitary farmhouses dotted the horizon. Warm summer breezes pushed gently over the crops, their song the only noise to disturb the quiet. The farm was a sanctuary, a home, an oasis of stability for him and his family, and Glenn knew it was available to him because of hockey.

If he'd been close to retiring at the end of the previous year, Hall's National Hockey League salary was certainly part of the enticement to return. But Glenn would never have gone back to the net if his passion wasn't still there, if he didn't truly believe he could play at his best. So Hall returned to the Chicago Black Hawks, although he did report late to training camp for the first time in his career. By this time, he felt about camp much as he did about practice. Hawk coach Billy Reay already knew this, and along with management, gave Hall permission to report late. The team had Denis DeJordy and Dave Dryden in camp to tend the nets.

Not wanting to appear as he was giving preferential treatment, Reay publicly remained mum about his star goalie's absence. The late-season rumors of Glenn's retirement, coupled with his camp absence and Reay's silence, caught the interest of a reporter. When the reporter called the Hall residence to ask why Glenn was tardy, Pauline picked up the phone. She told Glenn that a reporter wanted to speak with him about why he was late to camp, and he told her to tell him he was too busy to talk, that he was out painting the barn. That barn and its need for paint eventually took on mythic proportions.

When Hall did report, he arrived in time to witness a battle for the backup role. DeJordy was not happy with the limited game time he'd been seeing over the past three seasons. He'd only been marginally effective in his role, so his contention that he needed to play 70 games to be at his best might have been accurate. But as long as Hall was present, the only way he'd see that much action was in the minors, an option he didn't want to exercise. The timing of his demands couldn't have been worse, as Dryden took the camp by storm with extremely sharp play and simply beat DeJordy out. The man once heralded as "the next Sawchuk" soon found himself toiling in the minors for the St. Louis Braves of the Central Professional Hockey League. Ironically he played in the St. Louis Arena, the dilapidated building that Hawk owner Arthur Wirtz had just peddled to Sid Salomon as part of his deal to purchase an NHL expansion franchise.

Hall started the season with sharp play and the team did as well. By late November, the Hawks were already in a neck-and-neck battle for the top of the standings with the Montreal Canadiens. They could have lost some serious ground in their quest to end the "Curse of Muldoon" when Bobby Hull went down with a knee injury. But Hall stepped up his game to make up for the missing offensive punch.

In the first three games that Hull missed, Hall put on a display of goaltending that, even for his high standards, was remarkable. In Detroit, the Hawks held a 3–2 lead going into the third period. The Red Wings mounted a furious attack, throwing 17 shots his way. He refused to crack, and the Hawks won by a goal. The Wings went back to Chicago, only to run into Hall's stone wall in a 3–1 win, the Hawks netting their last score with just seconds to go in the empty net.

After that game, the Hawks traveled to New York. The Rangers were the league's weakest team. They would finish the season dead last, 35 points behind the second-place Black Hawks. Two young and largely untested goalies, Ed Giacomin and Cesare Maniago, vied for playing time, so this should have been an easy game for the Tribe, even without Hull. But like so many games while he was in a Hawk uniform, Hall had to take the team onto his shoulders. That night he gave the Gotham fans a clinic in clutch goalkeeping. The game was scoreless after the first, the Rangers holding a 13–5 shot advantage. The game was scoreless after the second, the Rangers outshooting the Hawks 16–9. Speedy wing Ken Wharram scored on a power play late in the third to give the Hawks a 1–0 lead. That score marked one of the few times the puck crossed the blue line, as the Rangers drilled Hall with 18 shots in the third. Which was his best stop? The Rod Gilbert breakaway? Donnie Marshall's point-blank rebound try? Bob Nevin's chances from the slot? By the time it was over, Hall had turned in a 47-save, 1–0 shutout victory.

"It was just an incredible stretch of goaltending," said Billy Reay. "He singlehandedly won three games for us, and you can't ask any more than that of anybody."

DAVE DRYDEN FOUND HIMSELF in a remarkable position with the Hawks. Coming off his strong camp, he now backed the man he had idolized as a youth. Coming into the situation, Dryden might have felt a bit intimidated, but he soon came to admire Glenn Hall the man as much as the athlete.

"We roomed together, and he used to sleep like crazy after a game," Dryden recalled. "But sometimes after a game [Hawk center] Billy Hay, who was a good friend of Glenn's, would come up to the room too. They'd sit and maybe have a beer, and they'd talk about the West. Sometimes they'd call a friend out west and just ask him to describe the plains. Then Glenn started bringing encyclopedias with him. I'd say, 'What are you reading?' And he'd say, 'Tonight I've got A.' And the next trip he'd bring B. He got such delight out of it. He'd say, 'Do you realize such-and-such is the case? It's right here on page 36.' When I idolized him like I did, I didn't expect that from him. I had imagined this real hardened guy with no sense of humor. But he was just terrific.

"I always thought that Glenn must have had some real run-ins in Detroit with the way he played. He had just started to use the butterfly style, and I had the feeling from the way we talked that Detroit management didn't think that was the way you played the game. But it's the enduring style. Glenn was right on so many blessed things. He was the best that I ever saw play. There's no question . . ."

By this time in Hall's career, carrying the mail for more than 60 games was too much to ask of a goalie who was now 34 years of age. "I know the greatest thing for me was a day off practice," he said. Once in a while, a coach would ask if I could use one and I had a standard two-word answer: 'Of course.' That's frowned on today. Coaches think you're not working hard if you take a day off.

"Practices [have now become] nothing more than shooting galleries for the gang, and I'm the target. When I was younger, I used to bear down in practices, but not any more. You watch me before a game starts when we have that 15-minute warm-up. I come out with the rest of the team, but instead of getting right into the net I circle around and around and around for a good five minutes. Then, very slowly, I move closer to the nets, and finally I move in. That should give you some idea about how I feel about practices. The fewer times I have to face those pucks, the better I feel."

But every so often in practice, Glenn had some fun. Eric Nesterenko was teammates with Hall throughout the '60s. Nicknamed "Swoop" because of his long, lazy stride, Nesterenko had a very solid NHL career, although he never realized the big-time potential as a goal scorer once predicted for him. Nesterenko recalled: "[Hall] was almost unbeatable in a one-on-one situation. He had an uncanny ability to read your moves and anticipate where you were going to shoot the puck. To test his reflexes, Glenn would sometimes lean to one side during practice, offer an open net to the attacker, then thrust his glove hand *behind his back* to snare the resulting shot. Damned if he didn't get it two out of five times."

That year, Glenn earned the plaudits of goalies across the league for helping to pay back one of their most noted tormentors. The Toronto Maple Leafs' Eddie Shack was one of the NHL's most colorful players. With a jumping bean of a skating stride and a penchant for stirring the pot after the whistle, he was known as a guy who took more than the occasional liberty with a goalie behind the play. In a game at Maple Leaf Gardens, Hall was on the way to the bench on a delayed penalty when Shack spotted him. Unable to resist the tempting combination of Hall not seeing him and the referee well ahead of the play, Shack put his stick under Hall's skates, sending the goalie toward the ice. As he fell, Hall turned and whipped the big goal stick around, catching Shack in the side of the neck and thereby earning some more space for Hall and Co. in future encounters.

Hall had learned early on how to use his stick to send a message. "When I was a rookie," he recalled, "and a few years after, I used to have some troubles with opponents skating around my goal crease. Sometimes they'd spear me or run across the net to try to take me out of the play. It was done plenty of times and rarely called by the referee. But don't think I was Mr. Nice Guy when it happened. I'd give it back to them. I had the great equalizer, my big goal stick. A two-hand wallop on the ankles hurts enough so they don't come back so fast. Mind you, I didn't go after them on the same play they got me. I'd wait for the openings. I used to call it the 'self-preservation play.' Nowadays they don't bother me anymore."

Black Hawk alumni guru and longtime Hall fan and friend Jack Fitzsimmons recounted defenseman "Moose" Vasko's comments about Hall's dexterity with the goal stick: "When Moose would screen Glenn, Glenn would give him a whack as well. Moose always said he wore his shin pads the wrong way while he was playing in front of Glenn."

JUST OVER HALFWAY THROUGH the season, just like the year before, Hall asked for a break. "Glenn's an awful worrier," Billy Reay told the press. "He takes his responsibility very seriously and when three or four shots began to get by him in every game, even though most of them weren't his fault, he really got down." To make matters worse, the once-adoring Chicago fans showed no patience with any chinks in his armor. Despite his remarkable consistency, they began to boo mercilessly if he had an "off" game. "So," Reay continued, "I told him to take a week off and not even bother showing up around the Stadium for a week."

Glenn never admitted to hearing catcalls from the stands. "When I was playing, I'd only hear one guy in the stands," he said. "He was the guy who'd say, 'Beeeeer. Get your cold beeeeer.'"

The Halls spent the week at the Lake Lawn Lodge, a country resort a couple of hours north of Chicago in Wisconsin. Glenn's respite gave Dryden three starts, during which time the club went 2–1, losing the third game 5–2 in Toronto before a return match at the Stadium. Glenn came back for that one, winning 3–2 and looking refreshed.

"It was amazing to see how good Glenn was so consistently," said Dryden. "He was so agile on the ice, he could cover any shot. There were no 'gimmes' against him. And he was so intelligent. He knew everything about every goal. He could remember where every guy was and that was because he had the power of absolute concentration. He could feel the flow of the game. I think he was a 'flow' goalie. He had a very interesting philosophy. He wanted the defense to challenge the shooter, to force more passes. He felt that the more they passed, the more mistakes would be made."

The game was still all-consuming for The Ghoulie. Teammates kidded him about the fact that when he dozed on a team flight, his legs lashed out as if he were making a save. "I'd dream about hockey on the nights before I was to play," he said. "I'd wake up dead tired. I'd have to ask what day it was. I didn't know if I'd played. It was that real."

Glenn finished the year second in shutouts with four, a goals-against average of 2.63, and 34 regular-season wins to lead the league in that category once again. He was voted to the First All-Star team for the sixth time, with his three second-team nods, this made nine recognitions in his 11-year career.

"He gave up only one bad goal all year," stated Dryden. "I still remember it, a shot from the point by Tim Horton."

The Hawks finished second yet again, eight points behind Montreal, three ahead of Toronto, and eight ahead of fourth-place Detroit. For the third consecutive year, Chicago met Detroit in the semifinals. In each of the two previous matches, the team that finished lower in the standings won. This year proved no different.

When Glenn tended the net on April 7 for the opening game of the play-offs, he played across the ice from a goalie who was his mirror image. Roger Crozier was a southpaw who had grown up in the Black Hawk organization. As Hall had incorporated elements of the trade he'd seen in Chuck Rayner and Terry Sawchuk in his formative years, Crozier had done likewise with Hall. The Bracebridge, Ontario, native adopted an acrobatic, crowd-pleasing style that featured the V as its foundation. He was the first goalie who'd adopted Hall's innovative signature technique to reach the NHL. And, just like Hall, Crozier made his big-league debut with the Wings, who had acquired him in a minor trade with the Hawks in 1963, and he was promptly named the NHL's Rookie of the Year. The pressures of the game also tore at him as much as they did at Hall. Like contemporaries Worsley and Hodge, Crozier was small at 5 feet, 7 inches; unlike those two, he was paper-thin at 145 pounds.

Hall and the Hawks won the first game of the series 2–1, but the Wings pounded Glenn 7–0 in Game 2. The boo birds were in full throat. In Detroit, Hall put on a show with a 35-save 2–1 win, but Detroit pounded him again the next game 5–1. As Hall left his locker room after the contest, he was accosted verbally by a Detroit fan and a short scuffle ensued. It was an uncharacteristic show from Glenn, outward evidence perhaps of the inner pressures he was experiencing. Game 5 only made matters worse as, back at the Stadium, Detroit hit Hall for five goals again. When the fourth puck got past him, the boos poured down again from the rafters. Hall's facial expression as he cleared the crease went unchanged. For years now, he had proven to be unflappable and inscrutable, his expression never varying whether he'd just been touched for a goal or had made an impossible save.

"When things got rough, I would picture that hot shower after a game," he said. "With ten minutes left on the clock and there was a face-off, I could just imagine how good that water would feel on my forehead."

"[One of the things that makes him great is] his disposition," said former Hawk star Johnny Gottselig. "He doesn't show emotion when a goal is scored . . . Never shows disgust toward a teammate. We've had goalies who'd never think it was their fault when a goal was scored. They'd glare at a team-mate so everyone could tell who they thought was responsible. Not Glenn. He just goes quietly back to work."

"I couldn't understand why the Chicago fans turned on him so quickly," said Dryden. "It's not that it [their treatment of him] was that bad, but it should have been better. I had talked to all the other goalies playing in those days and they all knew how good he really was. I do think Glenn was frustrated by the fans. I think he was hurt that they didn't recognize that he was doing his best."

Crozier was playing brilliantly. Taking a page from Hall's book, he got better the more shots he faced. He was not just stopping the puck; he was stopping it with flair, bouncing around the crease to make back-to-back saves, dropping into the V, and popping back up onto his feet. He stymied the Hawks at every turn.

The sixth game in Detroit was a tough loss. Glenn had made 27 saves, and the Hawks were holding a 2–1 lead with less than four minutes to play in the game. Detroit had been pressing, but Hall had every answer until lightning struck in the form of Dean Prentice. The solid Wing forward beat Hall twice inside of a minute to turn a one-goal lead into a one-goal deficit from which the Hawks didn't come back.

The Wings went on to play Montreal (who'd swept Toronto in four games) in the finals, the Canadiens winning another Stanley Cup in a six-game series. For his part, Crozier was named the Conn Smythe Trophy winner as the playoff MVP. Though Montreal goalie Gump Worsley was brilliant in the finals, Crozier's work got Detroit there in the first place.

The Glenn Hall who returned home to the farm in Stony Plain looked decidedly different than the Glenn Hall who had broken into the league 11 years earlier. His face had aged well past 34 years; it bore the telltale scars of the trade. His hairline had receded, and a balding patch was growing at the crown of his head. The years of wear and tear had turned Hall's public persona from amiable to gloomy. Early in his career, Hall had been accessible to the press after games, happy to be quoted honestly. That year, he ducked out as soon as he was changed, pushing curtly past the outstretched pens and notepads. Years later, Hall would say the reason he wanted to get out of the locker room quickly was because he wanted to get into his car and out on the expressway toward home right away so he could accurately review in his mind the goals he'd given up. If he'd stopped and talked with the press, it might have tainted his recall of events in the days before video review and goalie coaches.

One thing was certain. When Glenn's playing days came to an end, he had no interest in taking a front-office job: "That would be worse than playing. I'd have to put up with sportswriters and fans, and I'd have to think of pleasant things to say. I couldn't stand that."

Below: Glenn and Bobby Hull share a laugh in the locker room. Glenn considers Bobby the greatest Chicago Black Hawk ever to wear the sweater.

Facing page, top: Glenn readies for combat.

Facing page, bottom: Posing proudly with the ultimate prize, the Stanley Cup, which the Black Hawks won in 1961.

Left: Jacques Plante and Glenn combined to earn the Vezina Trophy in 1968–69. Despite predictions that the pair would quarrel, they got along well and played brilliantly.

Below: Glenn congratulates teammate Ron Schock who'd just tallied the game winner in the second OT to propel the St. Louis Blues into the 1968 Stanley Cup finals.

12

Burying Muldoon

—————

IF ELEMENTS OF CHICAGO'S fickle fandom had begun to turn on Glenn Hall, management still backed him totally in 1966–67. At the end of the previous season, they had threatened a housecleaning, tired of finishing in second place, disappointed in not making it to the Stanley Cup finals. Publicly owner Arthur Wirtz said Hall and Bobby Hull were his lone untouchables. But that vote of confidence coupled with his First All-Star status were not enough to convince Mr. Goalie to continue.

"There have been nights when I almost wished I didn't have to go out on the ice," he was quoted as saying. "All I want to do is stand out in the middle of the 160 acres I've got near Edmonton and holler, 'Damn you! Damn you! Damn you!' until I'm good and hoarse and hear the 'You! You! You!' echo back across the field."

And with that, Glenn informed general manager Tommy Ivan that he would be retiring from the game. At first, Ivan assumed he was dealing with a contract-negotiation ploy. As the summer progressed, Ivan was still in denial despite Glenn's repeated stance that this time he meant it and he would not come back. Ivan was sure that once the leaves began to turn, Glenn would return.

THE EASE OF THE SUMMER MONTHS did nothing to change Hall's mind. He spent the off-season working his farm and enjoying life with his wife and family, which now included fourth child and second son, Lindsay, named after Glenn's former teammate, Ted. He had not threatened to retire in an effort to secure a larger contract. This time the barn wasn't in need of an extra coat of paint. This time it was for real.

Back in Chicago, Black Hawk brass was staring reality in the eye. They were facing life without Glenn Hall for the first time in nine years. Was Denis DeJordy ever going to be the next Sawchuk? Was he ready to fill the void that Hall's exodus created? And what about Dave Dryden? He had played well in his infrequent starts the previous season. Between the two of them, surely the Hawks could make do. Management harbored doubts, and a trade with Toronto was rumored. The Maple Leafs were looking for defensive help, and the Hawks dangled physical backliner Doug Jarrett in an effort to acquire none other than Terry Sawchuk, who had spent the last two seasons with the Leafs. Toronto also tried to trade Sawchuk to the New York Rangers for tough forward Orland Kurtenbach. Neither swap came to fruition, and Sawchuk was destined to have his last real hurrah later in the year for the Leafs.

In point of fact, the focus of the entire Hawk organization had been on winning the regular-season championship. That goal took precedence over winning the Cup, since the Hawks had won the latter in 1961. It became an almost obsessive quest for owners Arthur Wirtz and Jim Norris, and they'd seen it slip out of their hands late in the year four times in the past six seasons.

"I was good friends with Jim Norris," said Hawk center Bill Hay. "And I think Jim and Arthur Wirtz felt that a first-place finish was more of a reflection of who was truly the better team than was the winner of the Cup."

In their minds, and in those of GM Tommy Ivan and coach Billy Reay, the 1966–67 season was now or never. Bobby Hull was at the peak of his powers and Stan Mikita had become one of the premier forwards in the league. Mikita was centering the "Scooter Line" of Ken Wharram and Doug Mohns, a great combination of speed, grit, and skill. Hull's center, young Phil Esposito, had shown signs of becoming a great player in his own right. Management even coaxed Bill Hay out of retirement after the season started to help the offense. The defense was about to get a boost from rookie Ed Van Impe, and young Pat Stapleton had had a great year the season previous and was being tabbed for NHL stardom. All the pieces were in place.

Except one.

The Hawk brain trust's worst fears were confirmed in training camp. De-Jordy performed competently, but privately teammates wondered how heavily replacing Hall was weighing on the youngster's shoulders. Hall was the goalie they had counted on to hold the fort until they got untracked. Although the NHL goalie's basic job was to stop the first shot of every rush, Hall routinely gave them stops two, three, and four. All of a sudden, the players in the Indian Head sweaters realized they were more urgently needed back in the territory they knew distantly as the defensive zone. Perhaps some of them realized that the more time they spent backchecking, the less time they had to score and tally up their bonus money at season's end. To a man, the Hawk players, despite their general aversion to defensive commitment, deeply appreciated how much Hall meant to them while he was there. He was a unilaterally popular and respected teammate. "Glenn is treated with the respect most people show their mothers or sisters," noted Hawk beat writer Dan Moulton.

"Glenn performed very quietly," said Stan Mikita. "He wasn't about the fanfare. We were from an era where we didn't talk a lot, where we showed our mettle on the ice. Glenn was the main reason we were winners, and we knew it. The level of respect he got grew because he didn't want to look obvious, he didn't showboat. He took everything in, he thought about the game a lot, but even if there were a group of us out having a beer or two, he wouldn't say much until everyone was done talking. Then he'd give his opinion in a very quiet, thoughtful way. He'd have his say, and if you were smart, you took what he said to heart."

The organization felt it needed Hall back. As training camp concluded, Tommy Ivan made the phone call. Although Hall, who was within days of turning 35, had not been sitting waiting by the phone, he had discovered that finding a job in town while continuing to work the farm was easier said than done. "The only trouble is that nobody out there has anything for retired goalkeepers to do," he said. Ivan offered Hall a raise to $40,000, which kept him the highest-paid goalie in the league. Recalled Glenn, "I just couldn't afford to turn it down. I'm far from independently wealthy." He did not accept the offer immediately. "Don't get me wrong. I think hockey is a great game," Hall said. "It's tremendous for spectators and it's great for kids to play. But for me [now] it's just a job that I don't like having to do. I don't think my feeling toward the game ever has hurt my play. Sure, I have to drive myself, but I earn my money."

Years later, Glenn realized the Hawks had another reason for asking him back: "Expansion was coming the next year, and if I was back playing they could leave me unprotected and then they'd probably be able to keep DeJordy and Dryden."

DeJordy battled his weight. To keep fit, he had to do extra work on the bike, and in his French accent, he would bemoan his fate to Glenn: "It is not fair. Last night, Freddie [teammate Stanfield] and I split three beer and a half. Today Freddie weigh 1 pound more, I weigh 4 pound more."

The season was ten days old when Hall informed Ivan that he would return. Ivan asked him to get to Chicago as quickly as he could. Glenn and

Pauline packed the station wagon, ushered the kids aboard, and set out on the 1,800-mile drive. The Hawks sent Dryden down to the farm.

It took all of three practices for Glenn to convince coach Reay he was ready for a game. "He's always in shape," said the coach. Hall reported to camp at 172 pounds, 6 under his playing weight. "And he really doesn't need that much work to get his reflexes sharp," added Reay.

"I feel pretty good right now," admitted the goalie after that third practice. "But it's early of course. The days, and especially the nights, get a lot longer as the season wears on."

Four games into the season, Hall returned to the net in Boston against the Bruins and made 27 saves in a 4–2 win. His Chicago debut was against the Rangers. When his name was announced as the starting goalie, an enormous roar filled the Stadium; a second shout went up when he took his place in front of the net that he had tended for the past nine years. It was a fitting welcome from the fans whose fickle treatment of their once-adored hero had nearly driven the nails into his career's coffin. Feeling right at home, the Hawks were outshot 27–25 and won 3–1. Staying true to form, Glenn recorded his first shutout of the year against the Montreal Canadiens by a 5–0 score. The Hawks were outshot 31–24.

Coach Reay stayed with a two-goalie system throughout the year. He said, "We feel we have two major-league goalies and we intend to operate that way." Sometimes he waited until just before the pre-game warm-up to tell his men which one was starting. Hall always took the news that he was not playing well.

"Glenn never broods when he's on the bench," said Reay. "When you tell him he's not going to work, it's as though you offered him $1,000."

"When they told me I wasn't playing the next game, that night I'd drift off into a lovely, lovely sleep. When I was told I was going to play, I'd toss and turn and play the game in my mind that I was going to play the next day. But I always wanted to know if I was playing the night before a game," Glenn said. "While I got to like the two-goalie system, I didn't like the deliberate rotation. Take me out when I'm horseshit. Don't take me out when I'm going good. The two-goalie system could make you look bad."

Occasionally Reay pulled an unorthodox move with his netmen. In a home game against Montreal, DeJordy wasn't going well and he inserted Hall for ten minutes of the second period, then went back to DeJordy to finish the game. Twice when penalty shots were called against the Hawks, Reay yanked De-Jordy and put Hall in cold to face the shot. The shooters, Frank Mahovlich in one instance and Norm Ullman in the second, both scored. Was the strategy doomed to fail? Probably. There wasn't enough time for Glenn to throw up.

BESIDES KEEPING HALL well rested, the two-goalie system let DeJordy break into the NHL gracefully. To that point, Denis had played in only 40 NHL games in his career, but with Hall almost certain to retire for good next year and with the NHL expanding to 12 teams, DeJordy finally saw the light at the end of the tunnel. Early in the season's second half, Hall was injured by a skate as he stretched to stop a rebound, and it took 43 stitches to close the horrible wound just below his knee. DeJordy was forced to play in ten consecutive games, and he acquitted himself well, furthering the perception that he would soon be ready to take the reins.

With both goalies playing very near peak form, the Hawks, as they had done so many times in the '60s, stayed at or near the top of the league throughout the season. But this year, as February faded into March, they held a commanding lead over Montreal and Toronto, who were battling for second place. The Hall-DeJordy combo also led the pack in goals against.

With a couple of weeks still left in the season, the Hawks were home on a Sunday afternoon to play the Toronto Maple Leafs. Two points would clinch the long-awaited and much-desired first place. Hall got the call for the game and patrolled his net opposite the Leafs' Terry Sawchuk.

Much time had passed since their halcyon days: Sawchuk was 37, Hall 35, yet stylistically neither man had conceded much to age. As the Hawks bore down on Terry that afternoon, he assumed his deep knee-bent crouch. He moved slower laterally, but he was still intimidating with an eerie mask and a blocker that looked like an overgrown mail bag. He twisted his head slowly and moved very deliberately. When the puck went from one side of the ice to the other, The Uke glided effortlessly and tucked himself from one post to the other. There was never any unnecessary movement, but when it was time to respond to a shot with quickness, he still supplied the answer, just not as consistently. Since 1958, his goals-against average had ballooned over 3.00 three times. His once-prodigious shutout production had trailed off to a dribble. Only three times in the '60s had he recorded five blanks, the last time in 1963–64. He never had more than two in a season after that. He shared the Vezina in 1964–65 with partner Johnny Bower, but each year he'd been faced with a new medical drama. You could almost see the energy draining out of him.

If Hall had slowed at all, it showed only rarely. He played a little farther in front of the goal line than he had in the past, trying to work the angles to compensate for some of the reflexes that he seemed sure were deserting him. The Ghoulie still moved from the low, knock-kneed stance from which the V bloomed on any low shot. He was touched for more than three goals only three times all year. His hair was graying at the sides, and the lines on his face were more distinct. But the platooning system left him fresh, and on that March afternoon he was as sharp as ever.

The Stadium was packed with over 20,000; the Chicago fire marshall looked the other way. The Hawks attacked Sawchuk with a vengeance, and The Uke looked uncomfortable from the first drop of the puck. With each Hawk goal, the fans littered the ice with confetti and beer cups, and the home squad piled it on, topping the Leafs 5–0. Appropriately the score again did not reflect the play, and the 39-save gem would be Hall's last shutout in a Hawk sweater. The win clinched first place for Chicago for the first time in the team's history. The post-game locker room floated in champagne and reeked of cigars. Shouts of "We buried Muldoon!" echoed off the players' cubicles, the skaters recalling the legendary curse which, in actuality, was the creation of an imaginative sportswriter. Little Lou Angotti, a skater usually relegated to the odd shift and penalty killing, had scored twice that day, once directly off a face-off against the shaky Sawchuk. Angotti, Hull, Mikita, and Reay were surrounded by reporters. At the other end of the locker room, Hall quickly dressed and slipped out of the side door, nearly unnoticed.

"I'm going out to meet two friends and celebrate quietly," he told an inquiring mind. At season's end, he would have something else to celebrate as he and DeJordy shared the Vezina Trophy, the second of Hall's career.

The Hawks finished the season 17 points ahead of second-place Montreal and 19 points in front of third-place Toronto. While the championship was an aberrant achievement for the Tribe, the playoff tendencies of the '60s would hold true to form. The Hawks had lost every semifinal series they entered as a favorite during the decade, and they would now be facing Toronto and the old-age home on blades that coach-GM Punch Imlach had assembled.

The Leafs had creaked into third place on the strength of a roster filled with players closer to their 40th birthday than their 30th. In fact, they were nosed out of second place in the last game of the season. Punch Imlach was an irrascible authoritarian who believed you could accomplish anything if you worked harder. He would practice his players longer than any other NHL team, ignoring their advanced ages and reasoning that tougher practices made the games that much easier. He was notoriously reliant on veterans and on team defense, and his teams had won three consecutive Stanley Cups between 1962 and 1964. His goalies were Sawchuk and the 40-something phenom

Johnny Bower. Before the end of the regular season, Bower split a finger on his blocker hand, making it impossible for him to grip his stick with any strength. He sat out the first few games of the opening round.

Imlach's roster featured forwards such as George Armstrong, Red Kelly, Bob Pulford, and Larry Jeffrey, whose careers were in decline while the players on his backline—Tim Horton, Bob Baun, Marcel Pronovost, and Allan Stanley—were all longer than long in the tooth. But that core, surrounded by stars at the peak of their games, like Dave Keon and Frank Mahovlich, made their advanced ages work for them as they sensed this year was likely to be their last hurrah. Imlach fashioned a physical and defensive game plan he felt gave the Leafs their best chance to ground the high-flying Hawks.

Reay started DeJordy in the opening game at home, and the Hawks won 5–2 against Sawchuk, who looked as wobbly as he had in their regular-season 5–0 win. Imlach's strategy paid off in Game 2, as the Leafs won 3–1 against DeJordy again. When the scene switched to the Gardens, Hall returned and also lost 3–1. The Leafs dominated the game, and Hall was sharp, but the Hawks mustered only a few threats to Sawchuk. That was the first time all season Terry had played more than two games in a week. With Bower still unable to play, Sawchuk got the next start as well. Reay stayed with Hall in the crucial fourth game, and the move paid dividends.

Glenn, who was later voted the best visiting goalie of the decade by the Toronto press in a hockey retrospective, proved why he earned the honor that night. He'd made 34 saves, and with just minutes to go in the third period the Hawks were leading 4–2. Dramatically outdueling Sawchuk, who was looking fatigued, Mr. Goalie stopped Keon on a breakaway and thwarted the Leaf power play four times before Jim Pappin had the puck in front of him from 30 feet away. Pappin snapped off a drive that Hall leaped to stop. The puck rose quickly, crushing into his lips. Glenn's head snapped back as if he'd been shot; the puck opened a vicious cut, and blood streamed from Hall's mouth and formed a trail at his feet. The official didn't see the damage and play continued. Hall recovered from the face save and watched the puck go off into the corner, holding his stance the entire time. When the puck squirted back toward the side of the goal, Glenn dropped to the ice to smother it, forcing a face-off. In one fluid motion, the injured veteran recovered from his last save and headed for the locker room. DeJordy took over, letting in the first shot against him, but the Hawks held on to tie the series.

It took some 20-plus stitches to close the wound, and Hall lost a tooth on the play, the first dental casualty in his career. Glenn recounted, "The dentist who examined me told me that I was lucky. Through my swollen lips I said, 'I un fee wucky.'"

Reay was forced to come back with DeJordy. Although there was plenty of second-guessing for having played DeJordy in the first two games (Reay reasoned that the home games would be easier for Denis than the road games and he felt confident both goalies could win), Hall's disfigured face gave Reay no choice for Game 5.

The fifth game of this series has been referred to as the greatest single goaltending exhibition in hockey history. It was not. That game has never and will never be played. There are hundreds of truly remarkable and unique displays of goaltending over the decades that as individual games should be worthy of Hall of Fame enshrinement, especially when one considers that baseball pitchers are so honored for each no-hitter. What cannot be disputed is that this was one of those games. Terry Sawchuk threw a relief no-hitter against the Hawks on this particular Saturday afternoon in April on TV.

Leaf coach Punch Imlach decided to start Bower. It was the 44-year-old Bower's first game of the series, and he looked rusty. Nursing a 1–0 lead after DeJordy gave up a soft goal, Bower returned the favor when he misplayed a puck behind the net. Lou Angotti scored into the vacated net. Shortly thereafter, Bower struggled with a shot that he normally would have frozen with his quick and sure hands, but the resulting rebound was buried by Bobby Hull. DeJordy couldn't stand that brief prosperity, and the Leafs left the period tied at two. It was clear that Bower's injured stick hand was still bothering him.

After the first period, Imlach decided to lift Bower and went back to Sawchuk. Reluctantly Terry answered the bell. He was promptly greeted with a Bobby Hull bullet that caught him right on the sore shoulder, knocking him nearly unconscious with pain. When the Leaf trainer got to the crumpled goalie, he asked The Uke if he was all right. "I stopped the fucking shot, didn't I?" was the reply. Sawchuk recovered and stopped 36 more over the last two periods while the Leafs scored twice more, the first another softie and the second into the empty net for a 4–2 win.

DeJordy became the target of the vociferous and unforgiving Stadium crowd, and from that point on in his Chicago career, he never earned the trust of the local fans. Over those last two periods, Sawchuk stopped shots from every conceivable angle. For those last 40 minutes, he transformed himself back into the Terry of the early '50s.

Down 3–2 in the series, the Hawks called on Glenn. Hall's face was still swollen, but he was the team's best hope for victory in Game 6. "You never saw a player with more courage," said Stan Mikita. Hall fought valiantly, but the Leafs outshot and outplayed the Hawks, winning 3–1.

Toronto toppled the Canadiens in the next round to win their fourth Cup of the decade.

The latest Chicago playoff failure was post-mortemed as a case of too much emphasis on the regular season. For the Hawks, it was a year of mixed emotions in that they'd slain the dragon of regular-season futility, yet still they failed to live up to Stanley Cup potential. Mr. Goalie finished the season having played a relatively leisurely 32 games with a league-best goals-against average of 2.38. His strong work was recognized by the league once again as he was named to the Second All-Star team behind burgeoning Ranger star Ed Giacomin. During his ten-year stint in Chicago, he'd come into his own and carved a sure-to-be Hall of Fame career. A perennial All-Star, he came to the Hawks when they were nothing and became the catalyst for their rise to power. The demands of the game and the undeniable effects of aging, along with an increasingly jaded home fandom, appeared to have turned the game from a passion into a financially necessary evil.

"Hockey," he'd been widely quoted as saying by then, "was 60 minutes or so of pure hell."

The end of the 1966–67 season was the close of an era for the NHL. With expansion to take place that summer, the league would double in size. That the Hawks pulled themselves out of their NHL purgatory undeniably helped to popularize the game and push it west of Chicago in the United States.

Expansion also ended an era with the Black Hawks. Hall's age, and his near-retirement of the previous fall, made him the logical man-out in the Hawk goaltending projections for the new 12-team league.

Mr. Goalie had played his last game in a Hawk sweater.

ESSAY: GATE 3½

Gate 3½ on the west side of Chicago Stadium was as close to paradise as any 11-year-old hockey fanatic could experience. This was the portal through which passed the privileged: box-holders, Stadium working staff, and, of course, the athletes themselves. Upon discovering this, I set two goals for myself right away. First, I wanted to get into the Stadium through that gate when the teams were practicing, and second, I wanted to establish a solid territory outside that gate so when the teams arrived before a game, I owned the prime autograph-getting real estate.

Chicago of the 1960s was billed as the "City that Worked." It worked principally for those able and willing to grease the palms of politicians or city patronage workers who were in a position to "get things done." Even by the tender age of 11, I knew that to get something you had to give something.

When my father took me with him to work at the hamburger stand during the season, I always found a way to sneak across the street and observe the goings on surrounding that powerful door. I knew that one of the Stadium workers, a spindly old black man everyone called "Spider," hung around that gate and guarded it as if his life depended on it. Soon I began taking a sack of double hamburgers, fries, and a strawberry shake over to him and, just like that, I saw Chicago work.

By the third or fourth time I'd plied Spider with the greasy fare, he led me through the magic door. Open Sesame! He pointed me toward a box seat on the turn, told me not to be loud or make any trouble, and warned me not to go chasing after any pucks the Hull brothers were sure to shoot into the stands. When he left to eat his food, I sat there all alone. No one else was in the arena and no one was on the ice just yet. The eerie silence was disquieting, since every other time I'd been inside this building the noise was constant. And the Stadium looked even more enormous when it was empty.

For all the Hawk practices I managed to con my way into, I remember the Maple Leaf practices the most vividly. As an aspiring goalie, I attribute this to two factors: the post-practice routine of Johnny Bower and the intimidating aura of Terry Sawchuk.

Johnny Bower always looked to me as if he were someone's cool uncle, the kind you wished were your own dad. At family get-togethers he'd be the one to give you the warm hug, tell a funny joke. I enjoyed watching him play immensely. His poke-checking ability was legendary. That maneuver was his answer to almost every breakaway he faced. The onrushing forward knew it was coming, but Bower was so good that it didn't matter. Somehow he'd snake his stick out there and separate the puck from the skater, sometimes tripping the hapless opponent in the process. The genius of Bower's style was his stance. In his set position, he held the stick halfway up the shaft, not at the shoulder the way every other NHL goalie did. So he was always halfway to the fully extended poke-check position every minute of the game. Bower was a stand-up goalie, seldom leaving his feet. He could sweep rebounds away with a one-handed motion with remarkable ease.

After the Leafs finished practicing, Bower would pick a teammate or two and have them line up 25 to 30 pucks across the tops of the circles. He'd set himself and point his stick at one of the shooters, signaling he was ready. The shooter would blast away from 25 feet, and the moment the puck made contact with a part of Johnny's equipment, he immediately focused on the next puck as it became a missile. He'd repeat the drill a time or two, then finally retreat to the dressing room. I got the impression that if he hadn't had to catch the team bus, he'd have been perfectly happy to stay on the ice all day.

I met Bower many years later quite by accident. I was attending a hockey memorabilia convention near the Toronto airport, and as I walked to the Expo Centre from my car, I looked up and saw him 10 feet in front of me. My jaw dropped, but I recovered in enough time to offer my hand and blurt, "I'm a huge fan and I always wanted to meet you."

Clever, huh?

He extended his hand, and when I shook it, I discovered why he was able to hold the stick so high on the shaft and still be strong enough to control rebounds and loose pucks so well. My hand literally disappeared and was damn near swallowed up by his enormous paw.

"Well, that's very nice of you to say," he replied, smiling pleasantly as if I'd made his day, and then he continued walking. He just felt wonderfully familiar; the encounter did nothing to change my image of him as the "cool uncle."

If Bower's aura suggested accessibility, Sawchuk's was exactly the opposite. The mask he wore made him look like a zombie, some otherworldly creature to which close exposure might prove fatal. As one of the autograph hounds who hung around outside Gate 3½, I stared at Sawchuk anytime he made his way into the Stadium. As he strode in, he seemed to move in slow motion. What always struck me is just how much his mask looked like his face. His ears were pointy, his face a mix of flesh tone and ochre, discolored in spots by the scar tissue he'd amassed from flying pucks and slashing skates. His hair was a closely cropped crew cut, and his face seemed frozen in a constant scowl.

I never worked up the courage to ask him for an autograph. Looking back, all he could have said was no, but at the time I felt that at any moment he could disintegrate me with a burning, laser stare. I tried to get close to him though, inching my way a little closer each time I saw him, as if testing the limits of his force field.

After every game, I hung around the parking lot to see the home warriors walk toward their cars and the road warriors make their way toward the bus. After the first game of the 1967 playoffs, I was in my usual spot, about 50 feet in front of Gate 3½. I was watching Stan Mikita walk toward his car when I sensed something off to my right. I turned, and not 7 feet from me was Sawchuk. He'd played that night and had looked poor in the 5–2 Hawk win. Punch Imlach, trying to shake up his troops, actually pulled Sawchuk for an extra attacker with just over eight minutes left, which somehow felt vaguely insulting toward the goalie.

Sawchuk was talking with a couple of people. I know they weren't teammates and they certainly weren't press. Perhaps they were relatives. What I do remember clearly is that he was wearing a long tan overcoat of some sort. And he was saying, "I'm through. This is it. You saw me out there and I was shit." I remember it so clearly because I was totally shocked that an athlete would say *shit*. I didn't move. I just wanted to continue eavesdropping, but very soon he turned and disappeared into the night.

For the series' fifth game, I was in my family's seats. We were in the first row of the first balcony directly over the net the Hawks defended for two periods. I was right above Sawchuk when he entered the game, and I could clearly hear the Bobby Hull rocket that dropped him like a bad habit as it struck his shoulder just minutes after he took over for Bower. I don't remember many of the individual saves, but I do vividly remember him reaching over the back of the net with his stick once, his skates dangling above the ice as he rested most of his weight on the crossbar to try to freeze the puck against the bottom back of the cage. I also remember booing Hawk goalie Denis DeJordy.

Loudly.

The other fans booed him because he'd given up a couple of soft goals in a must-win game. I'm sure I was booing because he committed the ultimate sin in my eyes—he wasn't Glenn Hall.

The game was an afternoon contest, and it was warm and sunny. It was so sunny that for some reason I remember the sun casting an almost uncomfortable glare. I was in my usual spot after the game, and when I noticed those same people Sawchuk had been speaking with after the first game, I decided not to move an inch. Soon thereafter, Sawchuk was there. I don't remember seeing him walk up. He was just there. I remember him wearing a thin dark tie; I remember he was holding that overcoat folded over his right arm. The arm was slightly bent, a fact I remember because he kept readjusting the coat as it slipped down his limb. Later I learned the arm was bent because of a childhood elbow injury that had never fully healed. I also remember what he said to those people he was standing with.

"Hell, you saw me out there. I can play this game forever."

I remember that, of course, because he did.

13

No Sad Blues

THE DECISION TO EXPAND the National Hockey League was made in the summer of 1965, when it became obvious that a league of six teams was an anachronism. Football and baseball teams covered the United States from coast to coast, and both sports boasted impressive TV ratings. Although the six NHL teams were enjoying great attendance and selling out most games, the owners' coffers could only grow through ticket-price hikes. Hockey had great TV coverage with *Hockey Night in Canada*, which was a part of the Canadian Saturday-night culture, and CBS offered a playoff weekend game-of-the-week in the United States. Clearly the way to expand the financial pie was to increase the audience, both live and through television. And so the league mushroomed, doubling its teams from six to 12 and establishing a truly cross-continental look.

With the close of the 1966–67 season, the franchises that would come to be known as the "Original Six" set their sights on preparing for the NHL's first expansion draft, which was set for the first week of June in Montreal. It was a fitting site, as Montreal Canadiens GM Sam Pollock was the man the league commissioned to formulate the draft procedures. To stock the six new franchises in Los Angeles, Minneapolis, Oakland, Philadelphia, Pittsburgh, and St. Louis, the Originals were allowed to protect 11 skaters and one goalie. The expansion teams, in an order determined by lot, could then claim any unprotected player for their roster. Once a player was chosen from an Original, that team could then add a previously unprotected player to its list of untouchables.

Protecting the top 11 skaters from six teams basically meant that the first player drafted by an expansion team was the 67th man on the NHL depth chart, and the players the Originals left unprotected were the ones they felt were has-beens or never-weres. The only real concession was that the expansionists would play in the new West Division and the Originals would compete in the East Division. Teams would play most games within their division.

"That first expansion was a big joke," said Glenn Hall. "They [the Originals] gave up a bunch of kids who didn't know if they could play and a bunch of guys who were thirty-five or forty years old . . . they had no intention of trying to help anybody."

Actually two drafts took place within that original draft. The first selection was devoted to goalkeepers, the second to skaters. In the goalie draft, Los Angeles won the right to pick first, Philadelphia second, St. Louis third, Minnesota fourth, Pittsburgh fifth, and Oakland last. Interestingly that order almost exactly mirrored the teams' final standings that first year in the West Division.

It was no surprise when Chicago Black Hawks GM Tommy Ivan left Glenn's name off the protected list on June 6. Everyone in the Hawk organization assumed Glenn was going to retire. Unbeknown to the Chicago GM, Glenn had decided "to play for whichever expansion team drafted me, providing the price was right. I'd just say I'm another moonlighting farmer. This farmer will be able to afford a few luxuries that other farmers may not have." Some of the new teams contacted Hall before the draft to see if he was going to retire, and if not, what his asking price was going to be. Glenn was candid about his financial expectations with all who inquired.

Canadian Jack Kent Cooke was the owner of the L.A. Kings. A longtime admirer of Terry Sawchuk, Cooke was convinced Sawchuk's name recognition and his still-fresh Stanley Cup victory would help sell hockey in Southern California. Cooke, ignoring Terry's history of injuries, didn't anticipate that Sawchuk's playoff run would be his last best effort. With the first choice overall, Cooke chose The Uke. Next up was Philadelphia, a team that had contacted Glenn. Flyer management, in the person of Glenn's former coach in Edmonton, Bud Poile, was put off by Glenn's price tag.

"Bud called me and wanted to know my asking price," Glenn recalled. "When I asked for 50 grand, he said, 'Hey, Glenn, I don't make that much.' So I said, 'But, Bud, you're not a goalie.'" So Poile opted to go young by drafting Bernie Parent, who had 60 games of NHL experience with Boston.

St. Louis, a club that had not contacted Glenn, was up next. GM Lynn Patrick did not hesitate. "From Chicago, St. Louis selects Glenn Hall."

In 1955, Patrick narrowly missed trading for Hall from Detroit, getting Sawchuk instead. Twelve years later, Patrick was determined to build his new team around the soon-to-be 36-year-old goalie. "I'll tell you how much I want him," Lynn told a newspaper reporter who asked him if he was going to have any trouble with Glenn's supposed retirement plans, "I'll go out and help him paint that fucking barn of his!" Patrick didn't need to buy any turpentine.

"I figured my record last year warranted a raise," said Hall. "And I got no argument from St. Louis management. But I would only sign a one-year contract."

The contract negotiation didn't last long. When Patrick asked Hall what he was looking for, Hall didn't blink. "Fifty thousand."

Patrick's eyes widened. "Holy mackerel!"

"Well, what were you going to offer?" asked The Ghoulie.

"Forty-five thousand," came the reply.

"Holy mackerel!" said Hall. "Let's split the difference."

They did, and with that Glenn Hall became the highest-paid goalie in NHL history at $47,500. That salary also made him the third-highest-paid player in the league behind Bobby Hull and Gordie Howe. "I just couldn't resist that kind of money," he said. "If I wasn't playing hockey, I'd be lucky to make $100 driving a truck." Patrick also gave him permission to report late to camp.

As unfair as the initial draft was, Scotty Bowman, who was Patrick's assistant GM and assistant coach at the time, pointed out where the West was stronger: "The West actually had better goalkeeping than the East, and that would be very significant in keeping expansion hockey competitive."

Patrick and Bowman went about building a team that wasn't going to be pushed around and could play well in its own end. In that initial expansion draft, they chose sixth in the player-selection process and made Montrealer Jim Roberts their first pick. They also added shot-blocking specialist Al Arbour and tough Noel Picard to bolster the back line, and Gerry Melnyk, Don McKenney, Ron Stewart, Ron Schock, Terry Crisp, and Wayne Rivers up front. They traded for Ranger defenseman Bob Plager, right wing Tim Ecclestone, and forward Larry Keenan, and purchased the rights to 32-year-old journeyman Bill McCreary. To partner with Hall, they drafted Red Wing prospect Don Caley, but also invited Canadian National Team goalie Seth Martin to camp.

Looking back on the team-building process, Bowman understood what having Hall meant. "He was our only big-name player, and he gave our franchise instant credibility."

GLENN'S MOVE TO ST. LOUIS was another challenge for his family. "I was disappointed," recalled son Pat. "I was 11 years old, and Mom woke me up and said, 'St. Louis drafted Dad.' Well, here was another move to a strange place."

"It was tough to leave Chicago after 10 years," said Pauline. "I was baking bread when I heard the news on the radio, and I wrote it down in my cookbook. But, of course, [the move] turned out wonderfully. St. Louis was the first place we were that really treated the players with respect." By the time Glenn arrived in St. Louis, training camp was nearly over. He and Pauline set up house in the far reaches of the St. Louis suburbs, and the distance from the urban life that he was never completely comfortable with in Detroit and Chicago was only the first of many pleasant changes. Along with his new teammates, Hall learned firsthand he was working for the most unique owners in all of sport in Sidney Salomon Jr. and son Sid III. "The Salomons were the first of a breed that didn't treat you like cattle," he noted.

The father-and-son duo operated under the philosophy: "Treat your employees with respect, keep them happy, and give the public full value for its money." The first public evidence of this was the St. Louis Arena itself. They poured in $2 million worth of improvements, expanded the seating capacity from 12,000 to 14,500, kept the interior spotless and freshly painted, gave the exterior a dramatic face-lift, and established a Wives Room where the players' families could retreat to privacy during the games. They created the Arena Club, a posh restaurant underneath the stands that was within 100 feet of the home locker room, a precursor to today's luxury suites. After finishing their pre-game supper, fans could stand along the hallway and feel the breeze created by the players as they walked out of the locker room onto the ice.

Their unique approach was more than cosmetic. The Salomons developed relationships with their players. "They treated us like human beings," remembered Billy McCreary. "And they embarassed the old guard of owners out of the simple dignity they showed us."

McCreary remembered: "We'd been losing. We were working hard, but we were losing. There was this sauna room in the Arena and Mr. Salomon was in there with a group of us. Here we were, failing really, still losing more than we were winning and he looks at us and he says, 'I'd just like to be one of you.' This great man, with all his money, all the things he'd done in his life [Solomon was an insurance tycoon and major player in the Democratic Party], and he just wanted to be one of us, one of the guys. An athlete. Then he says, 'But I'm not. So play your best every game and good things will happen.' That's quite a message really, and it wasn't lost on us."

The season started with promise. An October 11 opening-night crowd of over 11,000 saw the St. Louis Blues tie the Minnesota North Stars 2–2. Having arrived in town just 10 days previous, Hall watched from the bench as Seth Martin played. Glenn was in goal for another historic occasion, the

Blues' first win over an Original Six team, a 5–1 pasting of Boston on November 1. The disparity between the Original Six and their expansion stepbrothers was dramatic, so much so that any time an expansion team won, it was considered a major upset. With a solid defensive work ethic and Hall (rested thanks to Martin's strong relief work) playing very well, the Blues weren't getting scored on much. But neither were they scoring very often themselves.

Quickly Glenn found that expansion brought another unexpected challenge, which was more exasperating than the might of the Original Six. Taking a thinking man's approach to goaltending, Hall knew his opponents and he understood how to play to their weaknesses. "When I was on my game, I always was two or three moves ahead of the forward," recalled Glenn. He had learned to "reel in" an opponent by showing him the part of the net he wanted the attacker to see. As soon as the player put his head down to shoot, Hall moved to protect that corner. But with expansion and an influx of more marginal players who didn't look for corners, much less picked them, Hall couldn't use this tactic. He'd give a player that corner, and the player would miss—into the area Hall had vacated. Said Glenn: "The guy would raise his stick and think he was a hockey player. We [goalies] all had trouble with that at first . . . Most goals used to come on good shots. Now they come on rebounds and deflections. They jam up the front of the net and they whack away at you."

Glenn continued to pick his spots in practice, always doing just enough to keep sharp. Teammate Gerry Melnyk recalled: "After practice, you know, sometimes we'd have breakaway contests. The winner would get a beer or a milk shake or whatever. Well, Glenn was as competitive as anyone alive, and I think that's probably one of the traits that made him so great. Anyway, once you put something on the line like that, why Glenn's face would get serious and it looked like he was playing in Game 7 of the Cup finals. Glenn never liked to lose at anything whether it was Ping-Pong, pool, or breakaways."

Just three weeks after their big win over Boston and their hope-filled start, the Blues and their toothless offense were in the West Division basement at 4–10–2 and in the midst of a losing streak.

The home crowds were dwindling into the 5,000 to 6,000 range. Hall had seen it all before. Exactly ten years earlier—Hall's first with Chicago—he experienced a losing start to the season on a team that was effectively being built from scratch around him. On most nights, the Chicago Stadium had had twice as many empty seats as fans. Like Chicago youth in the '50s, kids in St. Louis weren't exactly playing hockey in the streets. Above and beyond competing, the Blues needed to sell hockey in the South.

Glenn's son, Pat, recalled the slow start: "I was ready to give up in

November. The team was floundering. But Claire [Mrs. Al] Arbour told me not to give up hope, that you had to believe."

The Salomons were alarmed at the team's struggles, and they huddled with GM Patrick. Together, they decided to make changes and quickly. On November 22, Patrick gave up his coaching duties to concentrate full-time as the GM. He turned the reins over to Scotty Bowman. It was a gutsy move, as Bowman at 34 years of age was younger than many of his best players and he had no NHL coaching or playing experience. On November 26, in one of Bowman's first games behind the bench, the Blues lost a 1–0 decision to the New York Rangers that typified their early-season frustration. Hall was brilliant, the Blues played tough, but they just couldn't score. That night, Patrick, Bowman, and Ranger coach and GM Emile Francis met and talked trade.

Patrick gambled again, sending the Blues' leading scorer, Ron Stewart, to the Rangers. That Stewart made his reputation before expansion as a defensive forward but was the Blues' leading scorer spoke volumes. Francis wanted Stewart specifically to "shadow" Bobby Hull. The Rangers had always had trouble containing Hull, and Francis felt the Hawks were their biggest obstacle to a divisional title. In exchange, Francis gave the Blues young defenseman Barclay Plager (whose brother Bob he'd traded to the Blues the previous summer) and the man the Blues were after primarily, Gordon "Red" Berenson.

Berenson was a rare NHLer on two counts. First, he'd made his way to the big time through the collegiate ranks, starring at the University of Michigan. Second, he was one of the few pros who wore a helmet. Bowman knew Berenson from his days in Montreal, the team for whom Red made his NHL debut. He'd been on the Hab Stanley Cup–winning team in 1965, but in 30 games for the Rangers in 1966–67, he'd not scored a single goal. In the first 19 games of the 1967–68 season, he'd notched only two. His stats and scholarly demeanor had soured the traditional Francis, and Emile had been limiting Berenson's minutes.

Berenson, who would go on to earn NHL Coach of the Year honors in 1981 for the Blues and then helm Michigan to two NCAA titles, noted, "I was excited about the trade. I was looking forward to the opportunity to play regularly." He made the most of his chance and earned the nickname "The Red Baron" by becoming the first true superstar of expansion, going on to light the lamp 22 precious times for the Blues that year.

Plager, who would also eventually coach the Blues before succumbing to cancer at an unacceptably young age, was excited about the trade as well. He had another priority, however, after learning where he was going. "The first thing I wanted to see was if Glenn Hall really got sick before the games," explained Plager. "You know, you hear the stories . . . but I was so surprised that he did."

Berenson became great friends with Hall, and he quickly developed an appreciation for what The Ghoulie's stomach-churning pre-game preparation meant: "He was such a competitor. Just think of the agony he put himself through to perform each game, each season. Before every game and between most periods to get sick like that. That was proof of the pride he took in his game. It was how he showed his competitive instinct. He was totally dedicated to playing the game as well as he possibly could. It was his life."

Bowman pitched in to the mid-season makeover the next week by following up on a tip from a former Montreal compatriot. It seemed that retired speedster Dickie Moore was getting the itch to play again. Out of the NHL since 1965, he signed with the Blues on December 3 and a week later scored the game winner in a 2–1 win over Toronto. That win was an important confidence builder for the team and their revamped lineup, which was further bolstered by adding defenseman Jean-Guy Talbot off waivers from Detroit, a former teammate of Moore's on several Montreal Cup-winning teams.

Bowman was faced with one more major situation soon after signing Moore. "I had been the coach for five games, only one of which we had won," he recalled. "I gave the guys the day off in Oakland, rented cars for them, told them to forget about hockey." The next day, just before dinner, Glenn showed up at Scotty's hotel room. "He told me, 'Scotty, I'm sorry. I've lost my touch. I just haven't got it anymore. I'm packing up.' I died a thousand deaths in the next minute. Here was our major asset, hockey's greatest goalie, playing well at 36, and he was quitting."

"I felt my level of play had fallen off," Glenn explained. "I remember hearing that Turk Broda would tell his teammates to watch him to make sure his knees were bent. If he was standing straight up, he wasn't sharp. That's what I was feeling. I was standing up too much. I was 'hitching' in my movements. I wasn't smooth. I had new defensemen who didn't know what to expect from me, and I didn't know what to expect from them. I needed to read my defensemen and I wasn't doing that."

Bowman was floored, but he remembered a story Lynn Patrick had shared about when Terry Sawchuk walked off the Boston Bruins team in mid-season. Patrick had said, "When your goalie is fair, [tell him] he's good. When your goalie is good, [tell him] he's great. Never knock your goalie. If he wants to quit, stall for time. Do anything, but don't let him go home." Bowman convinced Glenn to finish the road trip. The next day he shut out Oakland, and two days later he was superb in a 2–1 win over Toronto. But that still wasn't enough. "The next day," Bowman recounted, "he came to me and said, 'Scotty, I was fighting the puck in both games. It's no use. I've lost my touch.'"

When a goalie begins "fighting the puck," he's suffering from reduced confidence and compromised timing. The game is no longer fluid to him, and because his confidence is not where it should be, he makes subtle, ultimately self-destructive adjustments to his game. He plays deeper in his crease than usual, feeling his reflexes have slowed down and reasoning that the deeper he is, the more time he'll have to react to the puck. In reality, he's giving the shooter a bigger target. He'll guess more and go down earlier than usual, and he won't fight as hard to see the puck; instead he'll simply try to take up as much room as he can in the hope that the puck will hit him. In doing so, he only becomes more predictable to the shooter. Savoring the challenge of facing the rush is replaced with the fear of failure. The only way out is an infusion of confidence, but confidence can only be gained through strong play, and digging out of the syndrome can seem hopeless.

Hall confided further that he feared his eyesight was failing. Bowman sent him to the team optometrist. The doctor was younger than Glenn, and when Glenn was given a clean bill of health, he showed little confidence in the diagnosis. "He probably hasn't seen that many eyes," Hall said, fretting still.

This time Scotty sent Glenn to the Blues' team physician, Dr. J.G. Probstein. Glenn confessed that the pressure of the game was getting to him.

"No job's perfect," said Probstein. "Suppose you go back to the farm. You'd still worry there. You'd worry the barn would burn down. You'd worry that the tractor would run over one of your kids."

"You make farming sound worse than hockey," said Hall.

"I'm just saying that you're a born worrier. You'd worry whether you were in a barn or at the rink. But in a rink, you can worry for a lot more money."

Pat Hall recalled Glenn's mood at home: "Game day was always charged with tension. Mom had to keep us kids down. In Chicago, that was easier because they played on school days and Sundays, but in St. Louis there were a lot of Saturday games and we were pumped up . . . running through the house . . . Dad reflected internally for hours," said Pat. "He only talked about hockey with me if I asked him specific questions. When he was around the family, I think he felt like he was escaping the fish bowl of pressure."

"It wasn't always easy, especially as I got older. I became more independent and sometimes felt like I didn't need to deal with it all," said Pauline. "I tried to make it as easy as possible for him at home . . . Glenn's a very high-strung, very opinionated, nervous individual. It's a good thing he wasn't a brain surgeon."

No one knew the importance of confidence better than The Ghoulie. "That's half the battle with goalkeepers," he would say. "When you're having trouble and figure you can't stop a football, you've had it. When I'm moving right, I'm stopping the puck. When you figure you can stop it, you go out there and just eat the puck."

Placated by Probstein, Hall felt his confidence return, and by January the feel of the season began to change. On January 3, he recorded the 70th shutout of his career, over Oakland, lowering his goals-against average to 2.30. "[That's] not bad for an old man, one shutout for every year of my life," he told the press afterward. That mark was even better than his career mark and black-and-white proof that his fear he was "losing it" just a few weeks earlier was exactly as Dr. Probstein had diagnosed.

The shutout put Glenn in a reflective mood: "I've been happy with St. Louis. When you move from one place where hockey's been around for a while to a town where it's new, you could think of it as a demotion, as if you're going downhill. It hasn't been that way at all, however. Everything about our operation here has been big league. It's a fine town and a good hockey town . . . I can tell you I had it a lot tougher many times in Chicago . . . I can honestly say that I think this Blues club is a harder working bunch [than his Chicago teams] . . . Now this Blues club is really defensive minded. They work and work, and nobody scores many goals on us . . . Maybe I've slowed down a little, but I still know how to play."

With the Blues' lineup beginning to jell, players on the team started to feel some confidence. With the baseball season long ended and football over as well, the Arena crowds swelled and the games took on the feel of an "event." St. Louisans who were used to the slower pace of those two sports began to catch puck fever, and on one pivotal night the Blues finally and forever captured the town's imagination. On January 27, a season-high crowd of some 14,000 was on hand for a Saturday-night contest against the Rangers. The New Yorkers built a 3–0 lead before the game's halfway mark, but Larry Keenan's second-period goal got the big crowd into the game. Before the end of that period, Keenan had scored again.

As the Blues took to the ice in the third period trailing by only a goal, organist Norm Kramer struck up the opening chords to "St. Louis Blues." The crowd responded as if on cue with a standing ovation, clapping along on beat to the song. The standing lasted until the drop of the puck, but even as the throng settled into their seats, the din continued. The Blues tied the game on the second shift of the period, eliciting another frenzy. McCreary then beat goalie Eddie Giacomin with 12 minutes to play for a lead. The clock ticked down in front of 28,000 sweaty palms and 14,000 pounding hearts. With four minutes to go, the Rangers tried to spring star forward Rod Gilbert on a breakaway, but the puck hopped over his stick. He raced into the Blues' zone after it, but Hall charged 25 feet out of his goal to win the race and smother the puck. The Rangers pulled Giacomin in the last minute, and the fans were on their feet again cheering. As time wore down, Gilbert directed a low shot toward the net from point-blank, but the puck met with the trade-mark butterfly and ended up in the corner. At the buzzer, the Blues raced off their bench to congratulate Hall on the win and, as they made their way the length of the ice to the locker room at the far end of the Arena, the standing ovation continued as Kramer pounded out "St. Louis Blues." From that night on, the Blues' fans greeted their team with a standing ovation every time they hit the ice.

That victory cemented the team's loyal fan base. Scotty Bowman remem-bered: "The Rangers were a strong club at the time. They were plowing through the expansion clubs with little trouble. Beating them meant some-thing to the people of St. Louis. Not only were the Rangers established, they were *New York*." Three weeks later, proving that their heroics weren't a fluke, the Blues spotted Montreal a 3–0 lead before forging a tie.

Organist Kramer began another St. Louis tradition around this time as well. Frank St. Marseille was a talented forward whom Bowman had brought to the team to add some offensive punch. He became a popular Blue and was later named the team's rookie of the year. One night, Kramer played "When the Saints Go Marching In" after a St. Marseille goal, and the crowd sponta-neously started singing along. Although he played the song at first only when the rookie scored, Kramer soon banged it out after every Blues score. The Blues' fans customized the tune, changing *saints* to *Blues* and each time the team dented the opposing cage, a wild serenade followed. Just as the team charged toward a playoff berth, the fans were earning a league-wide reputa-tion for their enthusiasm and loyalty—just as the Chicago fans had done while Glenn led that franchise's resurgence.

"You can't believe how that crowd could pick up a team," said Al Arbour. "When the fans started clapping and carrying on, you could see everyone on the team come to life."

On March 2, a new record crowd of over 15,000 saw the Blues author an-other come-from-behind tie with Chicago. The point gave the Blues a 4–4–2 record against the East Division. Hall robbed his former teammate Eric Nesterenko twice in the second period from point-blank range with sliding-glove saves. "Hall was just too much," said Stan Mikita afterward, shaking his head. Glenn also stopped Bobby Hull in Period 3. What did he think of playing against the Golden Jet after years of seeing him in practice?

"I started to think about us," Glenn said. "I figured that he had scored about 190,000 goals against me since we joined the Black Hawks together in 1957–58. That means he'd taken 200,000 shots. Now I knew that he wouldn't be taking 200,000 shots against me anymore."

The drama of those games was a metaphor for the season itself. The Blues were making up their early-season deficit in the standings, and were fighting desperately for a playoff berth. Bowman had brilliantly balanced the rookies with the veterans, bringing them together by getting them to understand that what they had in common was something to prove. They now played in front of large crowds with unbridled enthusiasm, and went into the last regular-season weekend in fifth place, a point behind fourth-place Pittsburgh, three points behind third-place Minnesota. The Penguins had one game left in their season, the Blues a home-and-home series with the North Stars.

Trailing through most of the Saturday-night game at the Arena, Blues GM Patrick sent a note to the organ loft. Kramer opened it and read, "Play 'When the Saints Go Marching In.' It seems to pick the boys up."

Kramer played, the fans sang, the Blues marched. Down by a goal with less than three minutes to play, the Blues tied the game then got a huge assist from North Star coach Wren Blair. Off the very next face-off, the Stars were penalized. Irate, Blair protested to referee Art Skov. During his tirade, Blair was wiping his brow with a towel that ended up on the ice (Blair says it slipped out of his hands; Skov saw it thrown in protest). Skov whistled two more minutes against the Stars, and Larry Keenan scored, clinching a spot in the playoffs. The next night in Minneapolis, the Blues went into the third period down 3–2 and, without organ accompaniment, scored three unanswered. Pittsburgh lost its game to finish out of the money, and the Blues leapfrogged the North Stars into third place. At 36 years of age, Glenn had played every game down the stretch drive. "Glenn was the backbone," stated McCreary. "We wouldn't have had any of our success without him."

"It's hard to explain just how much Glenn meant that season," remembered Bowman. "He was a totally unselfish individual. He never once even hinted that a goal might have been someone else's fault. I mean, he held us in through that whole run to the playoffs. Glenn was so respected that he had every player on the ice in front of him fighting for him. We got to expect his excellence. He rose to the occasion every time we needed him. The bottom line was that we went into each game knowing no team could match our goaltending."

At season's end, Glenn was honored as the Blues' most valuable player by their fan club, appropriately named the Goaltender's Club. "Of course, he was our MVP," said Bowman. "He still never got enough credit. Remember, only a few points separated first from fifth place that year. We won because nobody could match our goaltending. Glenn was the best in the game."

Still, that recognition was not enough to stem the seemingly annual retirement talk. Hall's tone was different this year though. In the recent past, he had seemed drained by season's end, tired of the pressures of the game he loved so much. But now it seemed as if the St. Louis experience had recharged the batteries. With St. Louis, Glenn had found an organization whose philosophy meshed with his own. "I've always felt that if you were prepared and made playing well the goal, the winning would take care of itself. That's what was stressed in St. Louis. Just play well. It was different in Chicago, and it made it a lot tougher mentally."

More relaxed in St. Louis, he was more accessible after games, gladly giving up entertaining quotes to the press and even cracking wise on occasion, something he hadn't done since the early '60s. He still left the room quickly, usually one of the first out, but in later years he confided that he wanted to get away from the rink without rehashing the game with others. He wanted to go over the game in his own mind without his perceptions of his play being clouded by the opinions of others.

After the last game, a reporter asked about his plans for next year, and he answered candidly. "I'll make my decision after considering two main items: how I feel physically and how much financial security I have. Money will not be a factor in St. Louis. They have treated me wonderfully. I would not complain if I was offered the same contract I got this first season with the Blues." Glenn continued. "I think we made a good showing for the first year and I'm sure a lot of people were surprised at how well the West Division did."

Still, no West Division team finished above .500. At 36, Hall ended the year having played 49 games and recording five shutouts with a 2.48 goals-against average. He tied for the best goals-against mark of any goalie in the West with 23-year-old Flyer Bernie Parent who'd played in 11 fewer games for first-place Philadelphia. In contrast, Terry Sawchuk started 33 games and had a 3.07 mark for the second-place L.A. Kings, and Denis DeJordy had a 2.71 average with the Hawks who'd finished six games above .500.

The goalie, who halfway through the season was convinced he was losing it, had finished the season at the top of his game, enjoying hockey once again. And Glenn was poised to make the Blues' inaugural "second season" a memorable one.

14

The Road to the Smythe

NO AMOUNT OF RESEARCH can explain why the National Hockey League had a playoff system that saw the team finishing second in the regular-season standings face a team that was statistically worse than the opponent of the team that finished first. But that's the way it had been, and that's the way it was in this first year of expansion. The St. Louis Blues' third-place finish seeded them against the first-place Philadelphia Flyers in the opening round of the Stanley Cup playoffs. For the first time in history, it would take three playoff rounds to earn the Cup, with each division determining its playoff champion in the first two rounds, and the two winners playing off against each other in the grand finale.

Goalie Bernie Parent and his Flyers had topped the West Division with a 31–32–11 record, a scant three points ahead of St. Louis. Growing up in Montreal, Parent had idolized the now-retired Jacques Plante and played with a style extremely reminiscent of the famed Canadien goalie nicknamed "The Snake." Even Parent's mask was a carbon copy of the "pretzel" mask Plante wore in his last two years in Montreal and his two subsequent years with the New York Rangers. The comparisons extended further. Plante was always the first to tell people exactly how good he thought he was, and Parent, despite his youth, was gaining a similar reputation for self-promotion. Bernie shared the Flyer goal with another young goalie who was his polar opposite in style and temperament. Doug Favell had actually bested Parent statistically that year, and he had a knack for taking the wind out of Parent's sails. Any time Parent threw a tantrum in practice or acted the diva, Favell shook his head and approached his flustered partner addressing him as "Barnyard" Parent. This elicited a snicker and diffused the situation.

The Flyers came into the quarterfinals as clear favorites since they'd amassed a 7–1–2 record against the Blues during the regular season. The lone Blues' win was a 3–0 Hall whitewash. Flyers GM Bud Poile predicted a sweep. Bernie refused to understand why Hall had gained so many All-Star selections ahead of Plante, and he let that emotion slip into his pre-playoff public comments.

"We shouldn't have that much problem with them [the Blues]," Parent told *The Hockey News*. "We're better than them in goal. I always thought Hall was overrated. If he's so good, how come he only won one Cup in 12 years?"

For his part, Glenn deflected the comments, telling newsmen, "I doubt that any goalkeeper would disparage another especially when my record is better than his. I'm sure he'd been asked a leading question, such as 'Do you think you fellows can beat Glenn Hall?' and he answered, quite properly, 'How many Stanley Cups has he won?'"

But Parent had been quoted accurately, and Glenn's teammates, who to this day are his best press agents, responded. When the series opened at the Spectrum in Philadelphia, Glenn defeated his young counterpart by pitching a 1–0 shutout. He only faced 14 shots in the game, as the St. Louis squad played furiously in front of him. All agreed it was the best rebuttal to Parent. But Bud Poile stuck by his prediction: "I still think we'll win it in four straight. But I'm not saying which four. I just think that when we win one, we'll win the rest."

The Blues would build and lose a 3–1 edge in the series, losing Game 5 in a fight-filled contest in Philly and Game 6 at the Arena, a crushing 2–1 double overtime affair, the winning goal accidentally tipped home by a Blues defenseman. To make the agony worse, the Flyers had tied it with only 15 seconds left in regulation and the goalie pulled. That was the second double overtime game of the series, the Blues having won the first in Game 3, 3–2.

The hectic end of the regular season, marked by the Blues' desperate rush just to make the playoffs, followed immediately by six games of up-and-down, emotional, and very physical playoff hockey ($3,800 in fines were meted out by the NHL for the brawling that had occurred in the series), would have presented a great physical challenge for a young team. So the strain on the older Blues should have been showing, and the veteran team actually arrived in Philadelphia for Game 7 discernibly older than when it left the Arena after Game 6. This was because it had added yet another old-timer from the Montreal Canadiens dynasty to its roster.

Doug Harvey was 43 years old. He'd made his NHL debut 20 years earlier for Montreal, and in a distinguished career with Les Habitants, he played on five Cup winners and won the Norris Trophy as the league's top defenseman six times. He added a seventh after he was traded to the New York Rangers. History tells us that Bobby Orr changed the game forever with his daring offensive forays, but before Orr there was Harvey. Masterful at controlling the tempo of a game once the puck was on his stick, he would speed up the attack if he saw his opponents were flatfooted. If a team was lined up in a strong defensive position, he'd deliberately slow down, shifting his weight backward while surveying the patterns in front of him. If he didn't like his passing options, he would circle back again until he did, never bothering to look down at the puck, never panicking, never rattled. If the smallest opening presented itself, he'd dart a pass through the seam, sending the Canadiens onto the attack. In the summer of '61, unhappy with Harvey's union-endorsing activities, the Habs shipped him to New York. He retired from the NHL in 1964 but kicked around the minors as a player-coach, hanging on to a career that was fading into a haze of alcohol. In 1967, he signed on with the Blues as a head coach and player at their farm club in Kansas City, and once that team was eliminated from their playoffs, he could legally be added to the parent roster.

If Harvey needed any incentive in his return to the NHL, he got it from his son. "He called me the day before the game," said Harvey, "and he told me to make sure I sat near the end of the bench so he could see me on TV." Harvey deplaned in Philadelphia, an aged gunslinger-for-hire coming to help rescue the besieged Blues.

Harvey's presence, like his former teammate Dickie Moore's, had an impact on and off the ice. When Moore had come onboard in December, he'd brought the Montreal championship tradition to the Blues' locker room. When a St. Louis teammate casually tossed his game sweater on the floor, Moore pinned that player against the wall and informed him that in the Canadiens' locker room, no sweater ever touched the ground. If you had pride in your team, you had pride in the sweater. It was your flag. The tradition was immediately adopted by the Blues. Harvey made his first mark before the team got to the rink for the seventh and deciding game. Scotty Bowman recalled: "At the team meeting in the morning, Harvey wrote something in Italian on a blackboard. When I entered the room, he asked me, 'Is that what you want tonight, Scotty?' He translated it, 'It's easy if you work.' And that's what we did."

So the league's best-ever defenseman started the crucial Game 7 of the quarterfinals in front of the best-ever goalkeeper. The unretired ex-Hab Moore assisted on the game's first goal, the unretired ex-Hab Harvey assisted on the game's second goal, and the unretired ex-Hawk Hall stopped 26 shots. That trio sparked the Blues' 3–1 win, vanquishing the Flyers. Glenn's best work came during two penalty kills in the second period, and in the third, with the game still at 2–1, he robbed Bill Sutherland from point-blank.

Glenn's work in the series changed one man's opinion rather dramatically. "This was my first playoff series," Bernie Parent said afterward in the losers' locker room. "I think I have a few more in front of me. I've heard this might be the last one for Glenn because he's thinking of retiring. If that's the truth, I hope the Blues go all the way because Hall was great in this series. It would be a real tribute to him if St. Louis went all the way to the Stanley Cup final."

Bud Poile sought Glenn out in the Blues' room, but he had already departed. "Where is that son of a gun?" asked Bud. "He's the best. You tell him that. He'll always be the best in my books."

Meanwhile, on the Left Coast, the other quarterfinal had also reached a Game 7. Just as the Blues had relied on Hall, the Los Angeles Kings had counted on Terry Sawchuk to get them into the playoffs. Sawchuk played 12 of the team's last 14 games prior to the playoffs, although his goaltending partner, Wayne Rutledge, had made more appearances over the regular season. And just as the Flyers held a lopsided regular-season edge over the Blues, L.A.'s opponent, the Minnesota North Stars, had gone 6–2–2 against the Kings. Like Hall, Sawchuk recorded a relatively easy shutout early in the series, but after a poor performance in Game 3, Sawchuk gave way to Rutledge. Rutledge played well through Game 6, and along with his teammates was stunned when Sawchuk was assigned the start in the deciding game. Terry could not reproduce the magic of the previous year, and suffered a humiliating 9–4 thrashing. That set up a Blues–North Stars semifinal, continuing a rivalry that had started to heat up during the regular season and culminated in the dramatic weekend sweep that got the Blues into the playoffs.

April in St. Louis is a warm, pleasant time. Oppressively hot and humid in the summer months, the city on the Mississippi in springtime is often shirt-sleeves and breezes and always baseball crazy. Just how hockey in the spring would compete against a Cardinal team that was a World Series contender was anyone's guess, but you had to figure the skaters would play second fiddle.

They did not.

A standing-room-only crowd greeted the Blues with the traditional standing ovation in Game 1, and the home heroes won 5–3. A scheduling fiasco at the North Star rink, the Met Center, forced the teams to play Game 2 in Minnesota, and then Games 3, 4, and 5 in St. Louis. The Stars won the second game 3–2 in overtime. More hurtful to the Blues than the loss itself was the injury to their top defenseman, Al Arbour, that saw him sit out the next four games of the series. The St. Louis team looked its age in Game 3 back home, losing by a 5–1 count. The Stars nearly took complete command of the series in Game 4, finding themselves ahead 3–0 with ten minutes left in the game. The veteran Blues refused to concede. Roberts scored to make it 3–1, and, 63 seconds later, Moore beat Star goalie Cesare Maniago. Time ticked down, and Hall went to the bench for an extra attacker. Twenty seconds to go . . . 19, 18 . . . the puck slipped to Barclay Plager at the left point. Fourteen, 13, 12 . . . Maniago got a pad on Plager's shot, but the rebound went right to Roberts who tied the game. Gary Sabourin won it for the Blues early in OT. The Blues authored a 3–2 OT win in Game 5. Game 6 in Minnesota was all Minnesota again as the Stars forced a Game 7 with another 5–1 win. Bowman, convinced the Blues had run out of comeback magic, pulled Glenn late in the game when the score was 3–0 to rest him for Game 7.

But Game 6 had shaken Hall's confidence. He sought out Bowman again and asked him what his plans were for Game 7. Bowman was shocked at the question. Glenn had started every meaningful game for the previous two months, and it had never occurred to anyone that he wouldn't get the call for Game 7. But Hall confided to Bowman that he was very concerned he was going to have a bad game. "I'm just not moving right," he told his coach. "Don't hesitate to take me out if you see I'm not going well."

The Blues held a light skate the day before the big game, and Bowman huddled with Doug Harvey, sharing the gist of Glenn's conversation with him. He had Harvey and some teammates shoot pucks directly at The Ghoulie's pads both then and in the pre-game skate the next day so Glenn would feel some confidence. "Keep your eye on him, Doug," said Bowman.

"I'll keep both of them on him," Harvey replied.

The seventh game of any playoff series has all the elements of great drama. Every mistake takes on Herculean proportions. Every power play is a chance for glory, every penalty is rife with the possibilities of disaster. The fans cringe each time the opponent crosses their blue line and go mad with hope when the home team is on the attack. The seventh game of this series was an epic contest, one of the great playoff matches of all time, witnessed by the participants and the record crowd of 15,556 fans at the Arena, heard by those listening to the broadcasts, remembered by the die-hard fans of both teams.

The atmosphere inside the Arena was frenetic. When the gates opened at 6:00 p.m., those who'd scored standing-room tickets raced to claim a spot in the aisles. By the time Norm Kramer thumped the deep bass introductory chords to "St. Louis Blues" at 8:00 p.m., most of the crowd had long been seated. Those notes signaled that the locker-room door had swung open and that it was time to stand and applaud. Glenn Hall started the short walk down the runway, leading his teammates—wearing the blue jerseys with the gold-and-white piping and the musical notes on their chests—to the ice. The fans were standing as one, their ovation shaking the Arena's ancient rooftop and nearly drowning out the organ. The Blues skated the length of the ice under the monstrous din, the white-wearing North Stars skating silently in the opposite direction. As was his custom, the veteran netminder circled his zone, his flat goal skates pushing out from side to side, the paddle of his stick cradled in his catch glove. His expression never betrayed the churning emotion within.

Minutes into the game, North Star Ray Cullen fired a low shot through a screen that Hall butterflied away. That save relieved Bowman. Glenn had his puck-stopping rhythm. Five and a half minutes into the game, a scrum developed between the prickly and talented J.P. Parise and Barclay Plager. Noel Picard stuck his two cents in, and all three were whistled off. Glenn was joined on the penalty kill by Doug Harvey, Al Arbour, and Jimmy Roberts, and the Blues held the fort. Minnesota kept pressing, holding a territorial edge until the Blues got a power play of their own. They only managed one shot on Maniago during the two minutes, and the first period ended scoreless, the Stars doubling the Blues' shots at 10–5. Each team killed a penalty in Period 2, which also ended without a goal, the Stars again with a shot advantage of 9–6.

With a feeble old air-conditioning system, the Arena was starting to feel like a hothouse by the second intermission. As the teams took to the ice for the third period, small puddles had formed at various spots on the ice. Fans wondered at what point the 13 previous playoff games (five of which were OT contests) and the heat of the Arena would get to the aged (seven players on the team were 35 or older) squad in blue. Billy McCreary remembered what it felt like on the bench: "We had Hall. We just knew that no matter what the circumstance, we were going to find a way to win."

The third period turned out to be the most wide open of the game, with the teams combining for 23 shots. Maniago stopped a great Berenson chance early on. Hall answered deftly with stops on Dave Balon and the West Division's leading goal scorer, Wayne Connelly. The minutes disappeared toward what seemed to be the inevitable overtime. But, with just three minutes and 11 seconds left to play in regulation, Minnesota defenseman Bob McCord sent a drive toward Hall from the point. Walt McKechnie was cruising toward the slot and extended his stick, redirecting the shot. The puck glanced off Harvey and then Barclay Plager and landed just inside the post behind Hall. As the Stars rejoiced at what would surely prove to be the series-winning goal, the Arena fell silent in shock. Glenn stood, swiped the crease clean with his stick, and never looked back into the net.

By the time the official was ready to drop the puck at center ice, the crowd had awakened with chants of "Let's Go Blues!" St. Louis responded immediately. Keenan moved the puck to Plager near the Stars' blue line. Plager hesitated just a second before passing it to Dickie Moore. Moore caught the pass and in one motion fired a shot. He didn't get all of the puck, but the change of pace fooled Maniago, and as the disc fluttered over his left shoulder into the top shelf, the disbelieving crowd exploded, drowning out Blues radio announcer Gus Kyle's call. All the KMOX audience heard was: "Here's Keenan over to Plager and—" It took several seconds for Kyle to break through the wall of sound and tell his listeners that Moore had tied the game. Neither team recorded a shot in the waning seconds, and overtime was a reality.

Only two people left the building at that point. NHL President Clarence Campbell and referee-in-chief Scotty Morrison departed to catch a flight to Detroit, where they were to attend the funeral of Jack Adams, the man who signed Glenn to his first NHL contract, who had died the day before.

Hall had made 29 saves in regulation, the 29-year-old Maniago, 22. Maniago, who'd had cameo appearances as a youngster with the Toronto Maple Leafs and Montreal Canadiens before playing a couple of years with the New York Rangers, had started 47 games during the regular season, two less than Glenn. A solid pro, he was a great example of a player given a golden opportunity because of expansion. At 6 feet, 3 inches, he was also the game's second-tallest goalie, and oddly, he used a stick with a very short paddle to ensure a good, low stance when facing an oncoming rush.

The humidity continued to build as the teams faced overtime. Minnesota attacked with a vengeance, looking as if they wanted to decide things early. Halfway through the first OT, a bouncing puck hopped over Picard's stick at center ice. Anticipating the favorable bounce, Wayne Connelly raced behind the Blues' defense and broke in alone on Hall. Glenn backed in quickly, too quickly it appeared, and Connelly shot toward the far post. Hall snaked his catch glove out far to his left and behind him to make the save, just a fraction of an inch before the puck would have crossed the line. He then turned away 13 more shots to singlehandedly send the game into the second overtime.

The Blues had looked their age in the previous 20 minutes. They'd been outshot by four but outchanced by eight. Bowman had cut down on the number of players he was using, and his veterans were hanging on by savvy alone. Still, confidence had been built on the back of the team's miraculous playoff run and many come-from-behind games. In this, the record fourth OT contest of the series, the Blues had to defeat not only their opponents but the heat in the Arena and Father Time.

If Scotty Bowman made any inspirational speech between periods, Glenn didn't hear it. "I never heard a coach between periods," he claimed. "I was visualizing. I knew their best shooters and I'm sure I was focusing on how to defend them. Pressure situations bring out the best in you. Boy, it gives you the chance ... to respond. And fatigue? You only feel tired when you lose. You just talked yourself out of feeling fatigued. We all knew what we had to do. We were prepared."

Somehow, when they took to the ice again, they looked like a team that was ready to determine its own destiny. "Red" Berenson and Terry Crisp had shots on Maniago in the first minute. With just two minutes gone, the Blues threw two more shots his way. The Stars countered with a low shot from the point. Glenn steered it to the corner, making his 44th save of the game.

McCreary got control of the puck and moved it up the ice to Gerry Melnyk. Linemate Ron Schock, who hadn't scored a single goal in the playoffs, saw a seam at center ice. He sprinted toward the Stars' line between two defenders, and Melnyk hit him with a perfect pass in stride. Schock made a beeline toward Maniago. Big Cesare took several strides out to cut the angle, but it appeared as if the speed of Schock's attack caught him by surprise. The nearest Stars defender raced after Schock, but he was too far behind to catch him. Maniago crunched his lanky frame into a small ball of a crouch as Schock snapped the puck toward the lower left corner of the goal. The quickness of the release overpowered the North Star goalie, and the vulcanized rubber stretched the netting behind him, triggering the flashing red light.

The Arena erupted in joyous bedlam. The fans seated along the ice leaped to their feet and pounded on the glass as the Blues raced off their bench to celebrate in a gleeful scrum. Programs, hats, confetti, and rolls of toilet paper rained down on the ice while the building was shaken to its foundation. Strangers embraced as the celebration rolled up and down the stands. The Salomons were reduced to tears.

"I never became so emotionally involved with a team or a sport in my life," said Sid III. "I was totally worn out."

Hall was waylaid by a circle of teammates who made sure he felt their appreciation. As the team joined the formal post-series handshake line, the din subsided and then rose again in tribute to the masterful series that had just been completed. When the first Blues player completed his route through the line and turned to skate back toward the locker room, the crowd thundered again and continued long after the last skater cleared the ice.

"It was crazy that night," recalled Bob Plager. "When we finally went outside after the game, there were people in sleeping bags all over the place waiting for tickets to the finals to go on sale. It was almost as wild outside as it had been inside."

The good news, of course, was that the Blues would be the first expansion team to play for the Stanley Cup. The bad news was the Montreal Canadiens were waiting. Toe Blake's team had finished first in the East with a sparkling 42–22–10 record. Goalie Gump Worsley recorded the best goals-against average in the league at 1.98, the Habs led the NHL in goals scored, and three Canadien players had earned 60 points or more (Berenson had led the Blues with 51) while six others had notched 20 goals or more (Berenson had led the Blues with 22; St. Marseille was second with 16). The Flying Frenchmen had dispatched the Boston Bruins in four games and the Chicago Black Hawks in five (outscoring Chicago 23–9 in the process) and had been home for a week practicing while awaiting the winner of the West Division. To make matters worse, the opening game of the series was scheduled for Sunday afternoon, May 5, a scant 36 hours after Schock's game winner. The Blues would open the series without Arbour who had aggravated his leg injury, and also without Harvey who had to fly home to attend his mother's funeral.

To keep things as competitive as possible, the expansion finalist held the home-ice advantage. Still, the Canadiens entered the series as favorites. The Blues had only one tie in their regular-season games against Montreal, and the Habs had been playing dominant playoff hockey behind their team's central spiritual force, the great Jean Beliveau. Le Gros Bill had led them in scoring during the regular season and was asserting himself mightily in the playoffs, with seven goals in nine games. The first winner of the Conn Smythe playoff MVP award in 1965, Beliveau was a threat to duplicate that feat. The one break the Blues got going into the series was that early in the first game Beliveau aggravated an ankle injury and couldn't play the remaining games.

CBS CAMERAS WERE POISED to televise the action from the Arena to the entire United States. It was only the second series to be televised nationally south of the border, and privately the NHL brass was worried that the series was such a mismatch that future television rights would be jeopardized. All the events that had led to the series pointed toward a disaster.

The St. Louis faithful did not share in that prognosis. The city had gone hockey-mad, the drama of the Blues' season temporarily obscuring the popular baseball Cardinals. Fans trekked to the Arena early that bright and sunny Sunday morning for the 1:00 p.m. face-off. Streams of fans who'd parked in the Forest Park area (the oasis of parks, zoos, and museums located across from the Arena) marched across the pedestrian bridges that spanned Highway

40 toward Oakland Avenue, the street that fronted the Arena. It was widely assumed that the game was a sellout, but that rumor held down ticket sales, and the game drew only 10,000 to the old barn to watch the opener.

"We were tired going into that series, no question," recalled Billy Mc-Creary. "But we still had that sense of confidence and the best goalkeeping in the NHL. Great goaltending lets you accomplish a lot of things."

But it doesn't score goals.

As Hall settled into his crease before the drop of the puck, Worsley did the same for the Habs. It would be the second time the two met in the finals, and the Gumper presented a sharp contrast to Glenn in style and appearance. Gump was the 5-foot, 8-inch, 185-pound fireplug. His short pads, which had no outside ridges at the knees, made him look even rounder. His rotund face was topped with a spiny brush cut, and his face displayed whatever emotions he was feeling. As a rush neared him and he charged out to cut an angle, his cheeks often filled with air as a shot was about to be taken. If a puck was being carried behind his net, he turned around completely to face the puck, his back to the blue line. But he was an incredible talent. His reflexes were spectacularly fast, and his anticipation made him one of the most accomplished in the league at defending against breakaways. His agility was special, and because of it he used the splits to make skate saves regularly.

Early in the game it became apparent that the NHL brass could breathe a sigh of relief. The flow of play was back and forth, and the Blues actually broke the ice first when Barclay Plager beat Worsley with a wrist shot from the medium slot. But the Canadiens answered just seconds later when Henri Richard stormed down the wing and cracked a shot home off the outside post over Glenn's catch glove.

The Habs dominated Period 2, but again the Blues scored first as Moore lit the lamp. With less than two minutes to play in the second, Yvan Cournoyer tied the game. The third period went scoreless, and Hall and the Blues forced the Canadiens into OT. Right off the opening extra-period draw, the Blues threatened. A nifty passing play created a quick opening to Worsley's right, and the Blues beat the Gump, the puck clattering off the post. The Habs got possession of the puck and drove the other way. Jacques Lemaire, catching the Blues on a line change, ended up with the puck alone, 25 feet in front of Hall, and tore a shot into the corner of the net, ending the contest.

Game 2 of the series was vintage Hall, a performance that showed why he was called "Mr. Goalie." A record crowd of 16,117 was wedged into the Arena, and it witnessed the Blues get badly outshot in Period 1. Glenn was at his fluid, acrobatic best. Slipping from side to side, regaining his balance by bouncing off the posts, reaching up and out to snare anything off the ice, he shut the door in a scoreless first period.

In the second, he made a couple of saves that nearly defy description. On the first, Montrealer Claude Larose broke down the right wing, and although he built up an imposing head of steam, he stayed at a fairly wide angle. Hall set himself outside the top of the crease, giving him nothing to shoot at. Larose shot anyway, gunning for the top left corner of the goal. Automatically Glenn dropped into the butterfly, reacting to the high shot with his blocker. The puck stung the big leather rectangle, the speed of the shot making the rebound difficult to control. Just after the puck made contact, Hall, immediately sensing danger, moved toward the center of the net. At the same time, Richard had been watching the play develop and was in full flight, attacking the slot. The juicy rebound went right to Henri's stick. Knowing that the only place Hall would have a chance to stop the shot would be low, Richard, like all natural scorers, did not hesitate, pounding the puck high. Already starting into a desperate stacking motion, Hall never lost sight of the puck. As Glenn thrust his left leg out along the ice, Richard raised his stick in anticipation of the game's first goal. But his celebration was aborted as, unbelievably, Hall threw his right leg high into the air, intercepting the shot and leaving the Montreal bench in awe.

"We were starting to wonder if we were ever going to score off that guy," said Richard teammate Dick Duff.

Minutes later, Glenn proved his 36-year-old catch hand was just as quick as it was back on the Humboldt ponds. Cournoyer held the puck below the goal line. A screen developed in front of Hall as Cournoyer neared the front of the goal. He passed the puck to the slot, but the intended receiver missed the pass. Hall saw a stick crank up and reacted with the butterfly, but there was no shot. The puck slipped all the way through to the left face-off dot. Glenn relocated the puck and, like a cat, drove himself to his right. Hab Gilles Tremblay caught the errant pass on his tape, and fired to where Hall had moved from. With all of his momentum moving to his right, Glenn shot his left arm backward, devouring the shot and preserving the tie.

The game was still scoreless in the third, when a defensive breakdown cost the Blues. The crowd was revved up as the men in blue went on an early power play. But on the rush, a Blues defenseman coughed up a loose puck. The Canadiens moved the disc to the front of the St. Louis goal, resulting in a multi-player collision. The momentum of the pileup pushed Hall backward and prone, and Serge Savard managed to tap the loose puck under the tangle of bodies for a one-goal lead, an edge that held for the rest of the game.

Hab coach Toe Blake called the first two games the "toughest we've had in the playoffs . . . We're not going back to St. Louis. There's no way we're going back." Down 2–0 in the series, the Blues headed to Montreal, where the margins of victory stayed the same. Game 3 was yet another OT affair, an NHL record eighth OT of the playoffs for the Blues. Bobby Rousseau batted home the second rebound off a Dick Duff breakaway to end the game. The Blues were outshot 46–15 in the contest.

"A number of Hall's saves were seemingly impossible," wrote Toronto scribe Red Burnett. "Experts walked out of the Forum convinced no other netminder had ever toiled more brilliantly in a losing cause. Rousseau's goal was a heartbreaker."

The fourth game followed a similar script. The Blues held a 2–1 lead going into the third, but the Habs weren't going to be denied. J.C. Tremblay's game winner with just over eight minutes left hit both posts before crossing the line, the 3–2 win earning Montreal the Stanley Cup. Glenn's work in the third period keeping the game close drew repeated ovations from the appreciative Montreal fans. In the four games of the series, Montreal had outshot the Blues 151–91. "We basically played every game in our end," recalled "Red" Berenson. "We owed Glenn more goals."

Toe Blake, who announced his retirement from coaching immediately after that fourth game, noted the importance of Hall's play: "St. Louis got great goaltending, and because of it, were rarely behind in the score for any length of time in the games. That meant they never had to open up." In the four games, two went to OT, and all were decided by a single goal, the Habs holding the minimum edge in goals scored at 11–7.

"Close was good," Hall would say later. "Too bad it wasn't horseshoes."

At 36 years of age, Glenn had started all 18 playoff games—a new playoff record—after 49 regular-season appearances, and in that 67th game of the year was as sharp as ever. His playoff goals-against average was 2.43; his playoff save percentage .930.

When the Blues' flight returned home to Lambert Airport on the outskirts of St. Louis, 2,000 appreciative fans were there to greet the team. The Salomons showed their appreciation for the squad by sending the players and their families on an all-expenses paid vacation to Florida. "The Salomons were incredible people," said Pauline. "A trip to Florida! Can you just imagine that. The kids had a great time there. I remember that Stan Fischler wasn't happy with how the Salomons were treating the players. He wrote that they were just buying their players' affections. Well, I said, 'Good for them!'"

While the Stanley Cup settled into familiar surroundings in the Province of Quebec, the Conn Smythe Trophy to the MVP of the playoffs ended up at the league's southernmost destination, awarded to a player on the NHL's youngest franchise. Glenn Hall became the first player on an expansion team to win a league-wide trophy. His teammates revelled in the recognition as much as Glenn did.

"Without Glenn Hall, a tremendous goalie and person, we would never have even been in the finals," said Dickie Moore.

Bob Plager, the nothing-is-sacred team practical joker (who rewarded Glenn's 43-save Game 3 effort by cutting his underwear in two while The Ghoulie was in the shower), turned serious. "I was the first to shake his hand. This was a great tribute to Glenn . . ."

Scotty Bowman said, "I can't talk about the playoffs between the so-called established clubs, but I know Hall won the deciding games for us against Philadelphia and Minnesota. He's the reason we went as far as we did . . . After all, a guy really accomplishes something when he goes into a series with the Canadiens as Glenn Hall did . . . and comes out of it with the Conn Smythe Trophy. Being the outstanding player in a series where you have so many great players is really something."

And, with typical modesty, Hall exclaimed, "I consider this more a team trophy than an individual honor. I think they must have considered the Blues' overall effort when they picked me. . . . It was one of the most satisfying honors I've ever received. I'd like to think that I've never worked harder than I did this season. And I'd like to think that no hockey team ever worked harder than the Blues." The fact that Hall deliberately included his teammates in those remarks is a reflection of why he is so universally well thought of as a teammate, above and beyond his abilities. He continued: "I was very enthused when I learned I had won the Smythe Trophy, but I would have traded it any day for another Stanley Cup. We're always looking for the collective trophy more than the individual award, but it certainly was nice to be recognized."

Hall was asked what the key to his great playoff run was. "I was more relaxed this year. In Chicago, they said, 'Win.' Here, they said, 'Play well.' When you're a farmer, if you miss a strip of field, nobody gets too excited. But in hockey if the puck gets past you, people get upset . . . [As for playing next year] I'll have to talk things over with the management of the Blues. You can't play forever you know . . . Right now I'm just tired . . . Beautifully tired."

While his pre-expansion image was of a man driven to play solely for the money, his opposite number in the finals saw through the facade. "You can't play that well and be playing only for the money," said Gump Worsley. "He still has to like it."

ESSAY: HEROES

Growing up in a house that was full of discord, I found solace and retreat in warmth and heroes. With a moody and unpredictable father and a distracted and cold mother, I was most fortunate to be able to hide in the comfort of perfect grandparents and the career of Glenn Hall.

My maternal grandparents owned our home and lived in the upstairs apartment. Yia Yia Eleni was a proud Greek woman with the cold edge of her daughter. She expressed love in her cooking, and the cedar stairway that led to the second floor was always filled with the aroma of something freshly baked. Weeknights, it could be *kuloodia*, the vanilla-flavored, doughy cookies of the old country. Weekends, thick loaves of warm bread were there for the asking. A typical meal featured egg-lemon soup, lamb, and dolmades with homemade yogurt for dessert. I often ate upstairs with Yia Yia and Papou to escape the screaming that bounced off the walls of the apartment I was growing up in.

Papou was my step-grandfather, my blood grandfather having passed away five years before I was born. He was a square figure, his block-shaped head resting upon his block-shaped body. A thick shock of white hair crowned his forehead, and he had a full pouty mouth with a bottom lip that often extended farther than the top one any time he took to pondering. He'd been retired from the Greek government for many years by then, but he still took the bus to the consulate in downtown Chicago four times a week. He was a brilliant man, a lawyer in Greece, and he was appointed as an ambassadorial aide in Washington, D.C.

He'd mastered 11 languages. And he hated sports.

To Papou, sports were a waste of time, a frivolous distraction from his passion: politics. He had the *Chicago Tribune* delivered every day, and each morning before going to school I ran to the front stairs and out the front door, brought in the paper, sat on the stairs, and carefully tore away the "worthless" sports section. I then delivered to him the rest of the paper, what I thought were the worthless business, news, arts, and political sections, which he read over a steaming cup of thick Turkish coffee. God, that coffee smelled good, but alas Yia Yia forbade me to sample it. Papou let me sit next to him at the table, and I read my section of the paper as he read his. When my grandmother left the room, he'd make sure the coast was clear before letting me take a sip from the tiny cup. I loved the taste, the way the strong flavor of the muddy liquid lingered long after the swallow, the forbidden aspect of the sip, the fact that we were partners in this intrigue.

After Glenn Hall left Chicago, getting news about him and the St. Louis Blues was a challenge. That morning paper was a lifeline for me, and I soaked up every bit of information I could. I had all the NHL rosters and stats committed to memory, but I didn't know where to buy any hockey publications of the day. I confided my frustration to Papou, and surprisingly he agreed to help. After his day at the consulate, he collected the latest magazines from a downtown newsstand, where he'd explained in his heavily accented English that he would tip the vendor to save a copy of every new hockey magazine that came in.

So after school I'd hurry home, throw my books on the stairs, and run upstairs to Yia Yia and Papou's apartment. From the second-floor window, I could see down the block and watch for the bus to stop, the doors to open, and the short, white-haired gentleman wearing the vicuña-wool coat and the perfectly knotted tie to step down from the big green vehicle. He walked purposefully toward home, with a dignity that told anyone who saw him that he was important. Chances were that in his briefcase, among the *Wall Street Journal*, the *New York Times*, *Time*, and various documents from the Greek government that needed his proofreading, were *Hockey Pictorial*, *Hockey Illustrated*, *Hockey World*, and *The Hockey News*. Every so often, he even got his hands on the gem of all gems, a *St. Louis Post-Dispatch*.

Papou broke with tradition one morning. When we sat at the kitchen table, almost never a word was spoken, Papou immersed in his reading as deeply as I was immersed in mine. He took a long sip from his coffee and said, "I see Bobby Hull is not scoring as much as last year." That sentence coming from his mouth was about as imaginable as Don Cherry announcing his intention to coach the Swedish National Team.

Dumbstruck, I looked at him, my chin dropping. "Why you think that is?" he asked. Gathering my senses, I started to answer, finding it difficult to talk about hockey with a man who hadn't a clue as to what offside meant. As I was talking, I figured out that he had started to read my sports sections after I finished. Here was a guy who loathed sports as the ultimate distraction from important issues, and yet he'd started to study this subject that had so totally captivated me, just so he could talk to me about it. Or maybe it was just so I could have someone to talk to about hockey. To be fair, I started reading about politics. I don't know if Papou ever got to really like hockey, but I really liked learning about politics.

That morning, we started a new tradition. From then on, we shared conversations about our particular passions. That he had taken an interest in hockey was amazing to me. It is even more so now, more than 30 years later. He knew I was alone in my family. And since he was not a demonstrably affectionate man—I don't ever recall him holding or hugging me to that point—this was his affection, his gift. This was something more we could share to enrich our already precious mornings.

A month or so before that particular morning, I had written my first fan letter to Glenn Hall. I had carefully scripted a note and a poem, which my English teacher helped me with. Then I drew a caricature of Hall robbing Beliveau, with the weeping Frenchman moaning, "Can't he let in just one?" I enclosed a self-addressed, stamped manila envelope and asked Glenn Hall if he could autograph the drawing and return it to me in the envelope. I mailed it to Hall, care of the Blues at the Arena.

The 1968 playoffs were in full swing, and I was glued to the TV during the finals, my heart breaking any time the puck ended up in the Blues' net. Papou found out before me that Hall had won the Conn Smythe Trophy. He bounded home one day from the bus, uncharacteristically enthusiastic, and shoved the *Sporting News* at me. "Look inside right away," he directed breathlessly. HALL WINS SMYTHE TROPHY was the headline of the hockey section. I couldn't have been more excited if I'd won the award myself, and Papou was ecstatic at seeing me so happy.

Two more weeks passed. It was a Saturday afternoon, and Papou had gone down to the front stairs to pick up the day's mail. "Tommy, Tommy," he called. I walked toward his voice, which was coming from the landing outside our front door. I'd almost forgotten about the fan letter by that time, figuring stars that big probably didn't answer their mail or that maybe he'd never gotten my package in the first place.

I opened the door, and there stood Papou, his thick lips in a pursed upturn, an expression I don't think I'd ever seen before. Looking at his outstretched hand, I saw the manila envelope with my address scrawled across it in my handwriting.

I accepted the envelope with the same care a jeweler would use to handle the Hope Diamond. Sitting down there on the spot, I slowly tore away the seal and opened the letter. There was my drawing, signed "To Tom, Very

Best Regards, Glenn Hall." Also in the envelope was a five by seven publicity photo inscribed, "Thanks for the poem, Tom. Sincerely, Glenn."

When I stood, I looked into Papou's eyes. I couldn't utter a word. Neither could he.

So he put his arm around me.

As I write this, that autographed picture hangs framed and preserved on a wall behind me. And as I write this, I am looking at a photograph of Papou. My passion for reading and writing was the lasting gift from Papou: the inspiration to write this book came from Hall. When it is my time to pass from this world, I hope that my last sensation will be the warmth of the hug on that one special afternoon that I shared with my heroes.

15

The Single Greatest Year of Goaltending

WHEN WILLIAM "SCOTTY" BOWMAN'S epitaph is written, his tenure in St. Louis will likely be no more than a sentence or two long. It will note that the Mound City was his first National Hockey League coaching and general managerial stop, and that his first three teams made it to the Stanley Cup finals three consecutive years. If the author of that epitaph is the least bit perceptive, a keyword will recur throughout his work.

Adaptability.

Having cut his teeth in the Montreal organization, Bowman must have felt a twinge in his heart when venerable coach Toe Blake decided to step down amid the tears and bubbly of the Cup-winning Canadien locker room the previous spring. Although he was officially head coach and assistant general manager under Lynn Patrick, Bowman's experience could have led him to expect consideration as a candidate to replace Blake. If he was disappointed to hear that the job went to Claude Ruel, a contemporary of Bowman's in his days with the Canadien minor-league system who had zero NHL coaching experience, Bowman buried that emotion in a frenzy of work. Before the end of the summer of '68, Bowman was elevated to head coach and GM.

Bowman sat at the table of the summer's annual draft meeting with that authority already in place, and he dropped a bomb at those meetings that would resonate for months. Few would have predicted his fateful words: "From the auxilliary list of the New York Rangers, St. Louis claims Jacques Plante."

"Jake the Snake," as Plante was known, had retired from the Rangers three years earlier to spend more time with his wife when she fell ill. Before that, Jacques had experienced knee problems in his last season and a half with the

Rangers, and had shuttled between their minor-league team in Baltimore and the big squad. He had an ongoing battle with the team's physicians, who disagreed with Plante's self-diagnosis that his knee problems were at the root of his increasingly ineffectual play. As it turned out, Plante did undergo surgery, but immediately after the operation—which the Rangers paid for—he retired suddenly. Ranger management suspected that Plante knew all along he was going to retire, and the circumstances left a bad taste in their mouths.

Plante had already had one aborted comeback effort with the Oakland Seals the previous September. Former Montreal teammate Bert Olmstead was coaching the team, and he hired Jacques to work with his goalies in camp. One of them, Charlie Hodge, had a contract dispute and was sitting out the camp, so Jacques put on the equipment in his place. He felt he was playing well enough to be considered for a place on the team and approached Olmstead about renegotiating his contract. Bert summarily threw him out of camp. Since then, "The Snake" had been making it known that he wanted back into the game.

Bowman was familiar with the risks Plante presented, but he desperately needed a goalie to provide Glenn with the proper rest and, more to the point, he needed a goalie he didn't have to trade a player to acquire. Wanting to add skill and depth to the roster in other areas, Bowman knew he'd have to use bodies as trade bait. He didn't want to trade for a goalie, but if he didn't get a goalie, he knew he was perilously close to losing his team's backbone, Hall.

Glenn's capable backup man the year before had been 34-year-old Seth Martin. He'd taken a leave of absence during the regular season from his job as a firefighter, and then claimed his vacation time on top of that just to stay with the team through the playoffs. Had he stayed another season with the Blues he would have lost his pension rights with the fire department, and so, not being able to afford losing out on these, he retired. Hall was prompted to say, "Now I will have to play all of the games, and I'm too old to do that."

Bowman had approached the Philadelphia Flyers about acquiring one of their three young goalies, Bernie Parent, Doug Favell, or their top minor-leaguer, Fern Rivard. Nothing happened there. Bowman liked Montreal prospect Gerry Desjardins, but L.A., desperate to replace Terry Sawchuk, whom they'd soured on, traded for him first. L.A. left Sawchuk unprotected in the draft, but Scotty wasn't interested in him. So he called Dickie Moore, who had decided to retire after the playoff run, and asked the ex-Plante teammate if bringing Jacques aboard was a good idea.

"I told him no," said Moore. "I didn't know how the team would get along with him. Jacques was a great goalie. No doubt about it, but he was different and I didn't think he'd fit in. I told Scotty, 'Hey, don't ask me, ask Glenn Hall. He's the one you don't want to offend.'"

Bowman did call Glenn, who agreed to the idea.

"Jacques didn't quit because he couldn't play," said Bowman, who had coached Jacques in his last game, a 2–1 exhibition win by Bowman's Junior Canadiens over the Soviet National Team three years prior. "People forget that. He's kept in shape playing with the Quebec Oldtimers."

Bowman called Plante after securing his rights and explained the situation. "I told him he would play between 30, and no more than 40, games. I said we'd always have a job for him in the St. Louis organization. He's an intelligent person, a good speaker, an excellent teacher. All this impressed him and he signed immediately."

The contract was reportedly $35,000, and Bowman had added his goalie without spending a body. But Plante, showing his thoughtful foresightedness, negotiated a unique deferred-payment plan in the contract that meant he'd be receiving the monies long after his playing days were over.

"My wife had regained her health completely, and she told me that if I wanted to go back to hockey, it was fine with her," said Plante. "I appreciated the three years away from the game. I was relaxed and confident that I could play again. I'd maintained good conditioning and the St. Louis offer was a good one."

Plante's next statement after signing did not disappoint the drooling press. "Besides, Hall will be the best backup man I've ever had."

"That," said colorful Boston Bruin forward Derek Sanderson, "was like telling a Muslim that Allah was the best backup god in the world."

Bowman immediately stepped in and made sure Plante knew what was what. "Plante knows that Glenn is number one around here, and Jacques is just happy to get the opportunity to play again," he said.

The next day, Plante's tone softened dramatically. You could almost see Bowman's lips moving as Plante said, "I am very grateful to the St. Louis Blues for giving me this opportunity. In today's long schedule two netminders are a necessity. It will be an honor to share the goal with Glenn Hall." Later, some vintage Plante seeped through. "I know the St. Louis organization is one of the most solid in the league . . . I'd have to say that with Glenn and me on the same side, we're going to have the best goalkeeping in the West Division, maybe in the whole league."

With half the goaltending situation handled, Bowman turned back to Hall. Scotty called Glenn, whose son, Patrick, answered the phone.

"How's your dad?" Bowman asked.

"Oh, he's in great shape," said the boy.

When Hall picked up, Bowman said, "So I hear you're coming back."

"Who says?"

"Your son," Scotty coolly replied.

Bowman had already decided to pay Glenn a visit at the farm. As it happened, Lynn Patrick had run into Glenn's former Junior and Red Wing coach Jimmy Skinner at the NHL draft meetings. When the conversation turned to Glenn and Lynn's concern that Glenn might hang up the pads, Skinner suggested that Scotty make a personal visit.

"Glenn will respond to respect," advised his former coach.

With St. Louis Blues owner Sid Salomon playing in a golf tournament near Edmonton, both Sid and Scotty made the drive to the Hall spread to offer a contract.

"Glenn was sitting on the stoop of this little shed he had on the property, sipping on a cold one," Scotty recalled. "I wanted to see that barn he was always painting, but I never saw one. As far as I know, there was no barn." The contract Bowman and Salomon brought to the Hall farm had a raise in it to $55,000, keeping him the highest-paid goalie in the league. Glenn accepted the offer.

Hall's public comments were a contrast from Plante's. "[Signing Plante] was good news to me. You can't play all the time in this league anymore, not with the shooters they have and with those crazy curved sticks. Because I only played in 49 games last season, I was fresh for the playoffs. Plante will be a big help."

Bowman made his plans for using the two warhorses clear before the season. "We won't hesitate to use both men interchangeably. We're not in the least concerned with their ages."

Scotty had another ace up his sleeve though, a revolutionary idea he wouldn't reveal until after the season started, and one the NHL would have to legislate out of the game. In the meantime, he returned to the business of building the rest of the roster, assembling some more players considered over-the-hill, such as Camille "The Eel" Henry and Ab McDonald, and younger prospects, including Terry Gray; the third Plager brother, Billy; and goalie Robbie Irons, who soon figured into a most historical night.

"It was a terrific group of players," said Hall. "There were vast differences in our ages, but we were all friends."

PLANTE ARRIVED AT THE Blues training camp at the Ottawa Civic Centre on time and eager to get back into the NHL scene. Three other goalies were there, none of them Hall. Glenn had received permission to report late so he could harvest his grain crop, the delay in reporting prompting another round of "he's back home painting the barn" stories. He would join the team after the initial camp broke and the team headed south to St. Louis. The goalies skating with Jacques at that point were Irons and drafts Gary Edwards and Ted Ouimet. Jake was also joined by ex-Montreal teammates Doug Harvey and Jean-Guy Talbot as well as ex-Ranger mates Camille Henry and Bob Plager. Plante was in tremendous shape, and he impressed his new teammates early on with his work ethic and practice attitude, just as he had in New York.

"Maybe it's true what they say about life beginning at 40," he observed.

Winning over teammates on the ice was one thing; off the ice, he had a way to go. The Blues' camp moved to New Brunswick for a week, and Jacques, a notorious spendthrift, accompanied the boys to a local establishment for refreshments after a training session. The players took turns buying rounds, simply going around the table in the order they were seated. Just before it was Jacques's turn to foot the bill, he managed to make excuses and leave. After a couple of times of being had, Plager placed his money on the table as he ordered a round and directed the waitress, "And while you're at it, bring us another round right now." Pointing at Jake, he continued, "And that guy over there will pay for it."

The Blues made another significant addition at the beginning of the 1968–69 season. Although Gus Kyle, former Ranger tough-guy defenseman, continued to provide television color commentary of Blues games, Dan Kelly, an affable figure with an infectious love of hockey and a unique ability to convey the excitement of the action, became the Blues' principal play-by-play man. Kelly went on to a Hall-of-Fame career and stayed with the team, even when moonlighting as the voice of the NHL on national telecasts in the '70s and '80s, until he succumbed to cancer.

Plante got the starting nod for the games at the beginning of the season, and his official return to the NHL was at Chicago Stadium. Stepping onto the ice wearing a slightly updated version of the pretzel mask, Plante showed some rust but was solid in a 26-save, 4–3 loss. Jake's backup for the game was young Robbie Irons, the minor-league goalie the Blues were grooming for the future. Along with Irons, Edwards and Ouimet were being apprenticed to succeed Plante and Hall eventually, and Bowman split the season into thirds so that each of them could spend part of the season with the NHL club practicing and sitting on the bench as backup when one of the vets had the night off. The idea was that the vets would play two games and sit for two games, so the NHL grind of games and travel was kept at an absolute minimum. The youngster with the big club could be taught by the best in the game, and the non-playing veteran could enjoy the game from the comfort of the press box. And the other two apprentices got game experience by playing down on the farm club at Kansas City until their scheduled third of the season with the big club.

The Blues' season opener in St. Louis was a near sellout. The beloved baseball Cardinals had blown a 3–1 lead in the World Series to lose in seven to the Detroit Tigers, and the rabid hockey fans were eager to salute their heroes from last May, especially Mr. Goalie, who was being presented with the Conn Smythe Trophy in a ceremony before the game. Having just reported to the team two days earlier, Glenn wasn't ready to play, but he appeared at center ice to receive the award from Conn Smythe himself and was showered with a tremendous ovation. Immediately afterward, Jacques flipped the mask down and debuted with a 6–0 win over the Los Angeles Kings.

It was especially easy for the fans present that night to see Plante. No haze of cigarette smoke clouded the action, as the Salomons became the first owners in sports to declare their Arena smoke-free. Although it was a very controversial move at the time, all other sports and venues eventually adopted this rule.

The Blues defended the net farthest from their gate to the locker room. Before a game, the team could milk the traditional standing ovation as they skated 200 feet toward their net, and after the game, the team could bask under yet another prolonged tribute as they skated 200 feet to the exit. After this game, Plante removed his mask as he accepted congratulations from his teammates. (He never removed his mask after a loss until he was off the ice.) After the scrum around him broke up, and under the noise of the saluting crowd, Plante reached center ice as he was exiting and lifted his hands high in the air in a victory "V." A huge reactionary roar went up from the crowd, and that V became a post-win tradition during Jake's two-year stint in the Gateway City.

The Blues' fans had already earned the reputation as the most wildly supportive home crowd in the league, and six times in the opening game organist Norm Kramer struck up "When the Saints Go Marching In." Every time the Blues lit the lamp, the fans began a rhythmic serenade to go along with the standing ovation at the start of every period. Kramer had such a tremendous reputation for whipping the fans into a frenzy that Minnesota North Star GM Wren Blair threatened to pour glue on the organ's keys. The Pittsburgh Penguins sent their organist to scout Kramer and learn from him, and Penguin head coach Red Kelly once wore earmuffs on the bench at the Arena to muffle the din. "The crowd, and the acoustics in the building, gave us a 1–0 lead every game," said Glenn.

Jacques started the first four games of the year while Hall got into the swing of things at practice. Plante lost 4–2 to Montreal but beat Oakland 4–1. Glenn made his debut in Toronto, losing to the Maple Leafs 6–4. His next game was against the Boston Bruins at the Garden, a place he always sparkled in late in his career. He made 29 saves in a 2–1 win. Plante took over for the next two games, a 3–1 win over Pittsburgh and a 2–0 loss to the North Stars, and Bowman established the two-in, two-out rotation.

"You could always tell who was going to start the next game," remembered Red Berenson. "We'd have a light pre-game skate or a pre-game meeting the morning of game day and the guy sitting out was loosey-goosey. The other guy's face was white as a sheet."

Hall returned with a 4–4 tie against the Detroit Red Wings, the Blues erasing a 4–1 deficit harkening back to last season behind a hat trick from new Blue Camille Henry. Next, Glenn backstopped a 3–1 win over the Penguins. Plante was in the nets at Philadelphia on November 7 and recorded his second shutout of the season, lowering his goals-against average under 2. On any normal night, that would have made headlines, but that evening while the Blues beat Philly 8–0, Berenson set a modern-day record that still stands—and has since been equaled by Darryl Sittler—by scoring six goals in one game.

It was Hall's turn in the net as the Blues returned to Boston Garden, and he was magical in a 39-save, 1–1 tie. A St. Louis sportswriter described Hall's mastery over the Bruins: "Glenn Hall has a great circus act going for him. He skates out onto the ice and 18 Bruins roll over and play dead." Owner Sid Salomon was at the game and said of Mr. Goalie, "He's absolutely remarkable. His play never ceases to amaze me."

Days after setting his record, Berenson helped Glenn Hall to make the headlines for wearing a mask during a game. *The Hockey News* ran a picture of the newest masked marvel on its cover with the caption in bold print, LOOK WHO'S WEARING A MASK! Hall's protective device was designed a year earlier by Seth Martin, who had fashioned the mask for Glenn to wear in practice. It was white, nothing like the pretzel mask, and it had large triangular holes at the nose and mouth to provide ventilation, and eye holes that Hall had widened to allow for more peripheral vision. "I guess that was defeating the purpose of protecting my eyes," he later noted.

Berenson had confronted Hall one day, asking him, "Can you give me one good reason why you wouldn't wear the mask?"

Glenn couldn't. Simple as that. "I told him I had planned to try wearing a mask in games sometime and he said, 'Why sometime? Why not tomorrow?' So I said, 'Okay.'"

Hall debuted the mask the very next night at Madison Square Garden against the New York Rangers. Insanity ensued. Just a minute into the game, Ranger Vic Hadfield beat Hall with a long, unscreened drive from the blue line, a shot that dipped and curved. The goal frustrated Glenn. Very soon thereafter veteran ref Vern Buffey whistled a delay-of-game penalty against the Blues that Hall took emotional exception to. Hall left his crease to argue the call, and when Buffey rebuffed the newly masked man, Hall responded with a poke of his catch glove to the ref's chest, earning Glenn the first and only game misconduct of his career.

Plante was watching the game from the press box, and just minutes before had eschewed the offer of a hot dog. "No, thank you," said Plante. "I can't have the mustard, the hot dog . . . I am not playing but you never know . . ."

Backup man Irons left the bench to field some warm-up shots, but soon into the warm-up he seemed to turn an ankle . . . or hurt a knee . . . or bruise a thigh. Had Scotty Bowman told his young goalie to fake an injury and stall for time so that Plante could get dressed? Ranger coach Emile Francis sure thought so, and he was screaming that charge at the top of his lungs from atop the Ranger bench.

Bowman recalled the incident: "[Defenseman] Doug Harvey came over to me and said, 'Scotty, you know we can't go with this kid. Why don't we get Jacques? . . . You want me to tell him to get hurt?' I said, 'Okay, if you can.' So a couple of minutes into the warm-up Robbie Irons goes down, injured just like Doug told him to do. He's down and he won't get up . . . We had Plante paged on the PA system. He went down to the dressing room to get ready, and the whole thing took about 25 minutes. The worst part was that Bill Jennings, who was president of the Rangers, kept coming by my bench and so did Emile Francis . . . they wanted me barred from the league and everything else. I said, 'The guy's hurt. What are we supposed to do?' So Plante makes his grand entrance . . . and the big story is we won . . ."

Irons did, in fact, play three minutes of the game—the only NHL minutes of his career—and did not face a shot. It was Plante's first on-ice return to the Garden since 1965, and he shut down the Rangers the rest of the 55 minutes as the Blues took a 3–1 win.

After the game, Hall deadpanned to one teammate: "See, every time I wear a mask, I get thrown out of a game . . . Now I know what a starting pitcher feels like when he gets knocked out of the box in the first inning." But when asked by a journalist about finally adopting the mask, Hall turned serious: "I've had over 250 stitches in my head and face. I don't want my paycheck mailed to me at Good Samaritan Hospital . . . or Cemetery." Three games later, mask in place, Hall recorded the 74th shutout of his career in a 7–0 pasting of Oakland.

The Blues' early-season dramatics, led by Berenson's record-setting night and the Hall-Plante tandem, drew national attention to the Blues. *Sports Illustrated* did a feature article on the two goalies, and every week *The Hockey News* or *The Sporting News* ran a story about the entire hockey scene in St. Louis. Sellouts became commonplace, the crowds' college-like enthusiasm was unique to the sport—organist Kramer had the crowd chanting "Let's Go Blues!" in unison after every whistle—and the Salomons' ownership style made the Blues the envy of the league. Other franchise owners openly resented the Salomons, fearing their players would request to be traded to the Blues. That, in fact, did begin to happen. One sportswriter called the team a "floating old-age home," but the Blues were leading established teams left and right, and leaving their expansion brethren in their wake. Had ESPN or TSN existed in 1968, the Blues would have been a nightly feature: the St. Louis Blues sold expansion, their gaudy success legitimizing the NHL's growth from a cozy six-team circuit to a national sports phenomenon.

GOALIE GARY EDWARDS spent the middle third of the season backing up Plante and Hall. Like Robbie Irons before him, he was subjected to a team initiation masterminded by Glenn Hall. To welcome the rookie, Glenn invited him to share an evening of "snipe" hunting with the boys. Hall described their prey as a large bird for whom flight was nearly impossible. "We do it at night," Hall explained. "We chase 'em down corn rows and catch 'em in nets."

The safari members converged for the "hunt" at a nearby cornfield in Eureka, Illinois, just over the Missouri border. After dark fell, and emboldened by a few hours of sharing suds, Edwards was given a large fishing net and directed to hold a position at the edge of the cornfield. Hall and several teammates told him to stay ready as they headed to the far side of the field to chase and flush the snipe toward the waiting Edwards, who was to snare the snipe in the netting. In the distance, Edwards could hear his mates trying to intimidate the elusive bird, "Shoo, snipe! G'wan, big bird! Shoo!"

Squinting through the dark, Edwards saw little, but suddenly he felt the cold barrel of a gun pressed to his neck.

"What are you doing out here?" demanded a credential-waving conservation agent.

Silent for a minute, Edwards responded with an impaired, "Would you believe trying to catch butterflies?"

"Don't be impertinent," barked the agent. "You're arrested! I'm charging you with hunting snipe out of season with an oversize net."

"B-but," stammered Edwards, "I'm not the only one out here. There's 15 other guys out there."

Those 15, of course, had by now disappeared. The agent handcuffed Edwards and carted him away to a building where the Veterans of Foreign Wars (VFW) held their social meetings.

The town barber, wearing his bailiff hat, was waiting. "Bloody serious, this. You could go to jail or get whacked with a fine," he intoned in his most judicial timbre. No sooner had he started speaking than Hall and Co. appeared through the back door to listen and provide "support."

The bailiff continued. "See here, Edwards, we can't have you Canadians coming down here and ravaging our lands. That'll be a $300 fine."

Totally flustered, Edwards looked back at Hall, who generously offered to take up a collection for the troubled teammate. A total of $150 entered the hat, with Doug Harvey contributing 17 Green Stamps. The bailiff tallied the take. "Only $150 here, Mr. Edwards. You'll have to get up the other $150."

Sweating now, and well short of the $150 due, Edwards was finally tipped to the ruse when the bailiff gave him an alternative form of settling the debt. "We'll settle if you'll buy a round of drinks for the house."

JACQUES PLANTE TIED BOSTON 4–4 in his next game, so the ensuing set of games went to Hall, who topped Detroit 3–1 and then scored a 1–0 win over Philadelphia and Plante protégé Bernie Parent. In the second period, Glenn made a series of three point-blank, back-to-back-to-back saves that left play-by-play man Dan Kelly breathless. Flyer Simon Nolet started the assault with a wicked drive from the right circle. Hall made a catlike reaction with his right hand. The puck ricocheted off his blocker and went directly to Jean-Guy Gendron, who immediately sent the puck back at Hall. The Ghoulie butterflied, stopping the shot with his left pad in a mad stretch. Nolet had continued to the net and tried to stuff the puck back the other way, but Hall slid lengthwise out of his butterfly into a double pad stack and stabbed the rebound out of mid-air with his right pad before a Blues defender finally took possession.

Four games later, Hall lounged in the Chicago Stadium press box as Plante toiled for the Blues below. Leading 2–1, Plante was solid but not greatly tested until early in the second period when a Ken Wharram shot missed the pretzel mask but not the unprotected side of his head, ripping a 20-stitch gash. With a towel pressed to the wound, Plante was led from the ice, replaced by Gary Edwards. Edwards played four minutes, stopping two shots, before the door swung open at one end of the ice and Mr. Goalie skated out to take his place in the net. The fans gave a standing salute to their old hero, who was touched for five goals in the last two periods.

Plante used the injury to draw attention to the use of curved sticks. He was convinced the puck was jumping in different directions mid-flight because of the unrestricted curves, and he urged the league to do something. "I'll tell you what, if the league doesn't do something soon, someone is going to get killed," he said. "Shots off a curved stick dip and dive like a knuckleball. You never know where they're going. It's a wonder that more goalies haven't been hurt in recent years."

Hall chimed in, "It's open season on goalies now. The slap shot, the curved stick, the screened shots make it impossible for a goalkeeper. You don't see the puck half the time anymore. But you're not going to see any rule changes in the goalies' favor until one of them gets killed."

The league eventually regulated the depth of a curve, but the governors modified another rule first. Blues coach Bowman's three-goalies-in-a-game act inspired the NHL to rule that the only guys eligible to play in a game were those who were originally dressed. There would be no more calls to the press box for the cavalry and, if two goalies were unable to play through injury in a game, a regular skater would have to put the pads on.

Plante missed the next four games healing, but he returned in style, posting his fourth shutout with a 24-save effort over the Oakland Seals on the road. The Blues returned home against the Rangers, who were on a hot streak. Hall was in the cage and in top form, holding his travel-weary team close with 34 saves, and the Blues pulled out a 2–2 tie on a Berenson goal with Hall pulled and 12 seconds to play.

Up next was Minnesota, and not to be outdone by Jake, Glenn threw his third blank in a 2–0 win. Plante beat Minnesota the next night 3–2, then victimized the Kings again with a shutout, the scoreless tie his fifth zero of the year. Bowman gave the next three games to Glenn: a 3–1 win at Oakland, a 3–1 win away over Detroit, and then the final home game of the season's first half against Los Angeles. Glenn turned aside 30 shots, recording his fourth shutout and the pair's ninth.

At the halfway point, Hall had appeared in 20 games, Plante 19. Hall had a 12–4–3 record, Plante was 9–6–3. Plante had five shutouts, Hall four. Plante's goals-against average was 1.94 and Hall's 2.15. They won the first-half Vezina Trophy, and both were named to the West All-Star team, Glenn getting the First-Team nod. The pair had sparked a huge lead in the West Division, with the Blues 10 points ahead of their nearest competitor.

Even the established East Division noticed what was happening in St. Louis. The Blues were three games above .500 against them and, when bruising Montreal forward John Ferguson was asked the highlight of the NHL's first half, he said, "Those amazing St. Louis Blues and the terrific lead they've opened up in the West, and then kept so handily week after week. Above all, you have to give credit to the fantastic goaltending of Jacques Plante and Glenn Hall. Their shutout production has been a season highlight all by itself."

Teammate Billy McCreary reflected on what it was like to play in front of the two: "As a wing, with Jacques playing the puck so much and so well, I knew I didn't have to come back into the zone as deep as when Glenn was playing. With Jacques, your defensive job was to cover the weak side, because you knew he always had the strong-side angle . . . Glenn talked a lot on the ice. He was more involved with instruction and coaching. He told me, 'If I holler a direction, just go ahead and do it.' Glenn never blamed anyone for anything that went wrong on the ice in front of him. He never had emotional swings.

"Jacques mostly just thought about Jacques. When he wasn't playing, he wasn't very involved. I played with him a bit in Montreal. He was pretty quiet around the locker room, but supremely confident. And very, very bright. Clever. He was a very accomplished bridge player. He kept a book on the shooters, knew their tendencies well. Glenn was tremendously intelligent also. I don't think he liked to show that a lot. But he was. I think that's the thing they had in common. They were both so very clever. People talked about Jacques's skating, but there was no better skater than Hall. And he had such confidence in his catching hand. He'd dare you to beat him there. The fact is, we were playing on a team where we knew just about every night all we'd have to do is score three goals and we were going to win."

Red Berenson recalled the style-and-substance difference when the two played. "It showed up on two-on-ones," recalled the man St. Louisians called "The Red Baron." "Jacques always wanted the defenseman to hold the middle of the ice and take the pass away. Glenn wanted the defenseman to force the puck carrier into making a pass, thinking that the pressure would force a bad pass. One time [Blues defenseman] Noel Picard forgot about that and cheated to the puck carrier when Plante was in the net and Jacques was already out against that guy on his angle. So the player throws a pass across the slot and the other guy scores into the empty net, and Plante chases Picard all the way back to the bench because he wanted to make sure everyone in the rink knew that goal wasn't his [Plante's] fault! "Glenn was more of a team player, the consummate professional. He was very vocal in team issues. Plante was cordial. But he just wasn't a real 'team' guy."

McCreary remembered a last difference: "Jacques loved the attention, the whole V after each win. After a game, Glenn would sneak out the back way to avoid all the attention of the fans."

For all of the pre-season hand-wringing, it was clear that the two men respected the other. Plante remarked, "Glenn often was sick to his stomach before a game. Sometimes he was sick between periods. It was very surprising that he could endure all that and still be one of the very best goalies who ever played the position. I think the challenge of the job kept him going. There was no way he was going to let it get the best of him."

"I had no difficulty playing with Plante," said Hall. "I really didn't. We weren't going to teach each other anything new . . . He was different but he was a dedicated hockey player. So often your skill players are not dedicated, but Plante was. Plante liked to do different things, experiment, fool around with ideas . . . We were total opposites and we talked a lot about goaltending. For a while Jacques wanted to play the butterfly. But I told him that would be the worst thing that could happen to him. We were close to 40 years old and it was too late to change. We each had our own way and it worked, so why change it?"

With the Blues resting comfortably at the top of the West Division, the only regular-season question remaining was how far ahead of the pack they'd finish. After that, people wondered aloud whether this expansion club could legitimately challenge for a Stanley Cup.

Jacques opened the second half of the season with a 3–1 loss against the Chicago Black Hawks, but the Blues returned the favor the next night at home, pummeling the Hawks 6–1. Hall posted his second consecutive shutout, his third in his last four starts, in a 2–0 win over Minnesota. Both goalies were tied at five blanks for the season. Hall had allowed only one goal in his last 263 minutes of play, the second time during the season he'd gone over 200 minutes allowing a single score. It was the 78th shutout of his career.

"No shutout in the NHL is ever easy," he said, "but Jacques Plante and I have been getting a lot of help. Our forwards check like mad, and the defense plays a tight, smart game. It really makes a difference to have fellows like that in front of you." That same week, Hall was presented with the John E. Wray Award by the St. Louis baseball writers for outstanding contribution to sports other than baseball.

Jake had just turned 40 when he returned to the goal a game later to face New York, recording his second 40-plus save game of the season in a 2–2 tie. Since Hall had shutout Minnesota twice consecutively, Bowman went out of rotation to play Hall against the North Stars in the next game, a 3–1 win. That victory gave the team an amazing 15–2–4 record against their expansion brethren.

The All-Star game was held in Montreal that year, and for the first time it featured the West Division Stars against the East, breaking the old format of the Cup champions versus the rest of the NHL's All-Stars. Bowman added goalie Bernie Parent to the squad, and while the East outshot the West, the game ended in a 3–3 draw. Hall stopped 11 of 12 shots in the first period, Parent was ten-for-ten in the second, and Plante went 13 out of 15 in the third. At 37 and 40 respectively, Hall and Plante became the oldest goaltending tandem to toil in All-Star sweaters. Hall's 20 minutes of playing time were his last playing in the gala; it was his record 13th appearance, another record that is unlikely to be broken.

Right after the All-Star break, Glenn pulled ahead of Plante in the shutout derby when he blanked Detroit. Glenn recorded his seventh shutout of the season two weeks later, with a 30-save 2–0 win over Pittsburgh. Hall stopped two breakaways and slammed the door during a long five-on-three Penguin power play. Plante took over for the next two games, winning at Philadelphia, and then making 46 saves in a 4–1 home game against L.A. in perhaps his best match of the year.

Hall returned to the net at home against the North Stars. He'd allowed only four goals to them in four games. Early in the third period, the Blues leading 4–0 and the puck in Glenn's end of the ice, the referee signaled a delayed penalty. Hall headed for the bench and was ten feet inside his own blue line when the loose puck dribbled his way. Instinctively he decided not to go to the bench for an extra forward. Reaching his blade down to gather the puck in, he cut toward center ice and stickhandled the puck deftly toward the middle of the neutral zone, where teammate Terry Crisp was breaking between the North Star defensemen. Hall snapped off a perfect pass, hitting Crisp in flight. Terry split the defenders and drove toward the net, ripping a low shot past goalie Garry Bauman. The home crowd cheered with the bulge of the net and went into a second ovation when the announcer called Hall's name on the assist.

"Believe me, I thought of trying to score," said Mr. Goalie. "I wanted to be able to say that I got more goals this year than [defenseman] Bob Plager [who went the year without scoring once]." Crisp added, "I'd have cried if I had missed that one. Gordie Howe couldn't have given me a better pass."

The Blues went on to a 6–0 win. Hall's eighth shutout of the year, and the pair's 13th, tied the modern-day record for shutouts by one team set by Toronto's Harry Lumley in 1953–54. The 15-year-old record was set during Plante's sophomore year and one year prior to Hall's rookie campaign, in an age bereft of curved sticks and slap shots. To this day, the mark has only been equaled once in 1998 by Dominik Hasek and eclipsed once, by Chicago's Tony Esposito, who recorded 15 in 1970.

After the game, the press surrounded Glenn, talking as much about the assist as the shutout. From the other side of the locker room, with the skill of a ventriloquist, came a lone voice in the wilderness.

"Hey, who scored the goal?" When the question was ignored, it was repeated. "Who actually scored the goal?" The voice belonged to Crisp, whose head was turned the opposite way.

Plante was ready to take his turn in the net against Toronto at the Arena. Hall wasn't dressing and he was shooting a relaxing game of pool in the locker room when a tap on the shoulder interrupted the game. He was quietly informed that Plante's ankle was acting up and Jake wouldn't be able to play. Hall sat at his stall and looked at Plante, who had a towel covering his head. As Glenn began to undress, he detected some snickers coming from a few of the surrounding stalls and he soon realized he'd been had. Plante was fine; the call was a practical joke. For the Blues, Bob Plager was the culprit behind most pranks. Plager preferred to assault clothing: ties cut in half, underwear shredded, and toes cut out of socks were trademarks. This trick was a little more cerebral.

Hall got dressed again and went to the press box. No sooner had he sat down when another call came. This time Plante had injured himself in warm-ups, and Glenn would have to play for real. "It wouldn't have surprised me a bit if he hadn't come down the second time," said Red Berenson. "I probably wouldn't have. I'd have been thinking they caught me once, they're not going to catch me again." But Hall did come down and made 32 saves in a 1–1 tie.

On March 8, the Blues hosted Oakland with Glenn in goal, and the 5–2 victory clinched first place. For the team, which had been leading their division by some 20 points for the past month, the win was a bit anticlimactic. "We're really working toward the Vezina Trophy," said Bowman.

"We're playing every game with the thought of the Vezina for Jacques and Glenn in mind," agreed Berenson. "They deserve it for what they've done for this club all season."

The Blues were on the West Coast for their final two games of the regular season. Bowman brought the team out a couple of days early to train and relax in Squaw Valley, California, before the playoff run, which was just a week away from beginning.

By this time, some of Jacques's peculiarities had come to the surface. He'd been battling some tweaks in his knee, and he wasn't playing a lot. Indeed in the final 13 games, he'd started only four times. With Jacques' goals-against average sitting at 1.92, many around the team figured Plante was trying to get out of playing to keep his average below two.

Scotty Bowman wanted to make sure both men were prepared for the playoffs. With the division title already clinched, he split the last games down the middle so that neither man would be overworked or fatigued but would get just enough work to stay sharp. Hall and Plante split the game in Oakland, a 5–3 win. Hall had played the first half, allowing a goal, and Plante, the second half, allowing two, sending his goals-against average up a touch to 1.96.

"We went to Los Angeles to play the next night," recalled Scotty Bowman. "Plante was originally to play the whole game. That morning in the hotel, one of our players, Camille Henry, came to me and told me that Jacques didn't want to play because he said he had a twinge in his knee. I said that he was going to play. We went to the rink and came back to the hotel, and Doug Harvey also told me that Jacques really didn't want to play. I was kind of upset and I said, 'Well, he's gonna play.'

"About an hour and a half before the game, Doug and Camille came to see me and Jacques was with them . . . Jacques said, 'I don't think I can play tonight.' We had a third goalie with us, Ted Ouimet, and Glenn wasn't going to dress. The game meant something for Los Angeles in the playoff picture. The president of the league at the time, Clarence Campbell, was a big stickler on dressing your strongest lineup. There was no way you'd rest guys unless they were legitimately hurt. So I was obligated to play Glenn, and when I told him he was very upset. He said he had a sore back, a sore foot, a sore everything else. I said I wanted him to go in and if the game got out of hand Teddy would take over. We won 3–1 and Glenn played a terrific game.

"The players were upset with Plante, so they put all kinds of white tape around his luggage and painted a big red cross on it. Somebody wrote on it: 'Win [the game] for Jacques.' He came down into the dressing room about two minutes before the game was over and he was upset the players felt that way."

The duo finished the season with stats that were amazingly similar. Plante had 37 appearances, five shutouts, and an incredible 1.96 average. He went 16–14–5 on the season. Hall made 41 appearances with a 2.17 average, eight shutouts, and a 21–10–7 record. Glenn had drawn the tougher assignments throughout the year, a deliberate decision by Bowman. They posted the lowest goals-against mark in the league: their combined numbers brought them the Vezina Trophy, Hall's third and Plante's unprecedented seventh.

"If someone had told me that I'd share the Vezina Trophy with Glenn Hall when I was 40, I wouldn't have believed them. This has been an amazing season," said The Snake.

The Blues drew third-place Philadelphia in the opening round of the playoffs, just as they had the year before. This time, however, the regular-season standings were reversed. To prepare for the playoffs, Bowman holed up the team in a hotel just outside St. Louis the night before the first game. The coach had been wrestling with the issue of how to handle his goalies in the playoffs. Leaning toward going with Hall, just a year removed from his Smythe performance, Plante helped Bowman make up his mind.

"On Monday [the series would start Wednesday] Plante came in and told me he wouldn't be able to play [because of his knee]," Bowman recalled. "By that time we had all had it with him, I guess, so we went out of town to a hotel and told him to stay in St. Louis. The day of the game, we're getting off the bus at the Arena just as Jacques was pulling into the parking lot. Camille Henry, and I give him a lot of credit for this, came to me and said, 'I know how you feel. But he's not coming back, Scotty, unless we make a fuss over him, make him feel wanted. I know everybody's cheesed off with him, but I'm telling you I know what he's like. He'll coast right through the playoffs unless we appeal to his pride.'

"I thought that was a pretty good idea, so I talked to Plante and asked him how he felt . . . I tried to sympathize with him and that seemed to pep him up. He told me he thought he could dress as a backup that night, but he still didn't think he could play."

Before another packed house, Hall led the Blues to the ice. Mr. Goalie started the game brilliantly, fending off a couple of challenging rushes. The men in blue had been sloppy in their own end, and Hall stopped a 15-footer and the rebound just two minutes into play. The Blues built an early 2–0 lead but had been outshot 7–4 in the first ten minutes.

Bowman picks up the story: "When the game started, Plante didn't want to sit on the bench. He stayed behind in the dressing room and watched on TV . . . Gary Peters of Philadelphia broke in on Glenn Hall. Glenn made a great save, but he stretched right out to the limit and pulled his hamstring. It was terrible, really a tough injury. He came to the bench and said, 'Scotty, I don't know about this.' He was nauseated. He went back in, played about 30 seconds, came out again, and said, 'Sorry, Scotty, but I can't go.'

"So we had to go to Plante. I didn't know it, but he was in the dressing room with hardly any equipment on. So he had to put his pads and everything on and it took about ten or 15 minutes. Then he made his big entrance in the St. Louis Arena. He always had the crowd on his side, and they went for it as if he was Napoleon coming in."

This time Napoleon was not ready for Elba.

Plante surrendered a goal just a minute and a half after entering the game, but the Blues won the opener 5–2. With Hall on the sidelines and Plante feeling needed again, the ultimate showman responded to the spotlight. In Game 2, the Blues scored less than a minute into the game and never looked back, Jacques posting a 5–0, 21-save win. The scene moved to Philadelphia, and Plante was flawless again in the 3–0 win. The Flyers finally broke Plante's shutout string at 146 minutes in the second period of Game 4, but the Blues completed the sweep by winning 4–1. For the series, Plante had been beaten only three times in 230 minutes of play.

Hall's hamstring was responding very slowly to treatment. He tried skating again after the series ended, but he did not have full mobility, so Bowman decided to continue with Plante. Los Angeles, which had finished fourth in the division, upset Oakland in a tough seven-game series and visited St. Louis for the series opener. Despite their fatigue, the Kings threw 30 shots at Plante, who was perfect in a 4–0 win. It was his 13th career playoff shutout, tying him for the all-time lead with Toronto's Turk Broda.

The next day, *The Sporting News* announced its East and West All-Star teams as voted by the players. The official NHL team would be announced after the playoffs, and it would not differentiate between East and West Divisions. Hall was named the West's First All-Star goalie. Publicly Plante took it with class.

"We're represented," he said. "Glenn's there and that's all that matters." With Glenn still unable to play, Plante and the Blues closed out the series in four straight.

In the East, Montreal had crushed the Rangers in four and defeated the Bruins in a tough six-game series to reach the finals. They'd been pushed to three OTS in that series and won them all. Jean Beliveau had been the hero of the last series, and young defenseman Serge Savard was having an amazing playoff.

Hall was close to being able to play. Bowman considered opening the series with Glenn, Hall's Conn Smythe performance not far from Scotty's mind. "What is it now, about three weeks since Glenn's played?" asked the coach. Masking the extent of Glenn's injury, he continued. "He's fully recovered from his leg injury. He could have played in L.A., but we were leading 2–0 so I went with Plante. I may go with Jacques again Sunday." In reality, Scotty had no choice.

Jacques drew the start, but Scotty was hoping Glenn would be ready. Bowman had factored in Plante's history with Montreal. Prior to the season, Bowman had said he didn't want to play Plante against Montreal or Hall against Chicago because he felt it might give their opponents some extra incentive. In Plante's case, it was true.

Some sports traditions are sacrosanct. In baseball, it's the Yankees. In hockey, it's Les Canadiens and the wearing of the *bleu, blanc, et rouge*. Plante's rhetoric when he left Montreal for New York was six years in the past, but it still echoed in the famed Montreal locker room. He'd loudly criticized the Canadiens, their organization, and their players, predicting the Habs were on the way down while his new team, the Rangers, were the team to watch.

Speedy Hab forward Yvan Cournoyer summed it up: "We all knew how Plante shot his mouth off about Montreal. Every time I saw those beady eyes staring out from behind that mask, I wanted to shoot the puck at him out of a cannon."

The Blues played poorly in the early going and fell behind 2–0 before the five-minute mark. Plante gathered himself though, and held Montreal off the board the rest of the game. With the Blues behind 2–1 with three minutes to play, Montreal goalie Rogie Vachon made an out-of-nowhere glove save to rob Gary Sabourin. Montreal won 3–1, its final goal of the empty-net variety. The team outshot the Blues 25–17.

The next day, Hall and Plante were officially presented their Vezina at the annual NHL awards banquet. That same day, it was announced that Hall would start the next game. It would be Glenn's 104th playoff game, breaking the record for most appearances he'd shared with Terry Sawchuk. "I was still hurt," Glenn remembered. "I probably shouldn't have played."

Hall started the game, showing no rust from the layoff. He was sharp in the early going, not beaten until very late in the first. Montreal connected on two picture power plays in the second and went on to a 3–1 win, Glenn making 30 stops.

Despite the 2–0 deficit in the series, Bowman wasn't worried. "I don't know why everyone is so down in the mouth. Losing two here isn't the end of the world. I can't remember the last time a team came in here and didn't lose two. We know we're going to have to win one here to win the series, but right now all we're thinking about is the next two in St. Louis."

Both of the next two games were complete sellouts in St. Louis. Not a single standing-room ticket was to be had. The fans came to the Arena fully expecting their Blues could pull out a victory in Game 3. Their hopes took a hit early. Defenseman Savard's blast from the point beat Plante into the lower right side of the net, a shot he would have stopped handily on most nights. Jacques, who had managed three shutouts in post-season play, found himself on the losing end of a 4–0 game. Perhaps the heavy load was catching up with the 40-year-old who, for the first time in the playoffs, looked tired.

Hall returned for Game 4. Another monster crowd was on hand, and the fans kept the decibel level at maximum. Standing ovations that greeted the team at the first and second periods rocked the roof. Between stoppages of play, Norm Kramer pounded the keys harder and the fans screamed "Let's Go Blues!" louder. Over 16,000 fans did their best to be the sixth skater. Halfway through the game, they were rewarded. Terry Crisp caught the Canadien defense napping and hit Frank St. Marseille with a pass at center. St. Marseille was joined by Terry Gray, who broke for open ice on a clear two-on-one. St. Marseille threaded a pass through the Canadien defender to Gray, who chipped the puck behind Vachon for the Blues' first lead in the series. The Arena erupted in joy.

Hall was working his magic again. After the Blues took the lead, Montreal responded. Dick Duff attacked with a tough wrist shot that Hall steered away with his pads, and later in the period Glenn responded to a Serge Savard rising bullet with a brilliant blocker save that turned him completely around in the cage. He stoned Beliveau from 10 feet away.

But the Canadiens were still the Canadiens and, just 43 seconds into the third, light-scoring Ted Harris's screen shot found its way through a maze and landed behind Hall to tie the game. Three minutes later, tough guy John Ferguson somehow got around the defense and broke in alone off the right wing, deked to the front of the net on a breakaway, and slipped the puck through the five-hole to give Montreal a 2–1 lead. The Blues kept fighting, the crowd kept yelling. But young Vachon was matching Hall save for save. The clock ticked toward the one-minute mark, and with a face-off deep in the Montreal end, Bowman signaled for Hall to come to the bench.

Glenn left his net almost reluctantly, and the Blues fans began, slowly at first and then with building momentum, to rise and applaud. As Hall neared the bench, he lifted his mask and rested it on top of his head. By the time he stepped through the gate, 16,000 fans showed their appreciation. As they saluted him, they knew it was possible—perhaps even likely—that this would be Hall's last time in a St. Louis sweater.

The Blues attacked Vachon in a couple of waves with the extra attacker, but it was not to be, and the Canadiens swept their way to another Stanley Cup.

When the NHL announced its official All-Star team, players from all of the Original Six teams had made the cut. From the Cup-winning Canadiens were defenseman Jacques Laperriere and forward Yvan Cournoyer, both Second-Team selections. Two Black Hawks made the team: Bobby Hull on the First and Stan Mikita on the Second. There were three Bruins: First-Teamers Bobby Orr and Phil Esposito, and Ted Green on the Second. Red Wing Gordie Howe was a First-Team choice, and fellow Detroiter Frank Mahovlich made the Second Team. Toronto was represented on the First Team by defenseman Tim Horton and the Rangers on the Second Team by goalie Ed Giacomin.

Only one player made it from an expansion team. Glenn Hall was the First All-Star goalkeeper, the first player from an expansion team to make an All-Star squad. It was his seventh selection as the First All-Star, and the 11th overall of his career, both records. At no time in the history of the game has another goalie earned that number of All-Star recognitions. The honor also marked the first time any athlete in any major sport was named as a First All-Star playing for three different teams.

16

One Again

———

JUST BEFORE THE ANNUAL DRAFT meetings in 1969–70, St. Louis Blues coach Scotty Bowman received a phone call he was not anxious to accept. Glenn Hall was making it official and retiring from the game. The farm's charms had finally won out.

Mr. Goalie never liked to play at anything below his best. Having shared the Vezina Trophy the year before and having been named the National Hockey League's First All-Star goaltender at the age of 37, Glenn, unlike many athletes, was leaving the game on his own terms, and on top.

Pauline was unhappy about the decision too. "I wasn't ready to retire," she explained. "I liked the life. My kids liked the life. I remember asking Fitzy, 'What will we have to do? Where will we have to go?'"

Bowman kept Hall on the protected list, with the hope Glenn would eventually reconsider. To hedge that bet, Bowman traded the just-acquired Bob Schmautz and Norm Beaudin to the Montreal Canadiens for goalie Ernie Wakely, the Blues feeling that none of their trio of young goalies was ready to assume a full-time game-sharing role with Jacques Plante. Wakely, ironically, had played his first NHL game in 1962 as a substitute for Plante while the veteran was battling his asthma.

Summer passed into fall, and the Blues opened training camp with goalies Plante, Wakely, Gary Edwards, Robbie Irons, and Ted Ouimet in camp. Bowman fortified his roster further by adding forwards Phil Goyette and Andre Boudrias to the mix. The fact that the Blues had never scored more than a single goal in any of the finals games was not far from his mind. But the public was more concerned with Hall's absence.

Just before the season opener, Plante predicted Hall would be back. "What's he going to do when the crop's in?" asked The Snake. "That farming all summer is fine. But when the snow comes, Glenn will be pacing the floor. He'll be back with us." Until that day, Plante would hold the fort. "I'm ready to play however many games they want me to," he said.

Hall, who had just celebrated his 38th birthday, commented to *The Hockey News*, "I told Scotty Bowman before the season started that I would not return to the NHL unless the club was in a bind and needs my help through injuries. I haven't changed my mind on what I said then, and I still feel the same now."

He was looking forward to his first real winter at home since playing in the minors for Edmonton. "I love the cold, the snow, the Ski-Dooing," he said.

The Blues opened their first season without Glenn Hall against the Chicago Black Hawks. But starting in goal against Plante that night was Glenn's heir apparent, a rookie goalie making his first start for the Hawks. That night, he sported an ugly brown mask that harkened back to Plante's original Halloween special, but before long, he would adopt a carbon copy of Plante's current sleek white oval model. Over the next 15 years of his career, this rookie wore that very same white mask, adding bits and pieces of protection to it along the way and making it one of the most distinctive and recognizable masks in the history of the game.

Tony Esposito had been an All-American goaltender for Michigan Tech. He'd played some minor-league hockey in the Montreal farm system for Houston before being called up for limited but impressive action with the Canadiens during the 1968–69 season. His brother, Phil, was an All-Star forward for the Boston Bruins and had been a teammate of Hall's with the Hawks. Hawks general manager Tommy Ivan had obtained Esposito when Montreal left him exposed in the intra-league draft, and hoped to build from the goal out, as he had with Hall and his 1961 Stanley Cup–winning team.

Esposito was the second major NHL talent to employ the butterfly style after Hall originated the method. The other was Detroit Red Wing Roger Crozier. Like Crozier, Esposito caught with his right hand, but almost everything else about him was vintage Glenn Hall—minus the great skating ability. By mid-season, Blues coach Billy Reay remarked on the similarities of the two men, admitting that he sometimes thought Hall was back between the Stadium pipes. "He even sounded like Glenn," said the coach. "When he was barking directions on the ice, you'd swear it was Glenn."

Esposito also drew comparisons because he never blamed a teammate for a goal, was more than intense in his pre-game preparation, and admitted that being scored on or playing poorly was a far greater source of fear than being hurt.

But it was Esposito's popularization of the "V" that is his most lasting legacy. That he could employ it successfully proved it was a legitimate puck-stopping weapon, not a method that would only be unique to Glenn. Chicago's road games were televised during the last years of Hall's career, and a generation of Chicago-born goalies were avowed butterfly stylists. Canadian kids saw Hall play in some televised playoff contests and NHL games of the week or on *Hockey Night in Canada*. His stylistic influence was gaining a foothold in Canada, but its exposure in Glenn's native country was limited. In both countries though, the butterfly faced a challenge from a new, more hands-on generation of coaches, none of whom knew much about goaltending, who preferred the stand-up and skate-save style of stopping the puck. "There's nothing wrong with falling to the ice if you do it with a purpose in mind," Hall would rightly say. But many coaches actively discouaged it, because they didn't understand it. Hall observed: "Stand-up goalies are pretty to look at, but their goals-against averages aren't very good."

Esposito was one of the Canadian kids who'd seen Hall play. Tony's older brother, Phil, was a teammate of Glenn's and an unabashed fan who was often quoted as saying that Hall was the best goalie in the world. While he was still in college, Tony visited Phil in Chicago and caught a few exhibition games. During that time, he and Hall became acquainted and they talked goalkeeping.

"He would give me pointers. Over the years, I've tried to watch and maybe learn from him," Tony said.

"We talked a lot because he explained to me that his style was similar to mine," recalled Hall. "All I did, really, was try to explain the reasons behind the things I was doing. These things were still unusual, and I'd been criticized for them. What's important is to know the theory behind the moves.

"Let's face it, the people who tell you how to play goal aren't people who ever played goal themselves. Anything new bothers them. So they couldn't accept any goaltender who went down a lot. They couldn't understand that I was going down because I wasn't strong enough with my stick or because I felt you could handle the screen shots better from a lower position. Same thing with rebounds. You hear a goaltender criticized for giving up rebounds. If you're in tight, you just worry about stopping the shot. Let the defenseman clear the puck."

Esposito recognized the style's effectiveness, was greatly entertained by it, and incorporated it into his own. Since his heyday was in the '70s when TV exposure was everywhere, Esposito inspired a generation of goalies to adopt the butterfly simply because more kids got to see him than they did Hall. And, of course, because he was good. In his 15 years in the NHL, he earned a membership in the Hall of Fame. And in his very first full year, Esposito set a record that has yet to be broken in the modern era when he eclipsed Hall and Plante's single-season shutout production, recording 15 whitewashes.

In early November, Blues management announced a ceremony to honor Hall and Plante for winning the Vezina Trophy. The celebratory event was scheduled for Thursday, November 13, held prior to a game with the Pittsburgh Penguins. A day after that announcement, the Blues' fan club held a dinner honoring the team, and it presented Jacques with a new trophy that had been minted with him especially in mind. After receiving the "Blues' Most Colorful Player Award," Plante addressed the crowd: "I've been fortunate to win with all the teams in my career, first Montreal and then St. Louis [Jacques interestingly neglected his New York stint in this statement]. The fans here have been terrific, the best anywhere. But they have something to cheer about. They have a pretty good hockey team." Then, thinking of the upcoming Vezina presentation ceremony, Jacques declared, "I hope Glenn rejoins us." Plante soon echoed that sentiment directly to Hall.

BACK OUTSIDE EDMONTON, the Halls were seeing firsthand the perils of the farming life. Alberta had been hit with some terrible weather: the rain was so intense that Glenn couldn't get his barley crop out of the fields, and then the entire crop was buried under a foot of snow. As it was, his graineries were still nearly full with crops from last season, and the local economy was hit hard. Even faced with that adversity, Glenn had his mind made up that he would stick to his word and not return to play. "I've had enough," he said. "I just don't want to play anymore."

Ernie Wakely was set to start in goal against the Penguins on the 13th despite a bad back. When Wakely played, Plante didn't dress, so for the much-anticipated Vezina ceremony, Jake was in street clothes. That night, the Arena was festooned with signs heralding Hall: "WELCOME HOME, MR. GOALIE! COME BACK, GLENN."

The reception the fans gave the pair was genuine, warm, and loud. The chants of "We Want Hall" echoed throughout the Arena long after both Hall and Plante had retreated under the stands, replica Vezina trophies in hand. Both men watched from the press box as Wakely posted a very fitting shutout in a 4–0 Blues win. After the game, Hall reaffirmed his decision to stay retired to the press.

He said, "I can't just abandon St. Louis. This city has been too good to me. But the only way I would consider playing again is if the team had an emergency."

But Glenn was besieged by fans and well-wishers who wanted to make keeping that oath as tough as possible. After the reception, Hall planned to stay in St. Louis until Sunday the 16th before making a stop in Chicago to visit friends. Then he was heading back to Stony Plain. While Glenn was in St. Louis, his ex-teammates and coaches as well as the Salomons and the fans did not let up. Even Plante, who had never wanted to share the spotlight, got into the act. "I helped you last year," Jake told Hall. "Now you can help me this year."

But the real convincing came from the Salomons. They brought Glenn out to their expansive farm to stay while he was in St. Louis. Sid Jr. sat down with Glenn and offered him a contract. "I want you to sign this contract for yourself," advised the elder Salomon. "This money means you can build yourself a home." Salomon told Glenn the Blues would limit the number of games he'd play and then pressed home his point, saying, "You'll regret it if you don't accept this offer."

Long after he retired, Glenn completely understood the wisdom of what he'd been told. "He was exactly right," Glenn said. "I would have regretted it. That last contract provided my family with a lot."

The money was too good to pass up. The Blues announced on Monday the 17th that Hall had not only signed a contract, he'd signed a *two-year contract*. He was examined by the same team physician, Dr. Probstein, who two years earlier had convinced him that quitting mid-season was foolhardy. Said Probstein: "I've never examined a man in better physical condition." Glenn would report in two weeks. The contract terms were as remarkable as Hall's physical condition. The Salomons anted up $118,000 over two years, with no negotiating involved.

WITH HALL BACK in the fold, the Blues had three big-league talents on the roster in goal. Plante was named to the first-half All-Star team and shared the goal with Bernie Parent in the January game that was hosted by the Blues. Plante performed brilliantly in the 4–1 loss, but in the process reinjured his knee. Ernie Wakely and Hall played more and more while Jacques rehabbed, and Wakely was especially impressive in the closing months, finishing with a 12–9–4 record and a 2.11 goals-against mark. He also was undefeated at the Arena. With Wakely's strong play and Hall's arrival, rumors began to surface that the Blues were shopping the injured Plante around the league. Jacques's nettlesome habits, questionable and unpredictable health, and lack of team sense had certainly frayed the nerves of everyone around him, especially Scotty Bowman. But the trade deadline came and went, and Jake stayed put.

The Blues ran away with the division title again, and Bowman rotated his two veterans for the bulk of the first two playoff rounds, a 4–2 series win over the Minnesota North Stars and a 4–2 series win over the Pittsburgh Penguins. In the latter, Plante broke Turk Broda's career shutout record. Both Hall and Plante took 4–1 records into the finals against the Boston Bruins, Wakely having gone 0–2 in his only appearances, road games.

Boston had beaten New York 4–2 in the opening series and swept past Chicago 4–0 in the semis, earning the right to open the finals at the Arena. Before the series, Bowman had decided to go with Plante in the opening games at home where he was at his best, and Hall at the Garden where he'd always been masterful. The first period was scoreless until there were 15 seconds to play. Jake had been sharp to that point, but Johnny Bucyk scored on a nice shot to give the Bruins a big lift going into intermission. But the Blues answered as Jim Roberts tied the game less than two minutes into the second period. The Arena was a wall of noise, the fans frenetic with the tied score.

Just a couple of minutes later, with the game knotted at one apiece, Bruin Fred Stanfield found himself with the puck at the top of the circle to the right of Plante. He drew back his stick and fired a low drive. Plante moved his stick to his left toward the shot, when suddenly his mask jerked back, his arms flew up at his sides, and his body fell lifelessly on his left side. What had happened in front of Plante occured too quickly for the naked eye to see. Phil Esposito was stationed in the slot, and he tipped the Stanfield shot. The puck instantly changed directions, rocketing into the goalie's forehead, breaking the mask, and leaving the 41-year-old unconscious. Plante was carried off the ice in front of the silenced crowd and was replaced by Wakely, who was scored on in short order. The Bruins blew the game open, winning 6–2. The injury aborted any thoughts of victory the Blues' loyalists had.

At the hospital, Plante regained consciousness and the first words he uttered were: "The mask saved my life." It is not an exaggeration to say that had there been no mask, there would no longer have been a Jacques Plante.

In the next game, the entire hockey world expected to see Glenn Hall between the pipes. But Bowman made an uncharacteristic blunder and came back with Wakely. Although Glenn was nursing an injury to his catch hand that he'd sustained in the semifinals, he likely could have answered the bell. Defending his decision to the press, Bowman said that Wakely had not lost a home start all season (although Wakely was the losing goalie of record in that opening game) and that he deserved a chance. Hall was told he would play the two games in Boston, and Bowman didn't want to have to play him three games in a row while the team waited for word on Plante. Wakely was bad, and the Blues were embarrassed 6–1 in Game 2.

In accordance with the original plan, Hall was in goal for Game 3 at the Garden. According to history, Hall was brilliant. The Bruins knew they were in for a formidable battle. Boston coach Harry Sinden warned the troops that Hall would be ready. Phil Esposito said, "Glenn Hall is the best goalie in the world and we know what we are up against."

The Garden was uncomfortably hot, but so was Glenn. The Bruins attacked in waves, and Hall was at his acrobatic best. Derek Sanderson sent him sprawling backward with a shot, his legs flailing away at the rebound as he bounced off the crossbar to keep his balance. He stopped Esposito point-blank with a glove save in the second period, which prompted the center to ask, "Why me, Ghoulie, why me?"

The Bruins screened Hall to no avail, his V flaring out to turn sure goals into harmless face-offs. Boston outshot the Blues 32–10 in two periods, 19–7 in the second period alone, but clung to a narrow 2–1 lead. A shot from the slot found the back of the net in the third, and with just minutes to go, Boston scored on a fourth rebound after Hall had made three sprawling saves, the fourth shot ticking off the far post and just sneaking in. After the goal, Hall uncharacteristically lay on the ice, his head bowed in a very rare show of emotional fatigue. The final had been 4–1, and Hall had made 42 saves on the night.

The last game of the series was won 4–3 on the famous overtime Bobby Orr, flying-through-the-air goal. Hall put on another fabulous display between the pipes in a losing cause. It marked the third straight year he was defeated in the Stanley Cup–clinching game, all of those games lost by a single goal: 3–2, 2–1, and 4–3.

Years after Orr's goal, Hall, commenting on the famous photo of the goal, would tell Bobby, "I was showered and having a cold one by the time you hit the ice."

Right: Glenn holds the plaque commemorating the retirement of his sweater by the Chicago Black Hawks. Glenn is flanked (from the left) by legendary teammate Stan Mikita, friend and president of the Black Hawk alumni Jack Fitzsimmons, and longtime Hawk defenseman Keith Magnuson.

Below: The most important people in Glenn's life, his family. From the left are son Lindsay, daughter Tammy, Glenn, Pauline, daughter Leslie, and son Patrick.

Above: The well-painted barn, the building that took on mythic proportions in Glenn's career.

Facing page: Four of the greatest Black Hawks of all time at the dedication of the seventy-five year anniversary sculpture at the United Center in Chicago. From the left are Denis Savard, Tony Esposito, Stan Mikita, and Glenn.

17

Home

GLENN HALL PLAYED HIS LAST National Hockey League season, 1970–71, paired with Ernie Wakely. In the off-season, Bowman peddled Jacques Plante to the Toronto Maple Leafs in return for little-remembered forward Brit Selby. Glenn started the year in uncustomary fashion by attending his first full training camp, something he hadn't really done since 1964. In the 32 regular-season games that followed, he posted a 2.41 average, which was a number lower than his career mark and was fourth best in the league. He recorded shutout numbers 83 and 84 for his career, and shared a whitewash with Wakely in Boston, Glenn forced from the net after the second period when he was stricken by heat exhaustion. His best game of the year may have been against Toronto, when Jacques Plante came calling for his first game at the Arena since his trade from the Blues. Hall had 34 saves in a 2–1 win, the victory sealed when the now 39-year-old goalie thwarted a Dave Keon breakaway. At the halfway point of the season, Hall and Wakely led the league in save percentage and were in the thick of the Vezina race. The team finished fourth behind Original Six franchises New York, Chicago, and Boston.

Although his regular-season numbers still ranked him among the league's elite netminders, and peers such as Gerry Cheevers were still trumpeting him as the best in the game, Hall felt his days were certainly now numbered. The truth was that for some time, wife Pauline encouraged Glenn's decision to return to the goal, but now, not even she could persuade him to continue. In the playoffs, the Blues were defeated in the first round by the Minnesota North

Stars four games to two and Glenn lost all three of his starts. He did not play badly, but he did not play to the standards he'd set for himself and upheld consistently over the previous 16 years. His last NHL game was the fifth of that series, a 4–3 loss.

This time the retirement announcement was irrevocable.

Or was it?

After Glenn returned to Alberta, he was contacted by old friend Larry Regan, who was running the L.A. Kings. Regan told Glenn he wanted to sign him for a year, have him work with young Gary Edwards whom they'd acquired, and play maybe 10 to 15 games. Glenn was hesitant, but accepted Regan's offer to visit Los Angeles. The Kings and owner Jack Kent Cooke gave Glenn and Pauline the royal treatment, taking them to the studio where the long-running western *Bonanza* was filmed and introducing them to the show's lead actor and fellow Canadian Lorne Greene, entertaining them at exclusive restaurants, and putting them up in a posh L.A. hotel. In due time, Cooke broached the idea of a contract.

"I really don't care about the money," said Glenn.

"Well, I have to pay you something," replied Cooke.

Ultimately Glenn agreed to join the L.A. franchise as long as it didn't cost the Kings anything to get his rights from St. Louis. So Regan contacted Scotty Bowman, who demanded a first-round draft pick in exchange for Glenn's rights. Regan tried to massage the offer, but the Blues held firm and Glenn stayed retired.

"I was disappointed," said Pauline. "I would have liked to live in L.A." One could easily speculate that had they lived there, it would have been only a matter of time before Pauline had her own talk show. Pauline was always at the center of the off-ice activities, always the life of the party. In St. Louis, she coordinated the post-season banquets and wrote scripts for the sketches that lampooned the players and management. The shows went over so well, the baseball Cardinals asked her if she'd put on a similar deal for their club. Her casting left her with a bit of a guilty conscience though.

"For two years in a row, the husbands of the wives I cast to play Scotty Bowman got traded," she recalled. As it was, retirement was a tough adjustment for her.

"We'd moved so much that at first I couldn't pass up a packing box," she said. "I tried to get involved in various local events and activities, but it just wasn't the same. Glenn never talked about the adjustment very much. But I don't think you can do anything that well and not miss it."

Years later, Glenn summed up his feelings about leaving the game after

witnessing Calgary Flame Lanny McDonald's teary retirement press conference. Hall told the mustachioed wonder, "You never saw a goalie cry when he
retired."

Glenn returned to the farm life in Stony Plain, coaching his son's Junior
team for a time and loudly decrying the growing violence in the game. When
the World Hockey Association came to be in 1972, a franchise was granted to
nearby Edmonton and it was dubbed the Alberta Oilers. Head coach Ray
Kinesewich tapped Hall to work as his assistant and with his goalies.

The Oilers started the season playing good hockey, but Kinesewich soon
witnessed just how little Glenn's intensity had changed as he transitioned
from playing to coaching. The Oilers hit a slump that dropped them from the
top of the league into fourth place. After another loss, the head coach walked
into his office and said he heard Hall retching in the bathroom.

"I had a bad feeling about [the management] early on," Glenn recalled.
"We had an owner [Bill Hunter] who had his hands in everything. I wanted to
get out, but Ray said, 'Hey, don't leave me here alone.'"

Rumors surfaced that with the Oilers struggling, Hall might make a comeback. Although he had the team keep some equipment at the ready, he did not
don the pads until the All-Star break, and then only for a couple of practice
sessions. Still, once the pads were on, those present were sure that Mr. Goalie
had more hockey left in him, one witness describing his practice play as "dazzling." But Hall did not return to the goal and he did not last long in the assistant's job. Hunter fired Kinesewich and Hall in February.

EARLY IN 1973, Glenn faced an athlete's nightmare. The Quebec Police
Commission was conducting a province-wide inquiry into organized crime,
and it called small-time hood Theodore Aboud to testify. Aboud, who was in
the midst of serving a ten-year sentence for fraud, was called to talk about bet-
ting in sports. He alleged that he took action on some hockey games in the
early '60s because he got a tip from a bookie that the goalie for the Chicago
Black Hawks had placed bets on the New York Rangers to beat his own team
that evening, and then again a short time later in a game against the Boston
Bruins. Aboud also named four other games in which this fixing was alleged
to have happened. Aboud never named Hall, but in those days only one goalie
played for Chicago.

The presiding judge of the inquiry, Rheal Brunet, had barred the general
public from the courtroom, but not reporters. However, he never warned the
press that the type of third-person hearsay testimony that would be elicited
could have zero factual worth. The press ran with Aboud's allegation, which

was never researched or substantiated and was totally without foundation. Aboud was likely told about a goalie throwing a game to induce him to make bad wagers, a story crafted by a creative-thinking bookie who'd found an easy mark. Had the charges been leveled at almost any other athlete, the damage could easily have been long-term. But Hall, who'd never so much as played the ponies (a preoccupation with several of his teammates in Chicago), was so universally respected that the scandal quickly blew over.

The allegations were preposterous on their face. The Hawks lost both of the first two games cited, but the second was a 2–0 loss, the second Bruin goal scored into an empty net. The Hawks tied another of the games and won one of them.

An immediate outcry went up from some of hockey's most respected journalists, who came to Glenn's defense. League president Clarence Campbell did as well, issuing a statement: "I have no doubt whatsoever that Glenn Hall's conduct during his 16 seasons in the league is beyond reproach," the statement read. "Throughout his lengthy career, Glenn's reputation for absolute integrity among his fellow players, executives, and hosts of fans is so well established by his personal conduct that it is impossible to give any credence to the undocumented charge that was made against him at the inquiry."

Hall wanted to sue, but Campbell counseled against it, advising him to let it blow over. In retrospect, that was good advice, as that was exactly what happened. The greatest hurt Glenn felt came from the Players' Association, which he felt did not come to his defense in as timely a fashion as it should have.

By 1975, Glenn found himself back in hockey, when he returned to the Blues' organization as its goalkeeping consultant. Hall worked with the Blues' top prospect, Ed Staniowski, who had a brief and solid run with the team, and he also tutored a still-young John Davidson before he was eventually traded to the Rangers before embarking on a long and distinguished broadcasting career. Glenn traveled to St. Louis a few times a year to oversee his charges, but he never stayed away from the farm for very long.

That summer, eldest son Pat was working on a paving crew when a fellow worker flagged him down. "I just heard they're putting your dad in the Hall of Fame," the co-worker announced.

Glenn had been elected to the Hockey Hall of Fame on the first ballot of his eligibility. Because he'd played with three different teams, he got to choose which jersey he wanted to be pictured in for the official HHOF portrait. Logic dictated he would choose the Black Hawks: he was there the longest, won a Cup with the team, and finished the ironman streak while wearing the Chicago colours. But that wasn't the way it went. Instead, he was honored in the sweater of the team he said he most enjoyed playing for: the Blues. That decision made Hall not only the first expansion team player to win a major NHL trophy (Conn Smythe), the first expansion team member to be named an NHL First All-Star, and the first expansion team player to share the Vezina, but also the first member to be inducted into the Hall of Fame wearing an expansion team's jersey. At the ceremony, which was emceed by Blues play-by-play man Dan Kelly, Hall chose former Hawk teammate Stan Mikita to introduce him.

"I was very honored. It was a proud moment for me," Mikita recalled. "I didn't prepare anything because I wanted it to come from my heart. At the time Glenn and Pauline took me in, I didn't really appreciate just how much they were really doing for me. Now, after raising my own family and seeing the favors that people have granted my children along the way, I understand what they meant to me. I mean, how do you really say 'thank you' to someone you love? When I think back about his career though, I think, Jeez . . . I saw him get hit once in the jawbone with a shot. I mean, I heard the shot hit him and it opened him up and they took him to the dressing room and stitched him up and back he comes to finish the game. He used to wear the short goal pads because he liked to move around a lot, and I remember he took a skate above the knee and it ripped his thigh. It had to be an inch deep, and I nearly got sick seeing the cut, and he just gets stitched up and goes back out there. Stupid, eh? All he had to do was say, 'No, I can't go back out there.' I'll tell you, I've never seen more guts than he showed."

Glenn accepted the accolade with typical modesty. "I would like to have played a bit better [in St. Louis]," he said, "because the whole operation, the Blues' organization and the St. Louis fans, were so great. My years in St. Louis made more of an impression on me than anywhere else." Three weeks later, the Goaltenders Club of St. Louis honored Hall for his election with a lavish dinner. A short time later, he was inducted into the Saskatchewan Sports Hall of Fame and the St. Louis Sports Hall of Fame.

Hall stayed with the Blues as a consultant for another year, then in the late '70s signed on in a similar position with the Colorado Rockies. Around this time, Hall also consented to play a few old-timers' games in Chicago and St. Louis.

MR. GOALIE RETURNED TO Chicago to accept the NHL's Milestone Award for having appeared in more than a thousand games in the league. When the Rockies became the New Jersey Devils, he was hired away by the Calgary Flames to tutor their young goalies. Although he had to drive three hours from his home outside Edmonton, Hall professed to enjoy the time alone behind the wheel. Occasionally he hit the road with the team to evaluate the club's goalies. Former Chicago teammate Al MacNeil was also in Calgary management, and the two were seated next to each other in the Chicago Stadium press box during one trip. The Chicago fans had established a new tradition of applauding and cheering wildly while the national anthem was being played. The noise level grew continuously during the song, and the spectacle was enough to raise goose bumps on all in attendance. As the performance concluded and the assemblage began to be seated, McNeil leaned over to The Ghoulie and said, "It's almost enough to make you want to enlist."

As a coach, Glenn made an impact, particularly on the careers of Flames Don Edwards and Mike Vernon, and he was a member of the staff when Calgary won the Stanley Cup in 1989. Many years later, Glenn actively recommended that Scotty Bowman pick up Vernon for the Detroit Red Wings. He did, and Vernon helped the Wings to a Cup, winning the Conn Smythe Trophy on the way. Bowman, whose respect for Hall has no bounds, gave his son, Stan, the middle name Glenn, after Mr. Goalie.

"I never tried to change anyone's style," said Glenn, talking about his goal-keeping philosophy. "But I thought it was important to make sure you saw the puck. If you see it, you've got a chance to stop it, and to see it, you had to have good positioning. But I don't believe in all of this 'You have to be so far out of the net to challenge.' Lateral movement is very important. You have to be a good skater, you know, to be effective in the goal. And if you come out too far, you can't get there laterally when you have to. The chest should be upright of course, and you must be balanced. Balance is not talked about enough, but being well balanced is the foundation of everything. And that really goes back to your skating. If you skate well and have good balance you can explode back with the shooter, you can move laterally, you don't have to be 'locked.' When I played and I faced a breakaway, I had my little 'dance.' I rocked a bit side to side as the shooter approached, and that motion gave me an edge. Now I could go whichever way he wanted to.

"I have a lot of problems with some of today's thinking. Practice, for example. The poor goalies playing today face hundreds of shots each practice. Why? Hard work is good, of course, but too many of them are overdoing it. You can't leave your game at practice. You have to be fresh for the games, and now they make you play each practice like it's a game and that's just impossible. And when a game's over, what do the coaches have them doing? Riding the bike! Let me tell you something. If you've got enough energy left after a game to ride a bike, you didn't give enough during the game."

THE ACCOLADES kept pouring in. In the late '80s, Hall was inducted alongside the likes of Dick Butkus, Walter Payton, and Mike Ditka into the Chicago Sports Hall of Fame. Several years later, in 1993, Mr. Goalie was given the King Clancy Award by *The Hockey News* for meritorious service to the sport, and he was subsequently inducted into the Canadian Sports Hall of Fame. *Sports Illustrated* featured Hall prominently in a special issue devoted to the ten records in sports that will never be broken. Hall was honored for his consecutive-game streak, which was selected as the number-one record least likely to ever fall. When the NHL celebrated its 75th anniversary, Hall was selected as the All-Star goalie for the era from 1943–67. *The Hockey News* named him as their All-Star Goalie for the fifth decade (1957–67) of the NHL's history. In its millennium issue, a panel of hockey "experts" assembled by THN named Glenn the game's 16th-greatest player of all-time, and the third goalie behind Sawchuk and Plante.

"There was a real quiet period there for about ten years," said Pat Hall. "But then it was like a new awakening. Dad was getting all these honors, and in the late '80s it became clear that his career meant a lot to a lot of people's lives. It's been an incredible journey, like being around a retired rock star. We go to these signings and memorabilia shows, and you can see what Dad's career meant to all of these people. It's been great for me, because when I travel with him, I get to spend a lot of time with him, time that I didn't have that much of when he was playing. I'm just so proud of him and everything he did."

Perhaps the greatest honor was bestowed upon him in 1988. The franchise where he'd spent 10 years and where he'd been dubbed "Mr. Goalie," informed him it was going to retire his jersey. The ceremony was to be held November 20, the same night the Chicago Black Hawks were slated to retire the jersey of Hall protégé and successor Tony Esposito. It was the perfect symmetry. Hall had given the Hawks legitimacy, and he was the cornerstone upon which the Stanley Cup–winning team had been built. Esposito, a Hall clone, had lifted the Hawks out of their post-Hall doldrums and led them back to the Stanley Cup finals.

Befitting the magnitude of the honor, the entire Hall clan made the trip to Chicago, spending time at the home of Jack Fitzsimmons but encamping at the luxurious Drake Hotel, compliments of the Hawks. Glenn and family were joined by Stan Mikita and Bobby Hull at a pre-ceremony party at the Fitzsimmons home, when Hawk owner William Wirtz showed up accompanied by his dear friend, player rep Alan Eagleson.

"We all thought Al was a cool guy," recalled Pat Hall. "He was funny, had charisma, made a great impression. But I noticed that my dad wasn't as taken with him as the rest of us."

"Eagleson came up to me and said, 'You don't like me, do you?'" said Glenn. "I said, 'No. I like you fine. I just don't trust you.' He wanted to have a picture taken with me, and I told him I'd let him get that picture if he let me put *my* hand in *his* pocket for a change."

"Dad was right on the money on that guy," said Pat. "But at the time he had all of us fooled."

When Glenn and Pauline, and Tony and Marilyn Esposito, stepped onto the red carpet that had been rolled onto the ice for the pre-game ceremony, they received a heartfelt standing ovation from a standing-room-only crowd. Over 17,000 fans crammed the Stadium, drawn to the game principally because of the tribute, as the Hawks were struggling through a down season. Both men walked toward center ice where they were presented sweaters. Hall took off his suit coat and pulled the white Black Hawk jersey over his head, the black number one proudly stretching down the middle of his back. He took the microphone and looked around the arena he'd starred in for ten years.

A collector of pithy sayings, Glenn likely recalled one of his favorites that went, "No speech can be entirely bad if it is short."

He said simply, "Thank you for putting up with me all those years."

A banner was raised to the Stadium's rafters bearing the number one, the Indian Head logo, and the inscription GLENN HALL 1957–1967.

Afterward, Hall told reporters, "This is truly the greatest honor an athlete can receive. Like Phil Esposito told me, you know there are many people in the Hall of Fame. But there are only a few with their sweaters retired."

That his jersey is retired is not a comment on any future Chicago goalie's ability to wear the sweater. Indeed, anyone could manage that.

The truth is that there is no way another Chicago goalie could ever *fill* that sweater.

And understanding the difference between wearing a sweater and filling it is all the difference in the world. After all is said and done, the only man who could fill it was Number One, Glenn Hall. Mr. Goalie.

ESSAY: YOUTH AND SUNSETS

I WAS FIGHTING THE PUCK.

Just two weeks into the pre-season training for my college team in the fall of 1979, I couldn't stop anything. I was the returning vet, the team's number-one goalie who'd been the most valuable player of the national tournament the season before, and the expectations were wearing on me and showing on the ice. Guesses replaced my instincts. Fear overrode my confidence.

Last winter, the puck had looked enormous. I would move a part of my equipment into its path with ease, without a trace of fear. I'd hated when the puck was at the other end of the ice. "Come on, damn it. Let me show everybody how good I am," I'd muttered to myself. And when the other team got possession, it seemed as if every fiber of my being were completely focused on the puck. I could see the onrushing play in slow motion; I knew before the players did where they were going to shoot or deke. The goalie gloves and leg pads were a seamless part of my body.

This year the pads were heavy and ill-fitting. The gloves shifted uncomfortably from the sweat of my palms, sweat produced not from heat but from fear. As the blur neared, I flinched and blinked, hoping the puck would hit me, knowing it wouldn't. And I dropped to the ice too early, hearing again and again the sickeningly slight rustle of the puck pushing out at the back of the netting.

Well-meaning teammates came by, tapping my pads, and tried to say the right things. Their words were empty. Goaltending can be a lonely business when you play well. But when you struggle, the loneliness is absolute.

In those days, goalie coaches were rare at any level, and I was self-taught as it was. Growing up in Chicago and watching the Original Six was all the goalie coaching I had needed. But in 1979, the days when you could flip on the TV and watch Terry Sawchuk crouch behind that one-of-a-kind mask, see the maskless Gump Worsley sprawl to stop a breakaway, witness Johnny Bower make a poke-check, marvel at Jacques Plante's poise, or admire Ed Giacomin's passing were long gone. Gone also was my idol. Mr. Goalie.

But how do you go back to 1969 when it's 1979? I was in my dorm in suburban Chicago, wallowing in my sieve-based depression and listening to a Blues pre-season game. At one point play-by-play man Dan Kelly reminded his St. Louis audience that tickets were on sale for the pre-season exhibition game against the Hawks on Saturday, October 6. I didn't pay much attention until I heard that the opener would be an old-timers' game featuring the Blues' alumni versus the North Stars' alumni. My ears perked up. "Among the players returning for the Blues will be Doug Harvey, Jimmy Roberts, Frank St. Marseille, Red Berenson, Jacques Plante, and Glenn Hall," announced Kelly, but what I heard was: *If you build it, they will come.*

Two days later, Saturday morning, October 6, I jumped into my 1975 Chrysler Newport and started the five-hour drive south to the St. Louis Arena. If the game was sold out, I planned to buy a ticket from a scalper. I didn't really know if Hall or Plante would suit up, but as long as they were going to be there, something told me I had to be there as well.

It was a perfect autumn day. The drive down Interstate 55 as it cuts through the middle of Illinois is a lot like driving any Canadian highway. It winds through small, friendly towns and past fields that have turned from green to brown, soon to be gray covered in white. I filled the car with with loud Motown music, moving my shoulders to the Temptations and Diana Ross, and made my way across the state. As I neared St. Louis, I saw the Gateway Arch in the distance, its silver skin glistening in the sun. I crossed 55 over the mighty Mississippi River onto Route 40 and passed beyond downtown. I noticed Forest Park on my right, a green oasis of nature trails, small museums, and a zoo, and then just ahead on my left I caught sight of a structure that seemed oddly out of place. Looking like a cross between an armory and a medieval castle, with turret-like towers that served as the building's bookends, I approached the huge dark dome that hovered over white arched doorways.

St. Louis Arena.

I drove between wrought-iron entrance gates and down an incline, parked the car, and ran into the ticket office.

I bought the best ticket I could get, which put me about halfway between the ice surface and the nosebleeds. And when the lady behind the counter handed me the ticket, printed on it was a photo of Glenn Hall and Jacques Plante holding the Vezina Trophy.

This trip was meant to be.

I left the Arena only long enough to check in to a hotel and grab a Steak 'n Shake burger, arriving back just as they opened the gates. I was like a kid at his first game. I wasn't going to chance missing a thing, and as the building filled, I actually began to feel nervous. Maybe it was anticipation. Maybe it was a touch of fear.

No matter how we try, we can never really go back to our youth, can we? We can't go back to the days when heroes were really heroes, when the good guys wore the dark sweaters. What if Hall wasn't there? Even if he was, just exactly what was I hoping to get out of being there? What was I looking for?

The lights near the top of the Arena dimmed, and the crowd applauded. I inched a little closer to the edge of my seat. The PA announcer welcomed the fans and introduced the North Star old-timers, starting with the old Mutt-and-Jeff goaltending team of Cesare Maniago and Gump Worsley. An involuntary smile stretched my face as the rotund Gumper, more fireplug than athlete, skated to the blue line.

But when the organist struck up the strains of "St. Louis Blues," I rose to my feet with the rest of the fans, all of us clapping rhythmically, just as the crowds had done before every period back in the team's first days. The introductions began: Doug Harvey, Red Berenson, Jimmy Roberts, Bob and Barclay Plager, J.P. Picard. The names were magic.

Over the loudspeaker boomed the familiar refrain, "He came out of retirement in 1968 to join the Blues and shared the Vezina Trophy. I give you number 30, Jacques 'Jake the Snake' Plante!" Stepping out onto the ice was the Gallic legend, the man who gave us the mask and who was the first to go behind his net to gather loose pucks. His hair was sprinkled salt and pepper now, but the high cheekbones and the jutting chin were unmistakable. As he made his way toward the blue line, he threw his hands in the air, reprising his post-game victory salute and did a full 360-degree turn. All 16,000 of us present cheered.

Then, finally, came the words I'd been waiting for: "He was an original Blue, the first player chosen by the franchise. Playing from '67 to '71, he was the first West Division player elected to the All-Star team, he won a Vezina, the Conn Smythe Trophy, and he was the first player elected to the Hall of Fame to wear an expansion team's jersey. Ladies and gentlemen, Number One, Mr. Goalie, Glenn Hall!"

Around me the crowd erupted in the loudest ovation of the night. My breath shortened and my eyes teared as I clapped my hands raw. Amid the din Glenn smiled as he skated toward his former teammates. I was shocked. In all the years I'd watched him so closely, never once had I seen Glenn Hall smile on the ice. All of us were swept up in the excitement, clapping and whistling and shouting until Hall acknowledged our appreciation with a bashful wave.

As the players went into their warm-up routine, I watched Plante. With a nod to improved technology, he pulled on a cage/helmet combination instead of his trademark white mask. But when he went into the crease, assumed his catch-glove-scraping-the-ice stance, and faced an onslaught of shots with a relish equal to practice sessions in his playing days, I was transported back to the 1960s. True to form, Hall also attacked his warm-up with his usual gusto: he didn't take a single shot, opting instead to sign autographs along the glass and near the bench.

When the game started, Hall (also wearing a cage) faced his first shot as J.P. Parise fired one from the right side. Hall dipped his knees together and fanned his skates out, perfectly executing the V and shipping the puck harmlessly into the corner. When Plante's turn came later in the game, he chased down a loose puck into the corner to his left and laid a perfect pass onto Picard's stick.

With one minute left in the game, which was tied at three, both benches emptied for a riotous 15-on-15 scrimmage. Hall was the last over the boards, and he made a beeline for the net, joining Plante in the crease.

There they were, together again, the most important goalies ever, now literally side by side.

A 13-year-old boy watched the game that day. The boy was trapped inside the 23-year-old college goalie, but he was there. As I watched Hall and Plante through misty eyes, I rediscovered the feeling that had me put on the pads in the first place, made me really love the game.

I drove home the next day and returned to practice the day after that. I stopped just about everything in that practice and went on to have a great year, backstopping my team to a national championship.

The most important lesson I learned on that trip, though, was that I should never go anywhere or do anything without taking the time to consider and appreciate that 13-year-old boy, ever again.

And I never have.

ESSAY: WEST TO MECCA

THANKSGIVING WAS TRADITIONALLY a time of reflection, a day for giving thanks to God for the success of the harvest. Time and changing cultural values have obscured that meaning, turning the holiday into an orgy of overeating covered in a gravy of football. I'm not by any means religious—if anything the opposite is true—but Thanksgiving in 1999 coincided with a time when I was reexamining the meaning of many things in my life and feeling the need to thank people I hadn't. It is said that reaching middle age will do that to a man.

Some men buy Corvettes, others blondes. I wrote a letter.

It is said that if you love what you do, you never work a day in your life.

I'd been coaching hockey teams for 18 years, with a satisfying level of security doing it, and . . . I hadn't worked in years. Hockey was the one passion in my life whose flame had endured. And I had someone to thank for inspiring me to that path, someone who caught the fancy of a lonely kid who was desperate to be special.

So it was that the day after Thanksgiving '99 I sat down and wrote a letter to Glenn Hall. More than gratitude prompted my missive: I was outraged that Hall, the best of the best, had never been accorded his full due. I'd just read a wonderful biography of Terry Sawchuk. Although the book was insightful and greatly revealing, it fed the assumption that Sawchuk was the greatest. The more I coached goalkeepers, the more convinced I was of Hall's rightful, but not yet acknowledged, place in history. So as much as I enjoyed the Sawchuk book, it also angered me. I got upset every time I turned on the TV. At that time just about every NHL goalie was employing the butterfly, Glenn's eternal legacy, yet clueless announcers christened the move the "Quebec style" of goalkeeping.

Finally the combination of gratitude I felt to Mr. Goalie, fueled by my anger, moved me to write the letter. I thanked Glenn for his career, I built my case as to why I thought he was the greatest, I told him I was outraged that no one had written his biography, and I expressed the hope that I'd get a chance to shake his hand some day. Then I dropped the letter in the mail, and focused on my team's struggling power play and the angst of my approaching 44th birthday.

A week later, I reached into my mailbox to retrieve the usual mix of bills, advertisements, and the weekly allotment of fundraising propaganda from the college I'd graduated from. (That fine institution is apparently unfamiliar with the meager salary of a local hockey coach.) I was leafing through the envelopes on my way to my apartment when I quite literally froze in my tracks. There, among the rubbish, was a letter addressed to me, return address Stony Plain, Alberta, Canada, and above that in a hand I recognized instantly from years of collecting autographed pictures, the single word "Hall."

I don't remember much about how I made it back to my apartment or how I got to sit at my desk, but I vividly recall that I was still gaping, experiencing an emotional cocktail of wonder, joy, exhilaration, trepidation, and fear. What if the letter said, "Thanks, but don't bother me kid"? What if Glenn said I was a little old to be writing fan mail and should seek professional help? Breathing deeply helped bring me back to a semblance of clarity, and I realized I would indeed have to open the letter.

I turned the precious package over gently, with the care of a neurosurgeon. Ever so slowly, I slipped my pinkie under the flap on the back of the envelope, gingerly wedging apart the seal. "Slower, gently," I told myself. "Don't tear anything. This cannot be rushed."

The operation took several minutes, but it was a success. The envelope was now unsealed. With total focus and a deliberateness of purpose that I had displayed only when I was completely on my game, I reached inside the envelope, took the edge of the enclosure, and pinched it gently between my thumb and forefinger. I inched the paper from its cocoon, saw that it was folded thrice, and set it apart from the envelope.

I stared at it for a moment, then I felt myself unfold the letter. It was handwritten.

Dear Chico,

Thank you for the very complimentary letter. If you're in the Edmonton area this summer, I do hope you'll look me up. Stony Plain is about 20 miles west of Edmonton. My phone number is . . .

The good news is I talk better than I write.

Sincerely,

Glenn

He sent me his phone number! He would like me to look him up! This reality was beyond anything I could have hoped for, and for the first time in my life I felt as if my entire body were smiling. It struck me that it was only a matter of time. It was going to happen.

I was going to meet Mr. Goalie.

A full three months after I received Glenn's letter, I'd worked up the courage to dial his phone number. I'd lifted the phone off the receiver many times, punched in the area code, then always put down the receiver again, positive I would fumble my words so badly that whoever was on the other end of the line would be convinced they were being stalked by a muttering fool. The day finally arrived when I admitted to myself that if I waited any longer, Mr. Goalie would have totally forgotten about my letter and his reply.

I neared the phone, lifted the receiver, punched in the numbers, and hung up. On my second attempt, I calmed my nerves by touching each number slowly, counting to three before pressing the next digit. After I tapped the final digit, it seemed like less than a fraction of a second before I heard ringing at the other end of the line. I prayed, hoping for a machine or for the continued ringing of an unanswered phone. But there was a click after the third ring.

"Hello." The voice was sparkling and female.

"Um, yes, may I please speak with Mr. Hall?" I felt as if I were floating outside my body, somewhere above my kitchen and that I was looking down at myself shaking and stammering, my sweaty palms fumbling with the receiver.

"He's not at home. May I take a message?" came the reply.

I wasn't prepared for this answer, but ad-libbed adroitly, "Is this Mrs. Hall?"

"Yes . . ."

"Um, Mrs. Hall, my name is Chico Adrahtas, and I wrote your husband a letter last November. He was kind enough to give me your number as I told him I may be in the Edmonton area this summer, and if our schedules worked out, I might get the chance to meet him. I was his biggest fan and—"

"Where are you calling from, dear?"

"Just outside Chicago."

"Oh, what a lovely city. We had some of our best years there. When were you planning on coming up?"

I was now thrown for a loop. I was planning on coming up any time he'd see me. I suggested, "Well, sometime in August . . ." That was generic enough.

"Well, let me see here. We're going to be away from home the third week in August, so if you're up before then, just give us a call the day before and we'll give you directions to the farm."

"Oh, that'd be great. I can't thank you enough, and I'll be sure to call." There was no turning back. It was going to happen.

"You're quite welcome, dear. What was your name again?"

I WAS SET TO ARRIVE in Edmonton on the first Sunday in August. In the interim, I'd sent Glenn a videotape and with it a note. The tape was a video of my goalie school, including some on-ice footage but, more important, the dry-land sessions in which I lecture the kids on goalkeeping history and tell them why every jersey at the camp bears number one on its back. The note acknowledged my conversation with his wife, told him when I would be in town, and thanked him gratefully for whatever time he could give me.

I'd booked a room in a hotel on Edmonton's western edge, having discerned that Stony Plain was about a 35-minute drive straight west. Once I'd settled in, I picked up and dialed Glenn's phone number. Worst-case scenarios flashed through my mind. What if he'd been called out of town unexpectedly? What if he was home but didn't want to see me? I suddenly felt sure that after seeing the video he wouldn't want to meet this crazed goalie coach who was teaching a new generation of "Hallites."

The phone rang, and Pauline answered again. "Yes, he's here. Just a minute."

The next voice was his. "Hello."

"Hello, Mr. Hall. My name's Chico and I sent you a letter back in November, and you were kind enough to tell me that if I were ever in Edmonton to look you up."

"Oh."

"Um, yes. I recently sent you a videotape and another letter . . ."

"I'm sorry, but I never received a video. Where are you now?"

I was close to panic. I'd sent the tape weeks ago, knowing it would be the clincher in convincing him to see me. It felt as if my chance were about to melt away. "I . . . I'm in Edmonton at the Delta," I stammered.

"Oh, I see. Well, you're about 40 minutes from Stony. When did you want to come out?"

Salvation! The panic bled out, replaced by elation. Poise . . . poise . . . calm . . . "Any time that's convenient for you, sir," I exclaimed.

"How about tomorrow around 2:00 p.m. I'm golfing in the morning, but I'll be home easily by then."

"Two's great, Mr. Hall."

"Please call me Glenn."

"Um, yes, uh, Glenn, 2:00 . . ."

"Let me get you some directions."

I copied his instructions to the letter, repeated them to make sure I got them right, and thanked him profusely, far too much most likely, but with total sincerity. When I put the receiver down, I performed an impromptu dance, punctuating it with several arm thrusts—a gyration more befitting a goal-scoring soccer player than a hockey coach.

I learned that night that it is extremely difficult to sleep when your eyes refuse to shut.

The next morning, I got into my rental car, leaving the hotel an hour and 15 minutes before I was expected at the Halls. Leave wiggle room in case of a flat, I always say.

The journey took me along a well-kept highway and past a series of quaint, rural burgs. Turning south off the highway, I entered Stony Plain, a town of immaculate streets, meticulously manicured homes, and flowers hanging from baskets hooked to the lampposts, bordering walkways, outlining front yards.

I drove along the main street then onto a rural route. After a right turn, I traveled along a two-lane road past rolling green fields, dotted with trees, occasional hay bundles, and farmhouses set back from the road. I slowed to a crawl as I got closer . . . and took my first look. The entrance drive was bordered with trees and clearly wound back some distance. I could see neither the main house nor the legendary barn. But this was the place.

I'd arrived at the Hall farm 15 minutes early. I drove slowly past, made a U-turn, passed the farm slowly again. I rehearsed in my head the questions I'd always wanted to ask and how to present my idea for Glenn's biography. Be prepared, get it all done in 30 minutes, I kept telling myself. Getting to meet Glenn was beyond belief as it was, and I figured I had no right to expect any more time than that. I drove past the farm again, killed a few more minutes, went over my questions again, and tried my best to gather my wits. Then I approached the drive and turned in.

The driveway wound past a small cabin on the right, and there on the left was the barn, as red as a stoplight and well painted indeed. Up ahead to the right was the main house, a car, and a well-worn pickup truck parked in front of the garage. What most caught my eye was a vast, hilly field off to the left, wooden fencing on its borders, cattle grazing contentedly, trees on the far-off ridge kissed by a gentle breeze. A pond, its waters motionless, sat between the pasture and the back land of the main house. I slowed to a stop next to the truck and saw the door to the house swing open.

Getting out of the car, I reached into the back seat where I had a couple of writing samples, some short stories with hockey themes, along with sweatshirts emblazoned with my goalie-camp logo for Glenn, and an arrangement of flowers for Mrs. Hall. Someone approached me, but I was still awed enough by the setting and intimidated enough by the coming encounter not to look up.

"Well, hello there."

The man approaching me had familiar hooded eyes, and a welcoming smile crossed his face as he extended his hand.

"Mr. Hall, this is such an honor."

"You found it okay?"

"The directions were perfect."

"Come on in."

I followed Glenn past a wooden carving of two birds painted as farmers with the inscription TWO OLD CROWS LIVE HERE. We entered the house and walked into the kitchen where I met his wife, Pauline.

"So you're a fan of Glenn's, eh?" she said.

"I'm *the* fan," I replied as I handed her the bouquet.

We moved into the living room which like the rest of the house, was modest and comfortable. After we sat and made small talk, I started to ask my questions.

"Mr. Hall," I began.

"Please, Glenn."

I knew I would never get used to calling him by his first name.

"When I was playing," I began, "I always tried to wrap my skate around the outside of the post when the puck was behind the net. Now everybody teaches that that's wrong, and I always got scored on when I did it. But you did it all the time. Why did you do it and how did you get away with it?"

Glenn's brow furrowed a bit.

"You noticed that about Glenn?" asked Pauline.

"I noticed everything about how he played," I said.

Glenn explained that he adapted the move from baseball, emulating a slide technique that he felt gave him better quickness and coverage.

"The other thing I always wondered about," I asked, "was that 360-degree turn you'd make after a save, especially going to your right. At first I thought when I saw you do it, it was just something that happened, but then I saw you do it several times. And I got some old footage of you playing for Detroit and you were doing it there, so I know it was for a reason."

Hall paused again, clearly taken aback by the question. "You know, no one's ever asked me that before."

We'd made the connection. We were both speaking the same language, the mother tongue of the society of goalkeepers. My 30 minutes became an hour, and the conversation turned to the current crop of NHLers. Glenn's genuineness, his quiet dignity, his obvious comfort with Pauline swept over me, and I decided to abandon any idea of trying to talk him into doing his biography. Bringing it up would have cheapened this experience. How many people get the chance to meet their heroes? I wondered. And how many people, when they do, are disappointed?

At 3:30 p.m., Glenn glanced at his watch. "Did you get a chance to drive through Stony Plain at all?" he asked

"Just the main road on my way here."

"If you're not in a hurry, you can take a ride with me. I've got to run some errands."

Minutes later, I was in the passenger seat of the beat-up old pickup that fit Glenn like a custom-built set of Kennesky leg pads. We cruised around Stony, Mr. Goalie showing me the local rink, the tiny downtown area, and the incredible murals depicting the town's history that are painted on the sides of selected buildings. He pulled up to the post office and hopped inside to retrieve his mail. When he got back into the truck, he placed the bundle of mail between us. There, on top of the pile, sat the package containing the video I'd sent weeks earlier. We both remarked about the eerie coincidence.

The next stop was the liquor store. "What kind of beer do you like?" he asked as we entered the store.

"I'm not a drinker," I replied.

Glenn grabbed a case of Busch and placed it on the counter. After the cashier totaled the bill, I picked up the case, intending to carry it to the truck.

"What are you doing?" I heard Glenn ask.

"Well, I thought the least I could do was help."

"Hell, no. You're not drinking it. You might drop it. I just can't take that chance."

THE 30 MINUTES I'd hoped for turned into a tour of the town, a dinner invitation, and after-dinner conversation. It was nearly 10:00 p.m.

As I was leaving to return to the hotel, Glenn and Pauline walked me to my car and, to my utter astonishment, asked me back the next day. Day 2 held more goalie conversation, another truck ride—this time around the rural backroads—and another dinner invitation. At the conclusion of that second day, Glenn shook my hand heartily, and I enjoyed a warm hug from Pauline. Although my dream was coming to an end, I felt absolutely no sadness: I'd had 48 hours I never could have imagined.

"I'm coming to Chicago in October," Glenn mentioned as we said our goodbyes. "The Hawks are dedicating a statue for the 75th anniversary of the franchise. I'll give you a call and maybe we can get together for lunch."

It was the kind of thing that is said politely between people, the kind of thing you do not hold someone to, especially when that someone is a Hall of Fame goalkeeper with plenty of demands on his time, especially when he's returning to the scene of so many of his triumphs to be reunited with a bevy of former teammates and all the reminiscing and catching up they were sure to do.

Still, I must tell you I wasn't surprised one bit when the phone rang one Thursday morning in October and I heard, "Well, hello, Chico. It's Glenn."

Postscript

Two Old Crows Live Here

THESE DAYS GLENN AND PAULINE HALL'S golden years center around family and close friends. Three of their four children, Pat, Leslie, and Lindsay, live within an easy drive, and Glenn and Pauline speak frequently with Tammy, who lives in Saskatchewan.

The Hall family stands as a remarkable testament to a simpler time when the term *family values* was more than a convenient political slogan.

Eldest son, Pat Hall, is the western regional sales manager for Pembridge Insurance. He and his wife, Debbie, have two children, daughter, Carly, and son, Ryan, who followed his grandfather into the nets.

"We were raised modestly," he says. "We never felt like we were wealthy. I could relate to every friend we had and it didn't matter what their parents did. Mom and Dad weren't interested in excess. They lived within their means and we learned to do the same. Just imagine what they went through to get where they got. I mean, they were just a couple of farm kids who found themselves in these big cities. They weren't intimidated, and they didn't allow themselves to be swallowed up by them. That's pretty amazing in and of itself.

"I respect [Dad] so much, the mental toughness he had. When I think of what he went through . . . when I go through tough times I feel like a sissy. He takes a puck in the mouth and goes back out there. How did he have the courage to do that? He's my dad, but he's also one of my favorite people.

"I wonder how I would have reacted if I'd been Dad's age when he got his first contract, if, in this day and age, someone handed me $400,000 and called me a superstar. How would I have handled it? But with Mom and Dad, nothing changes them. They're secure and comfortable and we always felt that."

Daughter Leslie is married to Tom Stevenson, and they are the parents to Michelle, Grant, and Megan. Grant plays Division I National Collegiate Athletic Association hockey in Minnesota.

Leslie flashes a warm smile as she recalls: "I'd be lying if I said I didn't consider myself lucky to be able to watch my dad play hockey in the NHL. As a kid, my attention was focused on the fact that I'd have to start classes at a new school every fall and make new friends. Looking back, I realize that our life was more than merely this routine. I certainly realized we had a different and somewhat more exciting lifestyle than our friends in that we traveled so much. There were definite perks. We enjoyed going to the games and practices and later, in St. Louis, the Florida vacation that the Salomons gave us.

"I was totally blown away by my dad's achievements. The NHL consecutive-game streak was so amazing, and then when you add the All-Star games and minor-league years, it becomes even more remarkable. It's even more impressive when you realize how inferior his equipment was compared with the suits of armor today's goalies wear. It's always made a big impression on me that he was able to own one of only six available goaltender positions in the NHL.

"As much as I admire my dad, I'm equally proud of my mom. Her sense of community has gotten her involved with so many different organizations and clubs everywhere we've lived. She feels she's just as deserving of recognition for her accomplishments such as 500th consecutive meal served or 1,000th shirt ironed, as my dad is for his. She hasn't quite mastered the humble part!"

Daughter Tammy is married to Kelvin Mennie, and she is the mother of Sadie and Cole. "When we went to the games, he was just my dad," remembers Tammy. "But I knew something was different because it took us 30 minutes to get to the car. All these people would be saying nice things to my dad and asking for autographs and I'd wonder, 'Why are they doing that?' We go places, and you realize by the reaction of people that he's famous. But to me, he's just such a wonderful guy. Growing up, I remember St. Louis the best. We lived on the Salomon ranch with wide-open spaces and horses.

"I don't know how [Mom] did it. I only have two kids and it's a challenge. And she didn't have any help. The Christmases with Dad not home . . . I think she deserves a lot of credit. She's so outgoing, and I think I got that from her. I love people, and my mom would open her house to anyone.

"Dad, well, I'm just so very proud to be his daughter. The records he earned that will never be broken, it's just amazing. I'm thankful that my kids got to know what he did. He's been out of hockey for so long and still everyone remembers. They are amazing people, my parents. I love them with all my heart."

Youngest son, Lindsay, and his wife, Angie, are the parents of the Hall's youngest grandson, Luke. Lindsay saw the least of Glenn's career, but he remembers St. Louis fondly: "I had the best childhood. I was able to see a lot. But I didn't really see my dad play. He really only took me to the games when [Jacques] Plante played because he was too nervous when he was playing.

"It was great to grow up in a small town. My parents were very caring. Mom and Dad always put us first. I think of all the things that they went through and then I think the worst that's ever happened to me might be being bitten by a dog!

"My childhood was very normal because Dad had retired from hockey when I was only six, and he was farming full-time. I'm proud of Dad for what he's done, and how he's remained so humble and sincere. You get the feeling Dad enjoys having a beer with me and my friends as much as spending time with anyone else."

"We lived vicariously through Dad," summarizes Pat. "We went to some wild places. But what means more than any of the stats is the fact that he's just such a genuine person. Mom and Dad's example taught us that your occupation doesn't make you special. We also saw that marriage was a team effort. There is a great balance between them."

In return, Pauline replies, "Our children have given us these wonderful accolades, but we want to express our love for them, as they've been a credit to us."

PAULINE HALL'S SELF-CONFIDENCE is unmistakable. But under the brash sense of humor and obvious strength is a vulnerability and a warmth that is both comforting and welcoming. A handsome woman who comes across younger than her years, she has eyes that still sparkle and she exudes a protective pride over her husband's accomplishments. When you talk to the contemporaries of the Halls, Pauline is brought up as frequently as Glenn.

And, after all these years, she is still the life of the party. Recently she oversaw a roast of Glenn as a benefit for Stony Plain's hosting of the Allan Cup competitions, the championship of senior hockey in Canada. Son Lindsay had played on the 1999 champions, the Stony Plain Eagles. She coaxed Stan Mikita, Gerry Melnyk, Lanny McDonald, Al Coates, and Keith Magnuson to Stony on their own dime to participate in the show, which she eventually stole. When it was her turn to do the roasting, she surveyed the dais and quipped, "I didn't know Glenn had so many low friends in high places. I bet you didn't know Glenn and I met on a blind date. The guy who set us up was blind."

Hockey is still a feature in their lives, though Pauline says, "My memories of the years Glenn played have more to do with the people. I think of how good everyone was to us, the great friends we made. My dad was Glenn's biggest fan and he'd come down from Saskatchewan to watch the games, and he and Bill Hay just got along famously. The game doesn't mean much to me. It's the people. The game is so overrated. It's so ridiculous. Someone is so famous for shooting a puck? Are we as familiar with the man who invented the polio vaccine? Do we know the names of the brain surgeons?

"Now, so much of [hockey] is show business. I don't like that it looks like today's athletes invented the game. The older guys had to sue just to get $100,000 [in the Eagleson case]. That's such a black mark on hockey. I don't begrudge the players for the money they're getting, but I do feel resentful. It would have been nice to have enough money so our kids didn't have to have any money worries. When Joe Sakic won one of those awards, he thanked his wife for holding down the fort. I thought to myself, 'What fort is she holding down? Fort Knox?'"

These days she claims, "I almost forget that Glenn played hockey. The other night, they were awarding the Conn Smythe Trophy, and I look out my window at the guy cutting grass in the front yard and he's won that very same award, yet we think nothing of it."

But she does feel that his accomplishments are often short-changed: "Of course we all thought Glenn was the best. But we couldn't say that. I do think they should have retired his sweater in St. Louis as well. If those teams hadn't been successful, expansion might have failed. And Glenn was the biggest reason for the Blues' success."

GLENN HALL IS A MAN fully at ease with retirement. He spends his days tending to his farm, woodworking, hunting, and getting in the occasional round of golf. He is passionate about the issues he feels are important in matters of politics and hockey.

In Glenn's opinion, the Canadian government has lost sight of the importance of the country's farmers. Behind this disgust with the government lies a true patriotism, a full and deep appreciation for what his country should be. It is similar to the way he views the hockey world.

"Someone should write a book about the wives," he insists. "The wives and the trainers. The athletes would be nowhere without them. The wives were so important to the success of the team. And so many of them that we knew were terrific. What words can describe what Pauline meant to my career? Every one of us who made it can say the same thing.

"The trainers were the other heroes. A good trainer on a team meant so much. We had Nick Garen in Chicago and Tommy Woodcock in St. Louis, and those guys were the true backbones of the teams. No one talks enough about how difficult their jobs are, and how much they really contribute."

Today Glenn believes: "The players have never been better, the speed of the game is unbelievable, but the game is not as good as it was even ten years ago. A large part of the blame goes to the interpretation of the rules. Defensive hockey is not hooking, holding, and interference. Defensive hockey is being in a position to make an offensive play more difficult. Defensive hockey is not making the goalie pads two inches bigger and, because there are not enough goals, proposing to make the nets bigger.

"Hockey is such a great game that it bothers me that the head office in the NHL is not a collection of hockey people, but a bunch of business people trying to sell overpriced seats in all the arenas. I would have to think it's the same people who dictate to the officials how the game is to be called.

"The huge number of injuries in today's game is partly due to the speed and size of the players, but mostly because charging and boarding are simply not called. Because the officials refuse to call charging and boarding [except if the wrong team is up in the last two minutes of a game], the league puts in the new "checking from behind" rule . . . which is a great rule, except for the fact that if charging and boarding were being called, the new rule would be totally unnecessary. Unfortunately the NHL rules and the enforcement of those rules filter down to minor hockey.

"In today's game, even the wimps are tough because they are 'gang tough.' There's no accountability for those actions. The goon coaches say, 'Let them play,' which of course is to the advantage of the goon teams. It bothers me that a goon is called an 'enforcer.' We give in to the Don Cherry mentality of 'If we're not goons or play goon hockey, we do not want to win badly enough.' The officials are simply not doing a good job. Who is telling them what to call and what not to call? We are not supposed to yell at the referees, but the health and life of the players are in their hands. Yet it seems they are rewarded for doing a poor job. A parent should not have to watch their child injured in the name of hockey.

"I've gotten to the point where I hope Luke and Cole [his youngest grandsons] never play. This great game is being pulled down to the level of World Wrestling Entertainment."

Glenn and Pauline remain the strong team that shepherded the Hall family through the trials, tribulations, and triumphs of Glenn's Hall of Fame career. Pauline busies herself tending to the vegetable garden while Glenn sees to the lawn care. Both make time to fawn over grandson Luke and attend the doings of their other grandkids. They speak with their children daily, the relationships warm, strong, genuine, and welcome. The humor that so many of their friends remark upon and appreciate is still strong.

While Pauline tends to burgers on the grill, Glenn relaxes in a lawn chair, sipping a cold Busch, regaling a visitor with tales of his youth. "Yes," he begins, after savoring a sip of the frosty brew, "I broke a lot of hearts back when I was single."

Without skipping a beat or looking up from the grill, one hears Pauline's voice. "I wish you'd broken one more."

A small smile crosses Glenn's face. "Can I help you at all?"

"I wish you could," comes the sarcastic reply.

Underneath his breath, Glenn gets the last word as he whispers, "As long as the answer was no."

Afterword

WHEN THE HISTORY of goalkeeping is considered, the usual comparisons pit Glenn against Terry Sawchuk and Jacques Plante to determine the best ever. Although I addressed those comparisons in the opening of this book, I don't want to overlook the modern goalkeepers.

Let me start by dispelling yet another myth. There is an automatic assumption that the National Hockey League today is far superior, and therefore more challenging to the modern-day goalie. I don't buy that for a second. Glenn Hall himself believes that today's goalies are a marvelous and supremely talented lot, at least the equal of him and his peers. Also, I am not one so lost in the long-ago days of my youth that I believe the game then was just as fast, the shots just as hard. But I'm convinced that legitimate factors made goalkeeping back in those days more challenging than it is today, even conceding that the game itself and the shots themselves are faster.

First, some players in the days before masks could shoot the puck in the area of 100 miles an hour. There weren't as many as there are today, but in those days the puck was hammered at goalies off blades with unregulated curves. The resulting shots were trickier than the truer shots produced with today's more consistently superior power. The backhand, one of hockey's most effective shots, was a regularly employed weapon, effective because of its unpredictable pitch and the power that could be mustered behind it. In the '50s and into the early '60s, the backhand was the shot of choice before it devolved in favor of the slap shot.

The players are more athletic in this day and age, the product of year-round training and technology. But the athletes back then were the best of their day, and if they had the knowledge, training access, and free off-seasons of today's athletes, those differences in fitness would all even out. So what then really sets the old guard apart from today's hulking techno-athletes?

How would today's goalies fare if they had to work another job over the summer to support their families? How much more of a mental strain would it be to play without long-term, guaranteed contracts? What effect would it have on the game of the modern goalie if he faced the reality that a few bad games in a row could mean the end of his NHL career? How much more taxing would it be to know there were only six NHL jobs in the entire world, that the line to fill these places was circling the block, and that the spots weren't being protected by an agent?

In comparing today's goalies with those of the '50s and '60s, it is an insult to the old guard to ignore those mental factors in this, the most mentally demanding of all positions in sport.

Now, mix in the very real threat of physical harm, a factor much more distinct and threatening back in the Golden Era of the game. The puck was just as hard back then, and it was the same size. Hall and Co. wore wafer-thin arm pads and a modified baseball-catcher belly pad. The catch glove had no padding, goalies' necks were totally exposed, and portions of their legs were bare, the skates were less protective, and wearing a mask was considered cowardly. Masks at that time protected the wearer from cuts, not from the concussive power of the shot. The ears, the back of the head, and the eyes were vulnerable. What protection goalies did wear, and it was a fraction of what is worn today, weighed four times as much as contemporary armor.

To sum up, the old guard wore equipment that protected them less but weighed more, and they didn't strength-train or have the modern advantages of conditioning. In other words, they handled that heavier burden while in lesser physical condition. They labored under the constant threat of losing their jobs, were never offered more than one-year contracts, had no agents protecting their interests, and were forced to support their families by working summer jobs.

What about the most basic element of the job, protecting the net? Today's goalies face shots that get there quicker, but they also protect a smaller area than their forebears. The reason? The equipment. Today's padding is so much more protective and covers so much more area than in the old days that any meaningful comparison is almost comical. The five-hole is a third of the size today that it was then. The upper-body protection is enormous, and when a goalie's angle is cut properly today, the shooter can see nothing of the net behind him. In the old days, the shooter could always see something, no matter how well a goalie positioned himself. So the old-school goalie still had to react to shots that today's goalie can simply respond to with a pre-planned defense (like the paddle-down). The butterfly is so successful today in part because so much of the net is covered, and when one realizes this, admiration for Hall's ability to develop this style and use it successfully—wearing equipment only a fraction of the size used by goalies today—grows exponentially. Simply stated, Glenn was, at the very least, as quick as today's quickest goalies, and probably quicker. Using the same style, he had to cover more net because the equipment was smaller.

How do some of the more frequently mentioned modern goalies compare in the bid to be considered the best ever?

We can quickly eliminate Soviet Olympian Vladislav Tretiak as a contender. In truth, it's a mystery to me how he ever got mentioned in the first place, although it's safe to say that he isn't shy when it comes to tooting his own horn. Tretiak has rightfully earned a spot as one of, if not *the*, greatest goalie outside the NHL. But that's the point. Outside the NHL. Tretiak didn't play so much as a single minute of NHL hockey. He did play in a few series against league teams, but we never once saw him under day-to-day NHL fire. True greatness is marked by consistency over time, and while I'm not ready to concede that the Soviet Union outgoaltended Canada in the immortal '72 series, even if I did, that was *one series*. With that logic, Steve Penny should be immortalized for his run in the playoffs with the '84 Montreal Canadiens.

Why shouldn't Tretiak and the Soviet Union's abysmal failure in the '80 Olympics be given equal weight, if we're going to elevate him based on that single '72 series? If you look at the model of international hockey and use that reasoning, U.S. Olympian Jim Craig would rate somewhere on the list, and he couldn't handle the transition from the international game to the NHL. Craig was not alone in that failure. *None* of the international goalies who tried their hand in the NHL from the '70s succeeded, and many of them, like Czech Jiri Crha, were considered very close in ability to Tretiak. It's quite a stretch to think he would have fared any better. So strike Vlad from consideration.

Tony Esposito, Ken Dryden, and Bernie Parent were the best NHL goalies of the '70s. No one gives them serious consideration when ranking the best ever, but they all had tremendous runs and are deserved Hall of Famers. Where they fail is in the test of time. Two of the three, Dryden and Parent, didn't last nearly as long as the big three of Hall, Sawchuk, or Plante, and only one of them, Dryden, had the type of consistency that must be considered a key to serious consideration. Esposito played heroically behind good and bad Chicago teams, but he hung on too long: the last years of his career were spent in bitter ineffectiveness. Parent's run at the top was far too short-lived, his career numbers always a direct reflection of the strength of the team in front of him.

In the '80s, there were some significant talents. Grant Fuhr would have been terrific in any era. In terms of sheer talent, I believe when he was at the top of his game he was as good as anyone ever. But his down years were lower than low, and when coupled with his off-ice issues (alleged drug abuse), any claim he could make to the top is suspect. Billy Smith was a tremendous clutch performer, another goalie whose place in the Hall of Fame is secure. But his numbers don't reach the impressive levels when we're picky enough to determine the best of all time, despite his clutch playoff performances.

From the '80s emerged a young goalie who dazzled the NHL from his first appearance on, and who has remained effective throughout a career that is growing in legend with each appearance he makes. Patrick Roy burst onto the scene in 1985 and has maintained a consistent level of excellence that places him in serious contention with the big three. He's won Stanley Cups, and he's won the Conn Smythe an unprecedented three times. But for all of his successes, he doesn't approach Glenn's number of All-Star nods, and that's significant because it means he wasn't considered the best goalie of the year as consistently among his peers as Glenn was. There are other factors. Roy doesn't compare with the big three in his puck-handling skills. He's been a disaster out of the net. If all else is equal, that's a tiebreaker. One can't be overly impressed with his ability to make the easy save look difficult.

I'm a goalkeeping traditionalist in the sense that I dislike the hotdogging Roy does. His "I just caught this shot at my knees, but I'm going to thrust my glove up in the air as if I'd made a superhuman stop" act is the type of showboating reminiscent of Jacques Plante at his worst. Announcers buy it, ESPN loves it. Television has furthered the Roy mystique more than Roy's goalkeeping has. Again, let me be clear. I don't want to say Roy isn't one of the best. I think he is. He won Cups with teams that weren't close to the strongest teams Montreal fielded. But the extra nonsense that got him much-deserved negative press, like the trade-inducing tantrum that signaled his exit from Montreal, was so undignified that it is rightfully another tie-breaking factor if all else is even. Glenn's consecutive-game streak couldn't be broken by physical injury or illness and certainly would never have been aborted over such juvenile antics, whereas Roy's pride and ego got the better of him. From a numbers standpoint, unlike Hall, Roy's goals-against twice went above 3. His shutout production doesn't compare with Glenn's (who incidentally averaged 5.25 blanks a season versus Sawchuk's 5.15 over their careers). The bottom line becomes a choice between which goalie you'd rather have on your side over the course of a season, and reliable, consistent, unassuming, dignified excellence wins out. Character must still count.

The '90s have brought some wonderful talents as well, the most obvious being Dominik Hasek. The first goalie to leave Euro-hockey and truly become a star, Hasek endured a start to his career not unlike Hall's. People took a look at his methods and were sure he couldn't last. Not only did he last, he was brilliant, and brilliant behind teams of varying strength. It is doubtful that Hasek's snow angels will leave the goalkeeping legacy that Glenn's butterfly has. Although I feel confident in my prediction, let time be the judge. Hasek's career hasn't lasted as long as the big three's, and that's a separating factor. But in terms of sheer talent, Hasek, like Roy, is worthy of mention in the same breath. But also like Roy, Hasek will fall short of the First All-Star measuring stick.

To get a sense of how good Glenn was, allow me a Dr. Frankenstein moment. Take Patrick Roy's basic style. Incorporate Hasek's agility, Fuhr's acrobatics, Martin Brodeur's puck-handling, Curtis Joseph's fearlessness, and Mike Richter's skating. Add a generous helping of humility, coupled with a large sense of responsibility to family and to team. What you've stitched together is the best of the best, the greatest goalie who ever played.

You've just created Number One, Glenn Hall.

Mr. Goalie.

Statistics

AMERICAN HOCKEY LEAGUE (AHL)
REGULAR SEASON

Year	Team	GP	W	L	T	SO	GAA
1951–52	Indianapolis Capitols	68	22	40	6	0	3.89

WESTERN HOCKEY LEAGUE (WHL)
REGULAR SEASON

Year	Team	GP	W	L	T	SO	GAA
1952–53	Edmonton Flyers	63	27	27	9	2	3.29
1953–54	Edmonton Flyers	70	29	30	11	0	3.70
1954–55	Edmonton Flyers	66	38	18	10	5	2.83
Totals		**199**	**94**	**75**	**30**	**7**	**3.27**

PLAYOFFS

Year	Team	GP	W	L	SO	GAA
1952–53	Edmonton Flyers	15	10	5	0	3.51
1953–54	Edmonton Flyers	13	7	6	2	3.37
1954–55	Edmonton Flyers	16	11	5	1	2.58
Totals		**44**	**28**	**16**	**3**	**3.15**

NATIONAL HOCKEY LEAGUE (NHL)
REGULAR SEASON

Year	Team	GP	W	L	T	SO	GAA
1952–53	Detroit Red Wings	6	4	1	1	1	1.67
1954–55	Detroit Red Wings	2	2	0	0	0	1.00
1955–56	Detroit Red Wings	70	30	24	16	12	2.10
1956–57	Detroit Red Wings	70	38	20	12	4	2.21
1957–58	Chicago Black Hawks	70	24	39	7	7	2.86
1958–59	Chicago Black Hawks	70	28	29	13	1	2.97
1959–60	Chicago Black Hawks	70	28	29	13	6	2.56
1960–61	Chicago Black Hawks	70	29	24	17	6	2.51
1961–62	Chicago Black Hawks	70	31	26	13	9	2.63
1962–63	Chicago Black Hawks	66	30	20	15	5	2.47
1963–64	Chicago Black Hawks	65	34	19	11	7	2.30
1964–65	Chicago Black Hawks	41	18	17	5	4	2.43
1965–66	Chicago Black Hawks	64	34	21	7	4	2.63
1966–67	Chicago Black Hawks	32	19	5	5	2	2.38
1967–68	St. Louis Blues	49	19	21	9	5	2.48
1968–69	St. Louis Blues	41	19	12	8	8	2.17
1969–70	St. Louis Blues	18	7	8	3	1	2.91
1970–71	St. Louis Blues	32	13	11	8	2	2.42
Totals		**906**	**407**	**326**	**163**	**84**	**2.49**

PLAYOFFS

Year	Team	GP	W	L	SO	GAA
1955–56	Detroit Red Wings	10	5	5	0	2.78
1956–57	Detroit Red Wings	5	1	4	0	3.00
1958–59	Chicago Black Hawks	6	2	4	0	3.50
1959–60	Chicago Black Hawks	4	0	4	0	3.37
1960–61	Chicago Black Hawks	12	8	4	2	2.02
1961–62	Chicago Black Hawks	12	6	6	2	2.58
1962–63	Chicago Black Hawks	6	2	4	0	4.17

1963–64	Chicago Black Hawks	7	3	4	0	3.24
1964–65	Chicago Black Hawks	13	7	6	1	2.21
1965–66	Chicago Black Hawks	6	2	4	0	3.80
1966–67	Chicago Black Hawks	3	1	2	0	2.73
1967–68	St. Louis Blues	18	8	10	1	2.43
1968–69	St. Louis Blues	3	0	2	0	2.29
1969–70	St. Louis Blues	7	4	3	0	2.99
1970–71	St. Louis Blues	3	0	3	0	3.00
Totals		**115**	**49**	**65**	**6**	**2.7**

KEY:

GP = Games Played   W = Wins   L = Losses
T = Ties   SO = Shutouts   GAA = Goals Against Average

AWARDS

1950–51 Red Tilson Trophy (Ontario Hockey Association MVP)

1951–52 Indianapolis Capitols MVP

1955–56 Calder Trophy (NHL Rookie of the Year)

1957–58, 1959–60, 1960–61, 1962–63, 1964–65 Chicago Black Hawks MVP

1961 Stanley Cup

1963, 1967, 1969 Vezina Trophy

1967–68 St. Louis Blues MVP

1968 Conn Smythe Trophy (Playoff MVP; first expansion player to win league-wide trophy)

1968 John E. Wray Award (Outstanding St. Louis athlete)

1989 Stanley Cup (Calgary Flames, as assistant coach)

ALL-STAR TEAMS

1953–54 Western Hockey League First Team All-Star

1956–57, 1957–58, 1959–60, 1962–63, 1963–64, 1965–66, 1968–69

NHL First Team All-Star (Only athlete in any sport to be a First All-Star on three different teams—Detroit, Chicago, St. Louis)

1955–56, 1960–61, 1961–62, 1966–67 NHL Second Team All-Star

RECORDS

13 All-Star game appearances (This is the most ever in history for a goalie)

502 consecutive games

115 playoff appearances (More than any other goalie in the pre-four rounds of playoffs)

84 regular–season shutouts (Third all-time highest recorded in NHL history)

HALL OF FAME INDUCTIONS

1974 Edmonton Sports Hall of Fame

1975 Hockey Hall of Fame

1987 Sweater retired by the Chicago Black Hawks

1991 Saskatchewan Sports Hall of Fame

1993 Canada's Sports Hall of Fame

Acknowledgments

GLENN HALL COOPERATED WITH and authorized this biography, but the person he least liked to talk about was himself. The time I spent interviewing him was a joy for me, and I suspect torturous for him. He loved talking about goalkeeping and all of the philosophies and intricacies of the position. He was completely at ease relating the terrific locker-room stories and reflecting on the positive traits of so many of his teammates and coaches. His conviction that athletic trainers aren't appreciated anywhere near enough is absolute. And he is convinced that it is hockey wives who are deserving of having a book written about them. But in the time I spent with him, never once did he toot his own horn.

To be sure, there is a quiet confidence about the man, and I get the feeling he knows his rightful place in history. The point of this book, however, is to make sure that *you*, the reader, know it. The desire to get that message across loud and clear comes completely from me.

If I have accomplished the depth I set out for in fleshing out the story of this remarkable man, I owe a great deal to those who shared their stories. Friends of Glenn's, such as Jim Kacourek, Graham Crossman, Murray Parker, and Pat Walker had crystal-clear memories of long ago. Thanks to the remarkable Jack Fitzsimmons, a dear friend of the Halls and a lifelong Black Hawk loyalist who understands the meaning of the proud Chicago sweater much better than current Hawk management.

When news of this project began to circulate, the line formed of former coaches and teammates who wanted to contribute. Thanks to Jimmy Skinner for his insights. Scotty Bowman's observations were fascinating to listen to and provided great perspective. Whenever I saw the late Tommy Ivan around the old Stadium or at the United Center, I pestered him for information and culled some wonderful material from the ensuing conversations. Great thanks to Glenn's teammates and peers, including Stan Mikita, Red Berenson, John McKenzie, Billy McCreary, Ed Litzenberger, the late Gerry Melnyk, Ted Lindsay, Gary Sabourin, Bill Hay, Gary Edwards, Dave Dryden, Charlie Hodge, and Dickie Moore.

Collecting and sifting through the right source material was a labor of love, and I wish to thank the staff at the Hockey Hall of Fame archives, especially Tyler Wolesowich. Thanks also for hours of patience to the staffs of the Public Libraries Microfilm and Research Departments in Detroit, St. Louis, and Chicago. Contributions were also made by the Humboldt, Saskatchewan, Chamber of Commerce.

The writers of the 1950s and '60s were the ESPN/TSN of the day, and I am indebted to the likes of Charles Bartlett, Red Fisher, Dan Moulton, Stan Fischler, Ken McKenzie, Ray Sons, Trent Frayne, Jim Hunt, Dick Beddoes, Geoffrey Fischer, and the greatest of them all, the *Chicago Tribune*'s Ted Damata. Also to the contemporary scribes who uphold the grand old tradition, specifically Douglas Hunter and Bob Verdi. I am deeply appreciative of the men whose voices painted the pictures that captured my imagination as they jumped through the airwaves. How fortunate I was to have Lloyd Pettit and the late Dan Kelly describe all the actions of my favorite teams.

For work above and beyond the call of duty in helping with the photographic work for this book, I am indebted to David Schachman and Justin Greenhause. For helping with all things computer that are beyond my understanding, thanks for the time given to Vic, the Rat, and Kiella.

On the personal side, I have many thanks to give. To Bob Murray, for believing enough to ask my opinion and for allowing me the privilege of sitting in the press box. To my friends, co-workers, players, and students with the Danville Wings, Team Illinois, and Midwest Goalie School programs, who helped make time for this project and who heard so many of the stories contained within. You were the choir to whom I've been preaching.

Those who know me understand that I live for my trips to Canada, and I am lucky to count some wonderful people among my Canadian family. Thanks to John Neville, who gave me the greatest coaching compliment when he said my teams played with the passion of Canadians. You and your family have made a welcoming country seem even more like home. Thanks also to Joan Lemons, "Mrs. L" of Bracebridge, Ontario, who opened her home to me and others during our college years. You will forever be my second mother.

To Eve Cooper, my lifesaver, for giving me the gift of summer.

Always, the memory of Uncle Al is with me. I am grateful I was able to thank him for teaching me the importance of time, for being the greatest of the greatest generation. To my legendary Aunt Ginny, for living up to impossibly high standards and therefore raising mine. Now that I'm done, can I finally get a tan?

"Losing family obliges us to find our family . . . not always the family that is our blood, but the family that can become our blood." I found Larry, Adrienne, and Matt Snyder who have always been there, and I know always will be. To Dan Cotuno who, along with Matt, gave me the greatest tribute any coach could receive. Joe and Kristine Locallo, so much more than friends, so much more reliable than family, I am so lucky to have you in my life. The same with Go Lee Cannon, my brother. To the Gee Man, my deepest thanks for Finding Forrester.

To Jim Gifford of Stoddart Publishing, for taking my letters and calls and steering a complete unknown the right way. Fullest and most sincere gratitude to Lonnie Herman of McGregor Publishing, for patience, guidance, and ultimately believing enough to make my dream come true. Special thanks to Lucy Kenward for her patience and thoroughness in editing this book, and to Rob Sanders of Greystone Books for his enthusiastic backing.

Most important, to the Hall family, who made me feel so at ease. Glenn's brother, Doug, was one of my first interviews and a wonderful resource. Particular thanks to Pat for his cooperation and friendship. This book would not have come together without you. To Pauline, an unforgettable woman whose humor and warmth make everyone around her better people. Thanks, for the time given and the obvious pride in Dad and Mom, to Leslie, Tammy, and Lindsay.

And finally, of course, to Glenn Hall. I hope this book is the right balance between your amazing career, the humor you treasure, and the family you covet. People who actually come to know their idols are so often disappointed by seeing feet of clay. My admiration for you only grew.

TOM "CHICO" ADRAHTAS

Index

Plante, Jacques *(continued)*
  with New York, 115
  with St. Louis, 180–82, 183–86, 189–98,
    202, 204, 205–6
Playoff system, 163
Poile, Bud, 40, 41, 44–45, 152
Pollock, Sam, 51, 151
Potvin, Denis, 51
Prentice, Dean, 133
Preston, Bill, 71
Probstein, J.G., 158, 205
Pronovost, Marcel, 144
Provost, Claude, 81
Pulford, Bob, 144

Rayner, Chuck, 30–31, 57
Reay, Billy, 116, 120, 139
Red Tilson Award, 37–38
Richard, Henri ("Pocket Rocket"), 90, 91
Richard, Maurice, 48, 51
Robinson, Larry, 51
Rollins, Al, 56, 71, 72
Roy, Patrick, 241–42

Sabourin, Gary, 167
St. Laurent, Dollard, 77
St. Louis, Missouri, 12–13
St. Louis Arena, 13–14, 154, 185, 221
St. Louis Blues, 152–54
St. Louis fans, 159–60, 185, 188
St. Marseille, Frank, 160
Salaries, 60, 78
Salomon, Sid, Jr., and Sid, III, 154, 156, 174,
    183, 185, 188
Sanford, Ed, 53
Savard, Serge, 173
Save percentage, 122–23
Sawchuk, Terry ("The Uke")
  with Boston, 23, 53, 63
  with Detroit, 36–37, 39–40, 43–44, 45,
    47–48, 51, 71
  with Toronto, 139, 142, 143–45, 147,
    148–49
"Scooter Line," 139
Selke, Frank, 95
Service, Robert William, 18–19
Shack, Eddie, 130
Shutt, Steve, 51
Simmons, Don, 63–64, 105, 108
Skinner, Jimmy, 27, 46, 53, 54, 65
Skov, Glen, 29, 52, 73, 87
Slap shot, 68, 73, 107, 238

Sloan, Tod, 77, 82
Smith, Billy, 51, 241
Sports Illustrated, 103–4
Stanley, Allan, 144
Stanley Cup, 97–98
Stanley Cup games
  with Chicago, 79–81, 90–95, 96–98,
    103–5, 124, 125, 132–33
  with Detroit, 58–59, 64–66
  with St. Louis, 166–70, 171–75, 196–97,
    198–200
Stapleton, Pat, 139
Stasiuk, Vic, 41, 53, 64, 65
Stevenson, Grant (grandson), 233
Stevenson, Leslie (née Hall) (daughter), 86,
    124, 233
Stevenson, Megan (granddaughter), 233
Stevenson, Michelle (granddaughter), 233
Stevenson, Tom (son-in-law), 233
Stewart, Black Jack, 21, 36
Stony Plain, Alberta, 127, 230
Storey, Red, 80–81

Talbot, Jean-Guy, 91, 184
Television coverage, 151, 171
Timekeeping, 67
Toppazzini, Jerry, 52
Toronto Maple Leafs, 143–44
Tremblay, J.C., 174
Tretiak, Vladislav, 240
Trottier, Bryan, 51

Ullman, Norm, 41

Van Impe, Ed, 139
Vasko, Elmer ("Moose"), 77, 80, 94
Vezina Trophy, 15, 56, 83–84, 88, 108, 119,
    143, 195–96
V split, 57, 76, 203

Wakely, Ernie, 201, 204, 205, 212
Walker, Pat, 81
Western Hockey League, 40, 47
Wharram, Ken, 77, 90, 139, 190
Wilson, Johnny, 71
Wilson, Lefty, 42
Windsor Spitfires, 26–29
Wirtz, Arthur, 102, 139
Woodcock, Tommy, 238
World Hockey Association, 214
Worsley, Lorne ("Gump"), 115, 118, 125, 172